# Rome

**Bloomsbury Sources in Ancient History**

The Bloomsbury Sources in Ancient History series presents a definitive collection of source material in translation, combined with expert contextual commentary and annotation to provide a comprehensive survey of each volume's subject. Material is drawn from literary, as well as epigraphic, legal, and religious sources. Aimed primarily at undergraduate students, the series will also be invaluable for researchers, and faculty devising and teaching courses.

*Athenian Democracy: A Sourcebook*, Luca Asmonti
*Christianity in the Later Roman Empire: A Sourcebook*, David M. Gwynn
*Food and Drink in Antiquity: A Sourcebook*, John F. Donahue
*Greek and Roman Sexualities: A Sourcebook*, Jennifer Larson
*Rome: A Sourcebook on the Ancient City*, Fanny Dolansky and Stacie Raucci
*Women in Ancient Rome: A Sourcebook*, Bonnie MacLachlan
*Women in Ancient Greece: A Sourcebook*, Bonnie MacLachlan

# Rome

## A Sourcebook on the Ancient City

Fanny Dolansky and Stacie Raucci

Bloomsbury Academic
An imprint of Bloomsbury Publishing Plc

B L O O M S B U R Y
LONDON · OXFORD · NEW YORK · NEW DELHI · SYDNEY

**Bloomsbury Academic**

An imprint of Bloomsbury Publishing Plc

50 Bedford Square
London
WC1B 3DP
UK

1385 Broadway
New York
NY 10018
USA

www.bloomsbury.com

**BLOOMSBURY and the Diana logo are trademarks of Bloomsbury Publishing Plc**

First published 2018

**British Library Cataloguing-in-Publication Data**

A catalogue record for this book is available from the British Library.

| ISBN: | HB: | 978-1-4411-0754-1 |
| | PB: | 978-1-4411-9419-0 |
| | ePDF: | 978-1-4411-4485-0 |
| | eBook: | 978-0-5673-1031-6 |

**Library of Congress Cataloging-in-Publication Data**

Names: Dolansky, Fanny, author | Raucci, Stacie, author.
Title: Rome : a sourcebook on the ancient city / Fanny Dolansky and Stacie Raucci.
Description: London : New York : Bloomsbury Academic, 2017. |
Series: Bloomsbury sources in ancient history | Includes bibliographical references and index.
Identifiers: LCCN 2017034499 (print) | LCCN 2017035794 (ebook) |
ISBN 9781441144850 (ePDF) | ISBN 9780567310316 (ePub) |
ISBN 9781441194190 (paperback) | ISBN 9781441107541 (hardback)
Subjects: LCSH: Rome–Civilization–Sources. | BISAC: HISTORY / Ancient / General.
Classification: LCC DG77 (ebook) | LCC DG77 .D65 2017 (print) |
DDC 937/.07–dc23
LC record available at https://lccn.loc.gov/2017034499

Cover image © Gismondi, Italo (1887–1974)/Museo della Civiltà Romana, Rome, Italy/ De Agostini Picture Library/A. Dagli Orti/Bridgeman Images

Typeset by Integra Software Services Pvt. Ltd.
Printed and bound in Great Britain

To find out more about our authors and books visit www.bloomsbury.com. Here you will find extracts, author interviews, details of forthcoming events and the option to sign up for our newsletters.

# Contents

# List of Illustrations

## Figures

## Maps

# Acknowledgments

This book was written with the support of many people. We would like to thank the editorial staff at Bloomsbury Academic for their guidance and patience, especially Alice Wright, Lucy Carroll, and Clara Herberg. We are indebted to the anonymous readers for the press who provided valuable feedback on the initial proposal and the manuscript as a whole. A number of institutions offered crucial funding and spaces to write: the Humanities Research Fund at Union College, the Mary Elvira Stevens Traveling Fellowship from Wellesley College, the Fondation Hardt in Switzerland, and the Humanities Research Institute at Brock University, which supported both an early period of research in Rome and reproduction rights for the images in the volume.

Special thanks to Eliza Burbano and Pierre Castro, extraordinary undergraduate research assistants at Union College, and to the students in our classes for being sounding boards for this book.

On a more personal note, Stacie would like to thank her husband Patrick Singy and her parents Joseph and Lenore Raucci for endless support. Fanny would like to thank Phil Venticinque for helpful critique and encouragement at the beginning of this project in particular, and her family, especially her parents Ben and Diane and younger sister Lila, for support throughout.

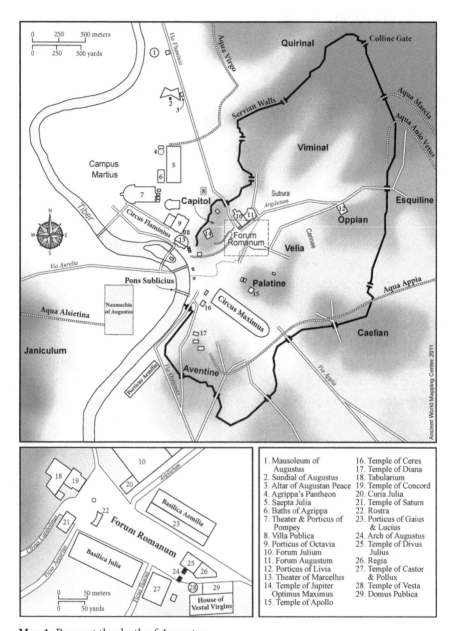

**Map 1** Rome at the death of Augustus

Legend:
1. Mausoleum of Augustus
2. Sundial of Augustus
3. Altar of Augustan Peace
4. Agrippa's Pantheon
5. Saepta Julia
6. Baths of Agrippa
7. Theater & Porticus of Pompey
8. Villa Publica
9. Porticus of Octavia
10. Forum Julium
11. Forum Augustum
12. Porticus of Livia
13. Theater of Marcellus
14. Temple of Jupiter Optimus Maximus
15. Temple of Apollo
16. Temple of Ceres
17. Temple of Diana
18. Tabularium
19. Temple of Concord
20. Curia Julia
21. Temple of Saturn
22. Rostra
23. Porticus of Gaius & Lucius
24. Arch of Augustus
25. Temple of Divus Julius
26. Regia
27. Temple of Castor & Pollux
28. Temple of Vesta
29. Domus Publica

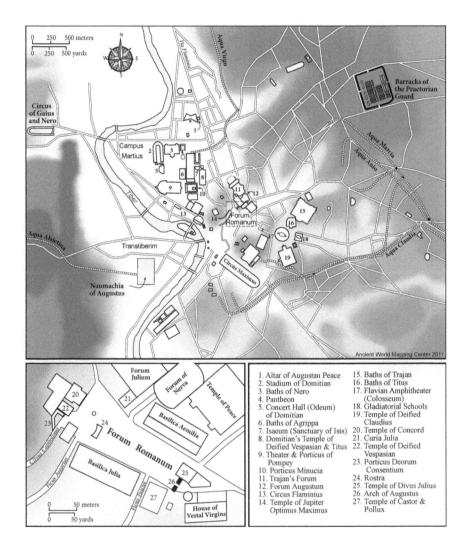

**Map 2** Rome at the death of Trajan

The map legend, left to right:

Labels on map: Via Flaminia, Aqua Virgo, Barracks of the Praetorian Guard, Circus of Gaius and Nero, Campus Martius, Aqua Marcia, Aqua Anio, Aqua Alsietina, Transtiberim, Forum Romanum, Aqua Claudia, Circus Maximus, Naumachia of Augustus, Ancient World Mapping Center 2011

Inset labels: Forum Julium, Forum of Nerva, Temple of Peace, Basilica Aemilia, Forum Romanum, Basilica Julia, Clivus Capitolinus, Vicus Iugarius, Vicus Tuscus, House of Vestal Virgins

1. Altar of Augustan Peace
2. Stadium of Domitian
3. Baths of Nero
4. Pantheon
5. Concert Hall (Odeum) of Domitian
6. Baths of Agrippa
7. Isaeum (Sanctuary of Isis)
8. Domitian's Temple of Deified Vespasian & Titus
9. Theater & Porticus of Pompey
10. Porticus Minucia
11. Trajan's Forum
12. Forum Augustum
13. Circus Flaminius
14. Temple of Jupiter Optimus Maximus
15. Baths of Trajan
16. Baths of Titus
17. Flavian Amphitheater (Colosseum)
18. Gladiatorial Schools
19. Temple of Deified Claudius
20. Temple of Concord
21. Curia Julia
22. Temple of Deified Vespasian
23. Porticus Deorum Consentium
24. Rostra
25. Temple of Divus Julius
26. Arch of Augustus
27. Temple of Castor & Pollux

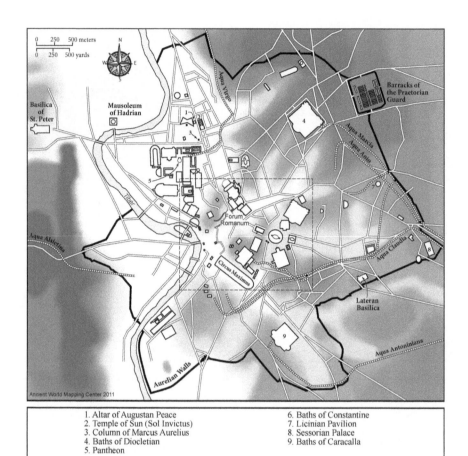

| | |
|---|---|
| 1. Altar of Augustan Peace | 6. Baths of Constantine |
| 2. Temple of Sun (Sol Invictus) | 7. Licinian Pavilion |
| 3. Column of Marcus Aurelius | 8. Sessorian Palace |
| 4. Baths of Diocletian | 9. Baths of Caracalla |
| 5. Pantheon | |

**Map 3** Rome in the age of Constantine

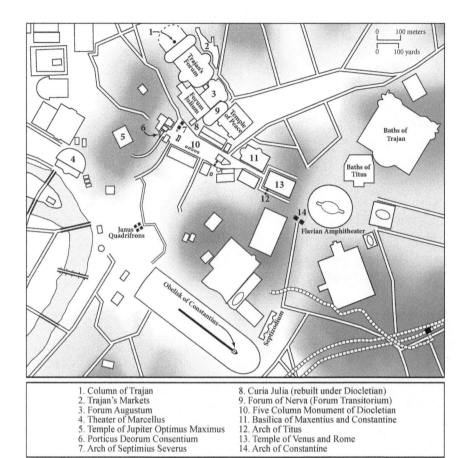

| | |
|---|---|
| 1. Column of Trajan | 8. Curia Julia (rebuilt under Diocletian) |
| 2. Trajan's Markets | 9. Forum of Nerva (Forum Transitorium) |
| 3. Forum Augustum | 10. Five Column Monument of Diocletian |
| 4. Theater of Marcellus | 11. Basilica of Maxentius and Constantine |
| 5. Temple of Jupiter Optimus Maximus | 12. Arch of Titus |
| 6. Porticus Deorum Consentium | 13. Temple of Venus and Rome |
| 7. Arch of Septimius Severus | 14. Arch of Constantine |

**Map 3** (Continued)

# Chronology of Rome's Rulers

## Kings (traditional dates)

| | |
|---|---|
| Romulus | 753–715 BCE |
| Numa Pompilius | 715–673 BCE |
| Tullus Hostilius | 673–642 BCE |
| Ancus Marcius | 642–617 BCE |
| Lucius Tarquinius Priscus ("Tarquin the Elder") | 616–579 BCE |
| Servius Tullius | 578–535 BCE |
| Lucius Tarquinius Superbus ("Tarquin the Proud") | 534–510 BCE |

## Emperors

| | |
|---|---|
| Augustus | 27 BCE–14 CE |
| Tiberius | 14–37 CE |
| Caligula | 37–41 CE |
| Claudius | 41–54 CE |
| Nero | 54–68 CE |
| Galba | 68–69 CE |
| Otho | 69 CE |
| Vitellius | 69 CE |
| Vespasian | 69–79 CE |
| Titus | 79–81 CE |
| Domitian | 81–96 CE |
| Nerva | 96–98 CE |
| Trajan | 98–117 CE |
| Hadrian | 117–138 CE |
| Antoninus Pius | 138–161 CE |
| Marcus Aurelius | 161–180 CE |
| Lucius Verus | 161–169 CE |
| Commodus | 177–192 CE |
| Pertinax | 193 CE |

| | |
|---|---|
| Didius Julianus | 193 CE |
| Septimius Severus | 193–211 CE |
| Caracalla | 211–217 CE |
| Macrinus | 217–218 CE |
| Elagabalus | 218–222 CE |
| Severus Alexander | 222–235 CE |
| Maximinus | 235–238 CE |
| Gordian I and II | 238 CE |
| Balbinus and Pupienus | 238 CE |
| Gordian III | 238–244 CE |
| Philip | 244–249 CE |
| Decius | 249–251 CE |
| Gallus | 251–253 CE |
| Valerian | 253–260 CE |
| Gallienus | 253–268 CE |
| Claudius Gothicus | 268–270 CE |
| Aurelian | 270–275 CE |
| Tacitus | 275–276 CE |
| Probus | 276–282 CE |
| Carus, Carinus, Numerian | 282–285 CE |
| Diocletian | 284–305 CE |
| Maximian | 286–305 CE |
| Constantius | 305–306 CE |
| Galerius | 305–311 CE |
| Maxentius | 306–312 CE |
| Constantine | 306–337 CE |
| Licinius | 313–323 CE |

# Introduction

The purpose of this volume is to lead you, the reader, on a journey through the ancient city of Rome via selected writings from antiquity. Inside these pages you will find passages from ancient Greek and Latin texts that we have translated into English and provided commentary on, where appropriate. This sourcebook is meant to provide you with an experience that is at the intersection of topography, social history, and cultural studies. This is why we have chosen to organize our book by themes rather than by geographical regions of the city. As you will see, there are chapters devoted to politics, spectacles, religion, and daily life, among other topics. Our overarching goal has been to place the sites of the city in the context of the lived experience of its inhabitants. In order to understand and appreciate the perspectives of the inhabitants as much as possible, we have provided chapters that explore the city at both ordinary and extraordinary moments of life.

Why take this thematic approach? We wanted to bring awareness to the symbiotic relationship between the city and its people. Diane Favro (1999: 205) aptly notes that, "Roman urban settings were not mere backdrops, but active participants in city life." She adds (206) that urban sites could "function as director, actor, and audience." While in this last phrase at least Favro is discussing the role of the city in Roman performances specifically, the idea can be applied to the city as a whole and is a useful framework to help us think about the living city.[1] The spaces of the city could facilitate certain kinds of activities and serve as witness to events. In turn, people could change the way urban sites were used through their actions. By mingling monuments with experiences, we hope that you will begin to see a vibrant relationship between the city and its inhabitants and thereby picture the *living* city.

Walking through the streets of Rome long after the time periods covered in this volume, many people have commented on the ruins we still see standing today, whether they are the easily spotted and magnificent remains of the Colosseum and the Roman Forum or the lesser noticed remains of the apartment complex of the Insula dell'Ara Coeli. Without careful thought, it is easy for the casual observer to view these remains as static old stones, remnants of a long-ago past now devoid of life and meaning. As you look today at the ruins spread across the urban landscape, it might also be tempting to gather ancient Rome together in your mind as a single entity. It would be a mistake, though, to see ancient Rome in such static and monolithic terms. As many have noted before us, the dynamics of the city were, and still are, constantly changing: the city of Rome has always been a living organism.[2] Rome's many layers of history are visible in its remains. This is why, as you engage with Rome's cityscape and the texts contained within this volume, you should try to remember that the marks left by people on the city have been made over many periods of time. Author André Aciman (2002: 3) writes that, "Rome is not about one path, or about one past, but an accumulation of pasts." In reading the literary, historical, and inscriptional sources in this volume, one should keep in mind that ancient writers were not all looking at the same Rome. They were writing in different time periods and therefore looking at different cityscapes from each other. And of course they were bringing different perspectives, too, based on their individual backgrounds and particular circumstances.

In this same spirit, many scholars have referred to the city of Rome as a palimpsest: something that has been written on, scraped clean, and reused many times over.[3] Sometimes traces of previous uses can still be seen. We mention this idea of palimpsestic Rome here as another reminder to the reader/viewer of the city to consider Rome's many pasts.

The voices contained within this volume are varied, ranging from the words of poets to biographers to historians, and include some of the words of Rome's most famous leaders. Nearly all of the literature surviving from the Roman world was written by men of means who were well educated and often well connected in social and political circles. Inscriptions, on the other hand, span the spectrum in terms of socio-economics, gender, legal status, and other defining features, and so offer unique glimpses of the experiences of the many others who lived and worked in the city, including slaves, freedmen, and women of all classes. Each passage should, therefore, be seen as a snapshot of the city framed by the viewpoint, goals, and biases of a particular author. An author writing in the genre of satire will not have the same goals as someone writing history. An inscription may seem more straightforward at a glance, but it too has its own aims. It is important to remember that the experience of the city and its monuments was different for different people based on age, gender, social status, and other markers of identity. Emily Gowers (1995: 24) refers to the range of voices on Rome as the "multiple consciousness of the city." There never was— nor is there today—only one Rome.

Given the large amount of ancient material on the city of Rome, the collection of texts from antiquity in this volume is by no means exhaustive. Take, for example, the epigraphic evidence. Scholars estimate that we have approximately 95,000 Latin inscriptions from the city of Rome alone.[4] In this volume, we could not reasonably include more than a sampling of the inscriptional evidence. The same applies to the literary record on the city and the experiences of its inhabitants. In truth, each topic in this sourcebook could have its own book devoted to it, as is often already the case. This book can only provide you with a good overview to start your studies—a taste of the ancient city of Rome to whet your appetite and hopefully encourage you to learn more. For anyone with a desire to find additional primary sources on specific sites, we recommend looking for more direction in any of the standard works on topography now available. Platner and Ashby's older *Topographical Dictionary of Ancient Rome* is available online.[5] Richardson's work, *A New Topographical Dictionary*, is an excellent place to begin, as well as Filippo Coarelli's *Rome and Environs*, and Amanda Claridge's *Oxford Archaeological Guide*. The *sine qua non* of work on the city of Rome is now the multi-authored *Lexicon Topographicum Urbis Romae* (often abbreviated as *LTUR*), edited by Eva Margareta Steinby. It is a multilingual volume with articles in English, French, German, and Italian. Without a doubt, the recently published (in English in 2017) *Atlas of Ancient Rome* by Andrea Carandini will also be indispensable for any study on the city, in particular for its maps and images.[6] A final source of use to students and general readers is Peter Aicher's wonderful *Rome Alive*; while it is also a sourcebook on the city, its approach is geographical rather than thematic.

Contained as well within the present volume are scholarly secondary sources that we have found useful and that may prove beneficial to you in considering specific topics or sites.[7] We have limited these further readings to English language publications and primarily to ones readily accessible to a student or general reader, but again, for those of you who have reading capabilities beyond English or want to explore farther, there are important scholarly works in other languages, as well as more specialized resources available.

Just as we have had to limit the sources translated and listed, we have limited the spatial boundaries and chronological scope of our examination. This book focuses on the city of Rome itself and only ventures to a few roads and religious sites on the outskirts of the city.[8] We begin with the foundations of the city and end in the fourth century CE, though because of the nature of the surviving evidence, especially literary, we concentrate on the final century of the Republic (the age of Cicero and Caesar in particular) and the first two centuries of the Empire. There are, of course, numerous writers and artists who document the city of Rome long after these time periods.[9]

Once you are familiar with the sources in this volume, what can you do next to "read" the city of Rome? How can you best consider the ancient city and not have it be simply words on a page? How can you make the connections between space and experience from such a distance of time and culture? A few scholars have created experiential journeys of the ancient city, taking their readers on thematic walks. These modern scholars explore the city much as some of the ancient writers take us on itineraries through the city (see **1.5** in this volume).[10] For readers trying to gain their own sense of how the space of the city influenced urban activity and vice versa, it can be useful to make your own digital map of the city (using any kind of mapping capability, such as Google My Maps). While not all of the sites have physical remains in the city, it can be helpful to have some sense of where things took place. One way to create such a virtual experience is to develop your own map based on one chapter in the book so that you can understand how particular thematic connections would have played out in the city. From there, if you would like to take this experiential approach beyond the bounds of the book, you might find themes that are of interest to you and explore sites connected to them in map form.

For viewing some of Rome's spaces, there are already excellent technologies available to you online. The American Academy in Rome provides a helpful summary of the mapping and visualizing resources available, including some of the most well known, such as the Digital Roman Forum, Rome Reborn, and Digital Augustan Rome.[11] There are numerous maps available online, such as those from the Ancient World Mapping Center (you can find three of their maps in this volume, as starting points for your spatial explorations).[12] Professor Sarah Bond's blog, *History from Below*, also has an excellent discussion of open-access resources.[13]

Our hope is that this book will be of use to you whether you are sitting in a classroom or walking the streets of Rome.

# Introducing the City of Rome

This first chapter introduces you to ways of looking at the city of Rome. It covers generic images of the city, showing how Roman writers often described its magnificence (**1.1**) and its status as *Roma aeterna* (eternal Rome) and *caput mundi* (head of the world) (**1.3–4**). Given the city's significance to an inhabitant of Rome, it is not surprising that those away from it recalled it with fondness and longing (**1.2**). This chapter also serves as an introduction to the site of the city (**1.6**), its mythological stories (**1.7–11**), and the ways in which authors create their own virtual versions of the city through their written texts (**1.5**). Not only did the places themselves serve as touchstones and placemarkers for urban travelers finding their way, but places were also imbued with the memories of what happened in those spots. Jennifer Rea (2007: 10) notes the importance of the monuments and places of the city as related to memory: "In brief, the Romans relied on visual narratives in their everyday life as well as their professional lives: they retrieved memories from recreations of physical monuments within their minds, but when they walked through the city, they saw a visual narrative of memories stored in specific monuments as well." Cicero, in a discussion not of Rome, but relevant nonetheless to a discussion of place and memory, describes the history we can encounter with every footstep through a place (Cicero, *On Ends* 5.5).[1] While we can certainly apply this idea to modern Rome with its palimpsestic appearance, the same held true for an ancient Roman. The chapter is ordered in a way to provide first an overview of impressions of the city, as told by ancient voices. Then it introduces the city's founding and myths.

## 1.1 The greatness of Rome

It is not uncommon to read about the greatness of the city of Rome in the works of ancient authors. In writings by many authors, Rome is referred to not as Rome, but as *urbs*, the word for city. It is clear that for these writers, Rome is the singular city, so there would be no reason to spell it out more than this.[2] The reasons given for the city's greatness vary. Pliny the Elder describes the gates, hills, height, and neighborhoods. Ammianus Marcellinus, writing in the fourth century CE, describes the emperor Constantius II's reaction to seeing the city for the first time. According to him, the diverse population and certain sites in the city stood out.

Vergil, *Eclogues* 1.19–25
Meliboeus, I was foolish and I thought that the city they call Rome was similar to our own, where we shepherds are accustomed to drive the tender offspring of sheep. Thus I knew that puppies were similar to dogs, that young goats were similar to their mothers. Thus I was accustomed to compare great things to small ones. But this city lifted her head high among the others, as high as cypress trees are accustomed to do among wayfaring trees.

Propertius, *Elegies* 4.1.1–2
What you see here, visitor, where greatest Rome is, was hill and grass before Phrygian Aeneas.

Ovid, *Letters from Pontus* 1.3.37
What is better than Rome?

Pliny the Elder, *Natural History* 3.5.66–7
Romulus left a city with three gates or, if we believe the ones relating the highest number, four. In the rule and censorship of Vespasian and Titus, in the 826th year of the founding of the city, walls surrounded the city, embracing seven hills, with a circumference of thirteen miles and 200 yards. The city itself is divided into fourteen regions with 265 crossroads with altars of the *Lares*.[3] With the measure running from the milestone at the head of the Roman Forum to individual gates, which are today only thirty-seven in number, counting the Twelve Gates once and passing by the seven old ones that no longer exist, the space of the city works out to twenty miles and 765 yards along a straight path. If we measure to the ends of the houses including the Praetorian Camp from the same milestone to the neighborhoods of all roads, it works out to a bit more than sixty miles. If someone should add the height of the houses, he truly would form a worthy estimation and would confess that the magnitude of no city in the whole world is comparable to it.[4]

Pliny the Elder, *Natural History* 36.24.101
But it is appropriate to turn to the marvels of our city and to "review the resources derived from the experiences of 800 years"[5] and to show also in this way [with the buildings of the city] that we have conquered the world.

Frontinus, *On the Aqueducts of Rome* 88.1 (see also **8.5** in this volume)
[Rome] queen and mistress of the world.

Martial, *Epigrams* 12.8.1–2
Rome is the goddess of lands and peoples. Nothing is equal to her and nothing second.

Athenaeus, *The Learned Banqueters* 1.20b
He says that Rome is the demos of the inhabited world. He says that whoever says Rome is the epitome of the inhabited world would not be far off the mark. You can see all the cities settled in it.

Ammianus Marcellinus, *Roman History* 16.10.5–6; 16.10.13–17
And when Constantius II was approaching the city, surveying with a serene face the attendance of the Senate and the revered likenesses of patrician stock, he was thinking, not like Cinaeus the lieutenant of Pyrrhus, that a crowd of kings was gathered, but that the asylum of the whole world was present. When he had turned to the common people, he was astounded in what great numbers every type of man flocked together to Rome from everywhere … Then he entered Rome, the home of empire and of all excellence. When he had arrived at the Rostra,[6] the most well-known forum of old power, he was astonished, and on every side where he turned his eyes he was struck by the number of marvelous things. He addressed the nobility in the Curia[7] and the people from the tribunal … Then surveying the parts of the city placed within the peaks of the seven hills and the parts with slopes and flat ground and the suburbs, whatever he had seen first he was expecting it to stand out among all others: the Temple of Tarpeian Jove, as much as divine things surpass those on earth; the baths, constructed to the measure of provinces; the mass of the amphitheater, made solid by the structure of Tiburtine stone, to the top of which human vision scarcely climbs; the Pantheon, like a rounded region vaulted with beautiful loftiness; and the raised peaks which rise with a platform of steps carrying the statues of earlier emperors; the Temple of the City and the Forum of Peace and the Theater of Pompey and the Odeum and Stadium and among these, other ornaments of the eternal city. But when he had come to the Forum of Trajan, a construction alone of its kind under the sky, as we think, even extraordinary by the agreement of the gods, he was astonished, standing fixed and turning his attention to the enormous buildings, not to be told with words, nor to be achieved again by mortals. And so with all hope removed of attempting anything of this sort, he said that he intended to and would be able to copy the horse alone of Trajan, located in the atrium, the horse that carries the emperor himself … Therefore, after he saw many things with astonishment, the emperor was complaining about fame as being weak or malicious, because in always embellishing everything, in respect to explaining these things that are in Rome, Rome loses value. After considering for a

long time what he should do there, he decided to add to the ornaments of the city by erecting an obelisk in the Circus Maximus, whose origin and figure I will point out in the appropriate place.

## 1.2 Thinking of the city while away

If Rome was seen as the center of the world, then it is not surprising that ancient authors found their time away from it heartbreaking. In particular, those people who were sent away from Rome involuntarily, as exiles, expressed the most distress at being away from Rome. The Roman poet Ovid and the Roman orator Cicero both experienced periods of exile, with Cicero being able to return and Ovid spending his last days away from it. The first letter of Cicero is from his time not as an exile, but as governor of Cilicia, and the second from Athens.

Further reading: Claassen 1999; Edwards 1996: 110–33; Gaertner 2007; Huskey 2006; McGowan 2009; O'Sullivan 2011: 83–4; van der Wal 2007.

Cicero, *Letters to Friends* 2.12.2
The city, the city, my Rufus, stay there and live in its light! Every travel abroad, which I decided from my youth, is dark and dirty to those whose diligence is able to be manifest at Rome.

Cicero, *Letters to Atticus* 5.11.1
Ah! So many times I have sent letters to Rome, when I sent none to you. But hereafter I will send a letter in vain rather than not send it, if it is possible to do so. While you are in Rome, take care of whatever you can, so that my time in this province not be extended! I cannot express how I burn with longing for the city, how I scarcely bear the insipidity of these circumstances.

Ovid, *Tristia* 1.1.1–2; 1.1.15; 1.1.57–8
Little book, you will go into the city without me—I don't hold it against you. Alas, that your master is not permitted to go ... Go, book, and greet the beloved places with my words ... Look upon Rome in my place. You are permitted to do so. Would that the gods allow me to be my book now.

Ovid, *Tristia* 1.3.1–4
When the saddest image of that night comes to my mind, that night which was my last time in the city, when I revisit that night when I left suddenly so many things dear to me, even now tears fall from my eyes.

Ovid, *Tristia* 1.5.67–70

My home is not Dulchium or Ithaca or Samos—to be away from these places is not a punishment—but Rome who looks upon the whole world from seven hills, Rome the place of empire and of the gods.

---

Ovid, *Tristia* 3.1.1; 3.1.23–32

Sent into this city, I come, fearfully, the book of an exile ... May the gods give to you what they have not granted to our poet: to be able to live in your own land. Come then, lead me! For I will follow, although I return, tired, by land and sea from a distant world. He obeyed and, leading me, he said: "This is the Forum of Caesar, this is the road which has its name from sacred things,[8] this is the place of Vesta, which preserves Pallas and the fire, this was the small palace of ancient Numa." Then going to my right side, he said: "That is the gate of the Palatine. Here is [Jupiter] Stator. In this place Rome was first founded."

---

Ovid, *Letters from Pontus* 1.8.31–8

Sometimes I remember you, sweet friends, now my daughter and dear wife come to my mind and from my house I recall again the places of the beautiful city and my mind looks upon everything with its own eyes. Now the *fora*, now the temples, now the theaters covered with marble. Now every porticus with leveled ground comes to mind. Now the grass of the Campus looking upon beautiful gardens and the pools and the channels and the water of the Aqua Virgo.

## 1.3 Eternal Rome and Rome as head of the world

Rome as the "eternal city" is a phrase that gets repeated often in modern advertisements to travelers. As clichéd as it may seem, it was an idea that was in existence in ancient Rome itself. Likewise, with Rome as the center of its empire, it was often called the *caput mundi* or head of the world, and discussion of Rome was sometimes the equivalent of talking about the world itself. The poet Ovid makes this connection between *urbs* and *orbis*, between the city and the world. Pliny the Elder mentions the bringing of the empire to Rome through the placement of a map of the world in the Porticus Vipsania.

Further reading: Boatwright 2014; Edwards and Woolf 2003; Pratt 1965; Richardson 1992: 319–20.

---

Livy, *History of Rome* 5.7.10

They said that Rome was happy and unconquered and eternal.

Tibullus, *Elegies* 2.5.23–4
Romulus had not yet fashioned the walls of the eternal city, not to be inhabited by his brother Remus.

Ovid, *The Loves* 1.15.26
While Rome will be the head of the conquered world …

Ovid, *Fasti* 2.683–4
The land of other nations has a certain boundary. The space of the city [of Rome] and the world is the same.

Ovid, *Fasti* 5.93–4
Here, where now is Rome, the head of the world, there was a tree, grass, and a few animals, and here and there a hut.

Pliny the Elder, *Natural History* 3.2.17
Agrippa was a very diligent man and above all careful in this work [the geography of the map]. Who would believe that he had made a mistake when he intended for the city to see the whole world? And with him the deified Augustus? For he [Augustus] completed the Porticus [Vipsania], begun by Agrippa's sister and that contained the map. He did so according to the design and explanation of Marcus Agrippa.

## 1.4 Rome as center and the center of Rome

There were spots in Rome that defined the city as the center of the world and others that marked the center of the city. Some of these sites, like the Mundus and the Umbilicus (the navel of Rome), remain mysterious. As Plutarch explains, the Mundus was set up as a trench in the Roman Forum that marked the foundation of the city. Other authors, like Festus, describe this site as a connection to the underworld that needed to be kept closed, except on certain days of the year. The Milliarium Aureum, the Golden Milestone, located in the Roman Forum, was a reminder by the emperor Augustus of the importance of the city, since it was the meeting point for roads from the city of Rome. The Umbilicus is sometimes connected to the Milliarium Aureum, due to its conceptual similarity. The Milliarium Aureum marked the center of the Roman world and the Umbilicus marked the center of the city (Coarelli 2014: 64). Other writers, such as the biographer Suetonius, depict Rome not only as a physical center, but as the center of intellectual life. The Capitoline Hill is also depicted by authors as the seat of the empire.

Further reading: Coarelli 2014: 63–4; Moatti 2013: 85; Newsome 2008; Richardson 1992: 254, 404; Woolf 2003.

---

Aelius Aristides, *Regarding Rome* 26.7
Wherever someone might be in the city, there is no hindrance to being equally in the middle of it.

---

Plutarch, *Life of Romulus* 11.1–2
A trench was dug in a circle around what is now the Comitium. The first fruits of all things, proclaimed good by custom or necessary by nature, were placed there. In the end, each person brought a small piece of the earth from where they came, threw it into the trench and mixed it together. They call this trench the mundus, by which name they call the heavens.

---

Dio, *Roman History* 54.8.4
At that time, Augustus was chosen as caretaker of the roads of Rome and he established what was called the Golden Milestone.

---

Plutarch, *Life of Galba* 24.4
Having gone through what is called the House of Tiberius, he walked to the Forum where stood a golden column at which all the divided roads of Italy come to an end.

---

Suetonius, *Julius Caesar* 42.1
He granted citizenship to all the people who practiced medicine at Rome and all the teachers of the liberal arts, so that they might more gladly inhabit the city and others might seek to do the same.

---

Suetonius, *Augustus* 42.3
Indeed at a time of great poverty and difficult remedy, he had expelled from the city the slaves for sale and the slaves of the gladiator trainers and all foreigners, except doctors and teachers.

---

Varro, *On the Latin Language* 5.41
Where there is now Rome, it was called the Septimontium from the number of hills that the city later held with its walls. From these the Capitoline was named because here it is said that a human head was found when they were digging the foundations of the Temple of Jove.

Livy, *History of Rome* 5.54.7
Here is the Capitoline, where once a human head was found, and it was said that in this place would be the head of things and the height of power.

# On writing the city

## 1.5 Written Romes and city walks

Our knowledge of the city of Rome is relatively limited when it comes to textual sources. These written texts need to be studied in combination with material culture, in order to make a more complete picture. Yet mentions of the city of Rome in textual sources are valuable and often go beyond the merely factual. Roman writers sometimes created their own written Romes, creating not necessarily carbon copies of Rome, but manipulated or idealized versions of it. Rome was their canvas onto which they could paint multiple meanings and refashion the city for their own purposes.

A number of ancient authors take their readers on virtual walks through the city. These walks are helpful to the reader in giving a sense of the space of the city and the possible journeys through them. They remind us of the living city, walking past monuments and streets, connecting the daily life of an urban walker to them. In his wide-ranging work on walking in Roman culture, Timothy O'Sullivan (2011: 6) refers to walking in ancient Rome as a "profoundly social activity." In literature, we rarely see the solitary urban wanderer, someone who just walks alone for leisure. Rather, a wanderer is typically accompanied by someone, whether or not we are aware of it. Horace 1.6 below seems to be an exception to this rule.

Although not included in the scope of this volume, a reader interested in urban itineraries might also consider looking at the regionary catalogues of the fourth century CE, the *Curiosum* and the *Notitia*, as well as the eighth-century CE Einsiedeln itinerary, an itinerary of the city written for pilgrims.

Further reading: Dyson 2010: 2; Edwards 1996; Ferriss-Hill 2011; Jaeger 1997; Macaulay-Lewis 2011; Newsome 2011; Östenberg, Malmberg, and Bjørnebye 2016; O'Sullivan 2011: 51–76; O'Sullivan 2016; Reitz-Joosse 2016; Rimell 2009; Vasaly 1993; Welch 2001.

Plautus, *Curculio* 467–83

I will point out in what place you will easily find each sort of man, so that one does not work too much if he wants to meet someone, whether someone full of faults or without fault or upright or not. Whoever wants to meet a perjurer, go to the Comitium. If someone wants to meet a liar and haughty person, go to the Temple of Venus Cloacina. Whoever wants to meet rich, married, and hurtful men, seek them under the basilica. In the same place, there will be male prostitutes[9] and those who are accustomed to bargain. The contributors to shared feasts are near the fish market. In the lowest part of the Forum, good and rich men take walks. In the middle, near the channel, are the real paraders. Confident and chatty and malevolent men are above the Lacus Curtius along with those who boldly speak insults to other people without reason and those who have enough that it could be said against themselves. Under the old shops, in that place are those who give and those who receive interest. Behind the Temple of Castor there are people you should not trust at once. In the Tuscan Way, there are men who sell themselves again and again. In the Velabrum,[10] you can find a baker, a butcher, or a soothsayer.

Catullus, *Poem* 55

I beg you, if perhaps it is not troublesome, to show me where are your haunts. I looked for you in the smaller Campus, in the Circus, in every bookseller's shop, in the sacred temple of highest Jove. In the Porticus of Pompey the Great, I took by surprise all the young women, my friend, whom I saw with a calm face.

Horace, *Satires* 1.6.111–15

Wherever there is the desire, I go alone. I inquire as to the price of the vegetables and grains. I wander often through the deceitful Circus and, in the evening, the Forum. I stand near the fortune-tellers.[11] Then I go home to a bowl of leeks and chickpeas and a cake of flour and oil.

Horace, *Satires* 1.9.1–4; 16–20; 35–6

I was going by chance on the Sacred Way, as is my custom, thinking about some trifle, completely focused on it, when someone known only to me by name runs up to me. Seizing my hand, he said: "how are you, dearest? ... I will follow you where you are going." [I replied:] "There is no need for you to wander about with me. I want to see someone you don't know. He lives far across the Tiber, near the gardens of Caesar." [He said:] "I have nothing to do and I am not slow. I will follow you all the way there." ... When a fourth of the day had past, we arrived at the Temple of Vesta.

Propertius, *Elegies* 4.1.55–7

She-wolf of Mars, the best of nurses for our subject, what walls have grown up from your milk. Let me try to lay out the walls in pious verse.

# The site of the city

## 1.6 On the placement of the site of the city and the Tiber River

Vitruvius discusses the ideal placement for an urban site, referring to the most worrisome issues for the health of the inhabitants. He provides the ideal setting needed for founding any city. Other authors specifically note Rome's placement. As part of that placement, the Tiber River is often mentioned. In Chapter Three, you will see the Tiber River as a crucial player in Rome's economy. In Chapter Ten, you will see it as a powerful natural force, able to cause much damage with its rising waters and subsequent flooding. Here it is a crucial part of the site of the city more generally. The authors help us to understand why Rome was founded at this site. Although the Tiber was useful to the Romans, it was not necessarily healthful, as Galen notes. In addition, there are other unusual events in the city associated with the river, such as the throwing of leftover food in it.

Further reading: Aldrete 2007; Aldrete 2009: 11–15; Mattern 2013: 113–27; Tuck 2013.

---

Vitruvius, *On Architecture* 1.4.1
As to the walls themselves, these will be the foundations. First the selection of the healthiest place. Moreover the site will be high, not cloudy, not foggy, and looking at regions of the sky neither hot nor cold but temperate, if the nearness of marshes is avoided. Then thus will proximity of the marsh be avoided … Likewise, if the walls will be by the sea and they will look toward midday or sunset, they will not be healthy, because through the summer, the midday sky grows hot with the rising sun. After the sun has risen, it grows warm, and at midday it grows hot and in the evening, it burns.

---

Cicero, *On the Republic* 2.10–11
How could Romulus, therefore, both embrace more divinely the maritime advantages and avoid the defects, than by placing the city on the bank of an everlasting river that is both consistent and flowing into a broad stream? Because of this the city was able to import what it needed and to export what it had in excess.[12] And by the same river, the city might not only transport by sea the things most necessary for sustenance and cultivation, but also receive the things carried in from the land. That man, Romulus, seems to me to have predicted at that time that this city would furnish the home for the greatest empire. For hardly could a city placed in any part of Italy more easily hold such great power over things. Moreover, who is so

unconcerned about the natural defenses of the city that he does not have them marked and plainly known in his mind? … And he chose a site both abundant in springs and healthful in an unhealthy region. Indeed there are hills that are both blown through by breezes and bring shade to the valleys.

Livy, *History of Rome* 5.54.2–4
Does the ground of our country or this land, which we call mother, hold us so little? Does the affection for our country hang on buildings and beams? Truly I will confess to you, although it pleases me to remember less of your injury and my misfortune, that whenever I was away, whenever my country came to my mind, all these things were coming to me: the hills, the fields, the Tiber, the region accustomed to my eyes and this sky, under which I had been born and brought up. Romans, now let these things move you with affection, that you remain in your dwelling, rather than afterwards when you have left it, that they distress you with longing. Not without reason have gods and men chosen this site for founding the city: the most healthful hills, the advantageous river, by which fruits may be conveyed from inland places, by which maritime provisions may be received, the sea nearby for conveniences, not exposed by too much proximity to the dangers of foreign fleets, a site in the middle region of Italy and singularly fit for the growth of a city.

Strabo, *Geography* 5.3.7
In the interior land, the first city above Ostia is Rome and it alone is situated on the Tiber. Concerning which, it is said that it was founded by necessity and not by choice. One must add that the people building some addition after these things did not have the authority for a better spot, but they were subject to what was already founded.

Galen, *On the Properties of Foodstuffs* 3.29 (6.721–2K)
As I was saying, it seems right to keep in mind this common thing, that the worst of all fish come from the mouths of rivers, as many of them clean out the latrines and the baths and the kitchens and the dirt of clothes and linens and of other things that need cleaning of the city, through which they flow, especially whenever the city is crowded. The flesh of the eel is found to be in the worst condition from spending time in such water. You do not find it going up inland or being born in marshy waters. But still the worst is from the mouths of such rivers, like the one flowing through Rome. On account of this, the fish is sold at a very fair price in that city.

Tacitus, *Annals* 15.18
But for the purpose of disguising his anxieties of foreign matters, Nero threw into the Tiber the grain of the people that was spoiled by age, by which he might maintain the security of the grain supply.

Sulla, offering up a tenth of all his property to Hercules, made costly feasts for the people and the preparation was so much more than was needed that each day a large amount of prepared food was thrown into the river.

# The mythical stories of the city

## 1.7 Aeneas and the founding of Rome

Aeneas, the Trojan man who fled from home after the Trojan War, traveled from Troy to Carthage to Latium, the region of the future site of Rome. His presence in Rome's early mythology provides a connection for the city to a long ago past. His story is told at length in Vergil's epic poem, the *Aeneid,* among other places. Aeneas was the son of Venus, the goddess to whom Julius Caesar and the emperor Augustus (Caesar's heir) linked themselves. The genealogical link gave authority to Rome's rulers, making a connection between Rome's mythological past and their present. Vergil takes the reader on a journey through the site of Rome not only at the time of Aeneas, but also of a future Rome.

Vergil, *Aeneid* 8.26–35; 46–8; 62–5

It was night and a deep sleep was holding the tired animals, the races of birds and cattle, through all the lands, when father Aeneas lay down on the bank under the pole of the very cold sky, disturbed in his heart by the sad war, and he gave his limbs a late rest. The god himself of the site, aged Tiberinus, god of this pleasant stream, appeared to him and raised himself among the poplar leaves. Light linen was enveloping him in a grayish cloak and a shady reed was covering his hair. Then thus he spoke and with these words he removed his cares ... "Here will be the site of the city, a certain rest from labors, from which in thirty years Ascanius[13] will establish the city Alba of illustrious name ... I am whom you see lightly touching the banks with a full river and reaping the fat fields. Sky blue Tiber, a stream dearest to the sky. Here is my great home, my head springs forth from towering cities."

Vergil, *Aeneid* 8.337–54

With this scarcely spoken, next Evander goes forward and shows both the altar and what the Romans call the Porta Carmentalis [Carmental Gate], which they remember as an ancient honor for the nymph Carmentis, the prophesying seer who first sang about the future great sons of Aeneas and renowned Pallanteum. After this he points out the large grove that brave Romulus restored as an asylum, and the Lupercal under an icy rock, in the Arcadian manner named after Lycaean Pan. He shows the grove of the sacred Argiletum and calls the place as witness and he tells about the death of his guest Argus. From this place he leads him to the Tarpeian Rock and the Capitol, now golden, once rough with woody brambles. Then already the fearful religion of the place was terrifying the timorous peasants. Then they were trembling at the forest and the rock. He says: "A god inhabits this grove (which god is uncertain), a hill with its leafy peak. The Arcadians believe that they have seen Jupiter himself when he has shaken his darkening aegis often with his right hand and stirred up the clouds. Moreover, you see the remains and memorials of the ancestors at these two towns with their walls destroyed. Father Janus founded this citadel, Saturn that one. The name to this one was the Janiculum, to that one Saturnia." With such things said between them, they were approaching the house of humble Evander and they saw herds of cattle scattered about, bellowing in the Roman Forum and in the elegant Carinae.

## 1.8 The brothers Romulus and Remus

The traditional founding date of the city is 21 April 753 BCE and is attached to the story of the brothers Romulus and Remus, as told below. The brothers were the sons of Rhea Silvia, a Vestal Virgin who claimed their father was Mars. Myths tell that they were abandoned at the order of the king, her uncle, then saved and suckled by a she-wolf, and eventually raised by a shepherd and his wife. They later decided to found their own city. In the struggle for the administration of the new city, Remus was killed, leaving Romulus to manage it alone. The image of the she-wolf suckling the brothers as babies is a familiar sight in the city of Rome today (see Fig. 1.1). The Casa Romuli, the supposed hut of Romulus on the Palatine Hill, was noted in later periods as being indicative of bad omens if it were damaged. The stories of the founding of Rome appear on the Basilica Aemilia, including a scene with Romulus, the rape of the Sabine women, and the story of Tarpeia. On April 21 each year, there are celebrations in the city, from parades to reenactments of historical events (see also **6.4** in this volume on the Parilia/Romaia festival).

Further reading: Albertson 1990; Mazzoni 2010; Rea 2007; Richardson 1992: 74; Wiseman 1995a.

Cicero, *On the Republic* 2.12
For he founded a city which he ordered be named Rome after his own name.

**Figure 1.1** Lupa Capitolina at the Capitoline Museums. © Vanni Archive/Art Resource, NY.

Plutarch, *Life of Romulus* 9.4–5; 10.1

After they started towards the founding of the city, right away there was a disagreement concerning the place. Romulus built a place called *Roma Quadrata*, which means square, and he wished to build the city in that place. Remus, on the other hand, built a strong district in the Aventine, which was named Remonium after him, but is now called Rignarium. They agreed to decide the quarrel with auspicious birds of omen. After they sat apart, they say that six vultures appeared to Remus and double that number to Romulus. Some say that Remus truly saw them, but that Romulus lied and that only when Remus came did twelve vultures appear to Romulus. For this reason, the Romans now consult vultures in taking omens from birds … When Remus learned of the fraud, he was angry and when Romulus dug a trench where the city wall was going to be, he mocked the work and hindered it. When he leapt across the wall, some say that Romulus himself struck him, others that it was a companion, Celer, and he fell dead there.

Livy, *History of Rome* 1.6.3–1.7.3

After the Alban state was entrusted to Numitor,[14] Romulus and Remus were seized by a desire of founding a city in the place where they had been exposed and reared.

And there was an overpopulation of Albans and Latins. Added to this also were the shepherds. All of this might make them hope that Alba would be small and Lavinium small in comparison to the city that they were founding. Then the ancestral evil, the desire of kingship, interrupted these plans. After that, a shameful contest arose that was mild enough at first. Since they were twins and a distinction could not be made between them based on age, so the gods, under whose protection were these places, would choose by augury who would give a name to the new city and who would rule it once it was established. Romulus takes the Palatine, Remus the Aventine for taking the omens. It is said that an augury had come first to Remus: six vultures. After the augury was announced, double that number appeared to Romulus. The respective groups greeted each man as king. Based on earlier time, one group was claiming the rule, but the other was claiming it by the number of birds. Then they engaged in an argument of words and because of a struggle of angers, they are turned to slaughter. There in the crowd, Remus was struck and fell. The more common story is that in mockery of his brother, Remus had crossed the new walls. Then he was killed by an angry Romulus. Romulus, chiding him, had added: "So then whoever will cross my walls." Thus he alone was in possession of power. The founded city was called after the name of its founder.

---

Ovid, *Fasti* 4.811–20; 4.837–48

It is agreed to gather the country people and to place the walls. It is undecided which of the two brothers should place them. "There is no need for any contest," said Romulus. "There is great faith in birds. Let us try the birds." The matter is approved. One approaches the rocks of the woody Palatine, the other in the morning goes to the peak of the Aventine. Remus sees six birds, Romulus twelve. They stick to the pact and Romulus holds the authority of the city. An appropriate day is chosen on which to mark out the walls with a plow. The sacred rites of Pales were at hand and the work is begun … Celer, whom Romulus himself had appointed, pushed forward this work. Romulus had said: "Celer, let these things be your concern. Let no one cross the walls or the ditch made by the plowshare. Put to death anyone who dares such things." Because Remus was ignorant of this, he began to disparage the low walls and said: "Will the people be safe with these walls?" Without delay, he leapt across them. Celer attacked the daring man with a shovel and Remus, bloody, lay upon the hard ground. When the king learned of these things, he swallowed his tears that sprung up within and he held the wound closed in his heart. He did not wish to weep openly and he maintained a strong appearance. He said: "Thus let it be for the enemy who crosses my walls."

---

Vitruvius, *On Architecture* 2.1.5

Likewise on the Capitol, the hut of Romulus, and on the citadel, the thatched rooftops of sacred buildings, are able to remind us and to point out the customs of antiquity.

Dio, *Roman History* 48.43.4

Many portentous things happened before this time, some olive oil spouted up beside the Tiber and many things at that time. The hut of Romulus was burned from some religious service that the priests had made in it.

## 1.9 Rape of the Sabine women

Romulus needed women in order to populate the new city. Livy tells the story of how Romulus and his men tricked women from neighboring areas to attend a spectacle at Rome and proceeded to capture them.

Further reading: Brown 1995; Miles 1995: 179–219.

Livy, *History of Rome* 1.9–13

Now the Roman state was so strong that it would be equal to any one of the neighboring states, but because of the scarcity of women, the greatness would endure only for the generation of a man, since at home there would be no hope of offspring nor would there be marriages with the neighbors. Then from the advice of the Senate, Romulus sent ambassadors around to neighboring peoples to seek an alliance and marriage for the new people. They said that cities also, as the rest, are born from the lowest place. Then, the cities that their own courage and the gods help, gain great power and make a great name for themselves. They said that it was enough to know that the gods had been present to the Roman origin and that excellence was not lacking. Therefore the men should not be worried about mixing their blood and race with these men. Nowhere was the embassy heard favorably. At the same time that they were spurning them, they were also fearing for themselves and their descendants that such a mass was growing in their midst. They [the ambassadors], when dismissed, were asked by many if they had also opened an asylum for women. That indeed would be the only way to have companions for marriage. The Roman youth suffered it with difficulty and certainly the matter began to look towards violence. Romulus, so that he might give a suitable time and place for this [violence], disguising the affliction of his mind, diligently prepared the solemn games for equestrian Neptune and called them the Consualia. He ordered that the spectacle be announced to the neighbors and [the men] celebrated it with as much splendor as they possessed so that they might make the affair brilliant and awaited. Many men came together, also with an enthusiasm for seeing the new city, especially the ones who were nearest: the Caeninenses, the Crustimini, the Antemnates, even the whole multitude of the Sabines came with their children and wives. Having been invited hospitably through the houses, when they had seen the site and the walls and the city crowded with houses, they wondered that the Roman state had grown in such a short time. When the time for the spectacle came and their minds had been given up to it along with their eyes, then, according to agreement, when the signal was given, the violence arose, and the Roman youth ran about to snatch the maidens. A great number of the women were seized by the men into whom they had fallen by chance. Some women, excelling in beauty, had been marked out for the chief men, and the plebeians, to whom the business had been given, were carrying them back to the houses. They say that one woman distinguished by far before the others in appearance and beauty was taken by the gang of a certain Thalassius, and with many inquiring to whom they were carrying her, again and again it was shouted that she was being taken for Thalassius, so that no one would violate her.

## 1.10 Tarpeia and the Tarpeian Rock

The story of the maiden Tarpeia is told with varied purpose by different authors. Livy and Propertius below offer two of these versions. Both depict her as a betrayer of Rome to enemy Sabine forces, but Livy represents the betrayal as a result of greed for material things and Propertius as a result of love for the enemy commander, the Sabine Titus Tatius. The spot of her death, the Tarpeian Rock, refers to a spot on the Capitoline Hill. This site is only one of many sites in central Rome with a link to the city's mythological history.

Further reading: O'Neill 1995; Welch 2005; Welch 2012; Welch 2015.

---

Livy, *History of Rome* 1.11.6–8
Spurius Tarpeius was in charge of the Roman citadel. Tatius corrupted Tarpeius's virgin daughter with gold to let his armed men into the citadel. By chance she had gone outside the walls to seek water for sacred rites. Once they were let inside the city, they killed her, crushing her with their weapons. They did this either so that the citadel would seem taken by force or for the sake of setting an example that there is no safety for a traitor. The story is added that she bargained for what they had on their left hands, because commonly the Sabines wore golden bracelets of heavy weight on their left arms and jeweled rings of beautiful appearance. Therefore in place of golden gifts their shields were heaped upon her.

---

Propertius, *Elegies* 4.4.1–2; 19–22; 81–2; 89–91
I will tell of the Tarpeian grove and the shameful tomb of Tarpeia and the captured threshold of ancient Jove ... She saw Tatius practicing on the sandy plains and raising his ornate arms over the golden mane of his horse. She was struck with amazement at the appearance of the king and his regal arms and the urn [of water she was carrying] fell from between her forgetful hands ... Tarpeia thought this her time and she went to the enemy. She made an agreement and she herself will be a companion to it ... But

Tatius said, for the enemy did not give honor to a crime, "Marry and mount to my royal bed." He spoke and he buried her under the massive arms of his comrades.

Varro, *On the Latin Language* 5.41
This hill earlier was called Tarpeian after the Vestal Virgin Tarpeia, who was there killed by Sabine weapons and buried. A memorial has been left of her name, since even now the cliff is called the Tarpeian rock.

## 1.11 Lacus Curtius

There are a number of legends surrounding this site located in the Roman Forum. All of the stories explain the reasons behind the chasm or swamp there. Varro below provides three stories in consecutive order. One version describes a Roman named Marcus Curtius who sacrificed himself to save Rome by jumping into the chasm. Another version describes a Sabine, Mettius Curtius, who was being chased by Romans and jumped into the chasm. A final version claims the spot was struck by lightning and was closed up by a consul with the name of Curtius. During the reign of Augustus, Suetonius tells that a coin was thrown into the hole for the health of the emperor. The spot in the Roman Forum is today marked by a copy of a relief of an armed man on his horse.

Further reading: Claridge 2010: 88–91; Richardson 1992: 229–30.

Varro, *On the Latin Language* 5.148–50
In the Forum, it is well known that the Lacus Curtius was named after Curtius and there is a threefold story about it. For Procilius has not reported the same thing that Piso reported nor did Cornelius follow Procilius. It was related by Procilius that in this place the land had split open and that by a decree of the Senate, the matter was referred to soothsayers. They replied that the god of the underworld demanded fulfillment of a forgotten sacrifice: that the bravest citizen be sent down to him. Then a certain brave man Curtius, armed, climbed onto his horse and having turned from the Temple of Concordia threw himself with his horse into the hole. It is said that the place closed up and buried his body by divine influence and left behind a memorial for his people. Piso, in the *Annals*, writes that in the Sabine war, which was between Romulus and Tatius, a Sabine man, the very strong Mettius Curtius, when Romulus along with his men had made a charge from a higher place, had withdrawn into a marshy place that was then in the Forum before the sewers were made and had gone back to the Capitol to his own men. From this the Lacus Curtius found a name. Cornelius and Lutatius write that this place was struck by lightning and by decree of the Senate the place was

enclosed. Since it was done by the consul Curtius to whom Marcus Genucius was a colleague, it was called the Lacus Curtius.

Livy, *History of Rome* 7.6.1–6

In that same year, whether by a movement of the earth or some other force, it is said that almost the middle of the Forum sunk into an immeasurable depth with an enormous pit. This pit could not be filled with the collection of earth that each person was bringing to it, until, because of a warning of the gods, they began to seek what makes the Roman people powerful. The seers were predicting that whatever it is should be consecrated to that place, if they wanted the Roman state to survive. Then they said that Marcus Curtius, a young man distinguished in war, chastised those questioning whether there was any good thing more Roman than arms and courage. Once silence was established, looking to the temples of the immortal gods which hang over the Forum, and looking at the Capitol, and spreading out his hands now to the sky, now to the exposed opening of land, they say that he vowed himself to the gods below. Sitting equipped on his well-adorned horse, he threw himself into the pit and gifts and fruits were heaped on above him by a crowd of men and women. The lake was called Curtius not from that ancient Curtius Mettius, soldier of Titus Tatius, but from this man.

Suetonius, *Augustus* 57.1

All the ranks of men yearly, according to a vow, were throwing a gift into the Lacus Curtius for his [Augustus's] health.

# The Lived-in City

It is impossible for us to know precisely what happened on the Roman street on a daily basis for average urban dwellers. Ancient writers tell us about the experiences of inhabitants living in the city, but they do so with different purposes in mind. Some are writing poetry, others satire, and others history. That said, any details we can cull about city life are useful in giving us as complete an image as possible. In addition to overall impressions of living in the city (**2.1–6**), its organization into neighborhoods (**2.8**), and the desire to get away from it at times (**2.7**), this chapter includes issues related to the daily life of the inhabitants, such as non-elite housing (**2.9–13**), elite and imperial housing (**2.14–17**), grain distribution (**2.22**), and public services like firefighting (**2.18–20**). When we examine these sources, we should remember that the experiences were different for people of different social classes, ages, and genders.

## Impressions of city life

### 2.1 The sound, smell, and noise of the city

The city was undoubtedly a busy space, with noise, dirt, and smells of all kinds. Many ancient authors describe the crowds of Rome and the general energy of a living city. Eleanor Betts (2011: 119) notes that past discussions of the city have focused on the visual aspects of it, but that more recent explorations have acknowledged that the "multisensory experience of the city is more valuable than this sanitized visualization." What sights did urban inhabitants see? What smells did they encounter? What sounds did they hear? There would certainly have been the smells of food, waste, various industries, and body odors, as well as the noises of vendors, the construction industry, and crowds, among other things.

Further reading: Betts 2011; Bradley 2015; Edwards and Woolf 2003; Hartnett 2011; Holleran 2011; Koloski-Ostrow 2015a; Morley 2015; Roman 2010; Scobie 1986.

---

Horace, *Epistles* 2.2.79–80
Do you want me to sing and to follow the narrow footsteps of the poets in the midst of nocturnal noises and daytime noises?

---

Horace, *Odes* 3.29.11–12
Stop marveling at the smoke, wealth, and noise of magnificent Rome.

---

Propertius, *Elegies* 4.8.1–3; 59–62
Learn what event panicked[1] the watery Esquiline last night, when the crowd, neighboring to the new gardens, ran, and when a shameful brawl sounded in a secret tavern … Proclaimed accusations[2] disturb the sleeping Romans. Every path resounds with raging voices. The first tavern on the dark road receives those girls, with their hair torn and tunics loosened.

---

Quintilian, *The Orator's Education* 10.3.30
Therefore, in a crowd, on a journey, even at a banquet, let our thoughts have solitude. What otherwise will happen when suddenly in the middle of the Forum you have to make an uninterrupted speech, with so many trials around, so many quarrels, so much casual noise, if we are not able to find anything to write in our tablets, except in solitude?

---

Juvenal, *Satires* 3.5–9
I prefer even Prochyta to the Subura.[3] For what place have we seen that is so wretched and so lonely that you would not think it worse to tremble at fires and the continual collapse of buildings and the thousands of dangers of the savage city and poets reciting in the month of August?[4]

---

Statius, *Silvae* 4.4.18
What gentler region takes you away from the noisy city?

---

Pliny the Younger, *Letters* 3.5.14
This [what he was doing each day] was in the middle of work and the loud noises of the city.

Juvenal, *Satires* 14.201–5
Do not let the loathing of any merchandise that must be sent off beyond the Tiber spring up on you, and do not believe that some difference must be made between perfumes and leather. The smell of profit is good, from any business.

## 2.2 On crowds

Juvenal and Seneca describe the streets of Rome as teeming with people and being difficult to traverse (see also **3.2** and **4.6** in this volume).

Juvenal, *Satires* 3.232–50
Here [Rome] very many a sick person dies from staying awake (but food undigested[5] and clinging to the burning stomach created the weakness). For what lodgings allow sleep? One sleeps in the city only if one has great wealth. That is the origin of the sickness.

The movements of carriages on the narrow bends of streets and the shouts at the drove of cattle standing still will snatch sleep from a Drusus and from seals.[6] If duty calls, the crowd will yield as the rich man is carried and he rushes above their heads in a huge Liburnian litter and while traveling within he will read or write or sleep (for a litter with a closed window produces sleep). Nevertheless, he will arrive before me. The wave in front of me hinders me as I hasten. The people who follow in a great mass press my organs. This guy strikes me with his elbow, another strikes me with a hard pole and this guy strikes my head with a log and that guy with a wine cask. My shins are smeared with mud. Soon from all sides I am trampled by powerful feet and the nail of a soldier sticks to my toe. Do you see how much smoke there is at the food distribution? There are one hundred diners and his own portable kitchen follows each person.

Seneca, *On Anger* 3.6.4
Just as someone hurrying through the crowded spaces of the city must clash with many people, it is unavoidable to slip in one place, to be held back in another, to be splashed in another, so in this scattered and unsettled motion of life, many hindrances occur and there are many complaints.

Seneca, *On Mercy* 1.6.1
Think about it, in this city, in which the crowd, flowing without interruption through the widest streets, is crushed whenever something blocks it to delay its path, as if it were a swift torrent.

## 2.3 Having to travel across the city

Considering that most people crossed the city on foot, the journey could be time- and energy-consuming. Martial is here addressing his friend Decianus, who was a lawyer in Rome (see also **4.3** in this volume on traveling the distance to a patron's home).

---

Martial, *Epigrams* 2.5

Let me not be well, Decianus, if I do not wish to be with you all the days and all the nights. But there are two miles[7] which separate us and they become four when I go and come back. Often you are not at home and even when you are, often you are denied or you only are free for your cases and for yourself. Nevertheless it does not annoy me to go two miles to see you. It annoys me to go four miles not to see you.

---

## 2.4 Finding your way in the city

How did someone find their way in the ancient city when it seems that people did not refer to specific house numbers? Literary and epigraphic sources point to finding one's way by referring to major monuments. As you will see below, there are instances in texts where someone gives directions in this way. In Terence's *The Brothers*, a Roman comedy, the speaker's directions include references to major monuments in the city, such as temples and porticoes, but also to spots of commerce, such as bakers and markets near major sites. The inscription in the *Corpus of Latin Inscriptions* directs you to find a barber by location. Martial personifies his book and directs it on a journey through the city by describing landmarks and he later depicts a view from a house in similar fashion.

Further reading: Holleran 2011: 247–8; Kaiser 2011: 9; Ling 1990; Richardson 1980; Richardson 1992: 400.

---

Terence, *The Brothers* 572–84

Syrus:   I don't know the name of that man, but I know the place where he is.
Demea:   Then tell me the place.
Syrus:   Do you know the porticus near the market down there?
Demea:   Of course I do.[8]
Syrus:   Go past, straight up the street. When you arrive there, there is a downward hill in front. Hurry down it here. After that, there is a sanctuary on this side there. Nearby there is an alley.

Demea:   Which one?

Syrus:   Where there is a large fig tree.

Demea:   I know it.

Syrus:   Continue this way.

Demea:   That alley is not a thoroughfare.

Syrus:   Truly by Hercules! Ah! I made a mistake. Go back to the porticus. Indeed you will go a lot closer. The wandering is lesser. Do you know the house of this rich Cratinus?

Demea:   I know.

Syrus:   When you have passed it, go to the left, go straight down the street. When you come to the Temple of Diana, go to the right. Before you come to the gate, near the reservoir itself, there is a bakery and a workshop across. There he is.

---

*Corpus of Latin Inscriptions* 6.31900
Barber near the Circus.

---

Martial, *Epigrams* 1.70.1–10
Go to give my greetings for me, book. You are ordered to go to the shining house of Proculus, dutiful one. You ask the way. I will tell you. You will pass the Temple of Castor near venerable Vesta and the home of the virgins. Then you will seek the revered Palatine by means of the sacred slope, where very many an image of the greatest leader gleams. Let not the shining structure of the amazing Colossus, which rejoices to conquer the work of Rhodes, detain you. Turn your path where there is the building of drunk Lycaeus and the dome of Cybele stands with its painted priest.

---

Martial, *Epigrams* 7.73
There is a house of yours on the Esquiline, there is a house of yours on the hill of Diana, and the Patrician Quarter holds your rooftop. From here you see the shrine of widowed Cybele, from there the shrine of Vesta, from there the new Temple of Jove, from there the old one. Tell me where to meet you, tell me in what part of the city to look for you. Whoever lives everywhere, Maximus, lives nowhere.

## 2.5 On urban sprawl

Dionysius questions where the boundaries of the city were. He is not referring to an official demarcation, but rather to the spreading of Roman life.

Further reading: Favro 2005: 258; Scott 2013: 101; Witcher 2013.

Dionysius of Halicarnassus, *Roman Antiquities* 4.13.4
And if someone wishes to examine the magnitude of Rome from the boundaries, he will be compelled to be misled. And he will not have any sure sign by which it can be discerned up to where it is still the city and from where it is no longer the city. So much is the city woven together with the country that it gives the notion of the city lengthened into indefinite space to the ones looking at it.

## 2.6 On window gardens

Urban dwellers clearly had limited space. For those not able to have a country home to which to escape, there is literary evidence of having a bit of the country in one's home in the form of window gardens.

Further reading: Linderski 2001.[9]

Pliny the Elder, *Natural History* 19.19.59
At that time, the urban plebs were offering daily rural settings to their eyes with the likenesses of gardens in their windows, before the savage robbery of a countless number compelled all the views to be walled up.

Martial, *Epigrams* 11.18.1–16; 23
Lupus, you have given me a country place near the city, but the country place is greater in my window. Are you able to say this is a country place or to call it that? In it, the bitter herb plant makes a grove of Diana, which the wing of a noisy cicada covers, which an ant eats in one day, an ant to whom the leaf of a closed rose is a crown; in which grass is not found more than the early leaf of Cosmus or a pepper; in which a cucumber is not able to lie straight nor is a whole snake able to live there. The garden nourishes one caterpillar badly and a gnat dies once it has devoured the willow and the mole is a digger and plowman for me. The mushroom cannot stand open, the figs cannot laugh and the violets cannot lie open … The cultivated harvest scarcely fills a snail shell.

## 2.7 Getting out of town

Sometimes Romans needed or simply wanted to get out of the city for business, pleasure, or in order to escape the heat that could bring on illness. The first two excerpts offer contrasting portrayals of traveling from Rome that suggest one's means could make a significant difference in how smooth the journey went. In Horace's satirical sketch of his travels from Rome to Brundisium, with several stops along the way including Aricia and Anxur, he is full of complaints as he and a companion travel on foot and on a small boat or barge pulled by a mule along a canal. Pliny the Younger instead reports with great pride about reaching his Laurentine villa, which was located close enough to Rome that he could conduct his business for the day and still arrive at his treasured retreat in the afternoon. Wealthy Romans like Pliny generally owned several properties outside the city of Rome including luxury villas and agricultural estates. In the last excerpt, Horace describes the ability of some people to escape the illness-inducing heat.

Further reading: Balsdon 1969: 213–22, 224–43; Scheidel 2003.

---

Horace, *Satires* 1.5.1–29

Aricia [sixteen Roman miles south of the capital] took me in with modest hospitality after I had left mighty Rome. The rhetorician Heliodorus was my companion, by far the most learned of all Greeks. From there we came to Forum Appii [twenty-seven miles beyond Aricia], boiling with boatmen and stingy innkeepers. Being lazy types, we split this leg of the journey in two but it is only one [day's journey] for more energetic travelers. The Appian Way is less tiring for slowcoaches. On account of the water there, because it was terrible, I declare war on my stomach and wait grumpily as my companions dine. Already night was preparing to draw shadows over the earth and spread the stars out in the sky. Then slaves heap insults on boatmen and boatmen on slaves: "Put in here!" "You're cramming in three hundred [passengers]!" "Whoa, that's enough!" While the fare is collected, while the mule is harnessed, an entire hour disappears. Pesky gnats and marsh frogs drive off sleep as the boatman, thoroughly sloshed on cheap wine, sings of his girlfriend and a passenger takes up the refrain. Finally the passenger, worn out, begins to sleep and the lazy boatman ties the ropes of his mule to a stone and sends him out to graze. Then he's lying on his back snoring! It was already day when we realize our little boat is going nowhere until one hot-headed fellow jumps out and beats the mule and the boatman on the head and the loins with a willow wood club. At last at the fourth hour [approximately 10 a.m.] we scarcely disembark. We wash our face and hands in your stream, Feronia. Then once we've had breakfast, we crawl three miles and climb up to Anxur positioned on her widely gleaming rocks. My fine friend Maecenas and noble Cocceius were going to come here, both sent as envoys concerning important business and accustomed to reconciling feuding friends.

---

Pliny the Younger, *Letters* 2.17.1–3

To his friend Gallus. You marvel at why my Laurentine (or if you prefer, my Laurentian villa) delights me to such an extent; you will cease to wonder once you get to know the charm of the villa, the convenience of the location, the expanse of the shoreline. It is seventeen miles from Rome so that once the necessary business of the day has been completed, you can stay there with the day left intact and settled. There is not one approach, for the roads to both Laurentum and to Ostia go in the same direction, but you must leave the Laurentine road at the fourteenth milestone and the Ostian road at the eleventh. The road that proceeds from both is sandy in some parts, a little more difficult and longer for a wagon, short and easy on horseback. On this side and that, the view changes, for now the road narrows as you encounter woodlands, now it widens and opens up through very broad meadows. There are many flocks of sheep and many herds of horses and cattle there; once they are driven down from the mountains in the winter, they grow sleek on the grass and in the warm spring.

---

Horace, *Epistles* 1.7.1–9

I promised that I would be in the country for five days. A liar, I am missed for the whole of August. And so, if you wish that I live healthy and strong, the pardon you give to me when I am sick, you will give to me when I am afraid of being sick, Maecenas, while the first fig tree and the heat decorate the undertaker with his gloomy attendants, while every father and little mother turns pale for their children, and while obliging officiousness and the petty work of the Forum lead forth fevers and unseal wills.

---

# Regions of the city

## 2.8 Neighborhood life

The ancient city of Rome was a city of neighborhoods. Individual neighborhoods (called *vici*) were known for certain characteristics, whether it was having residences, being the main location for particular industries, or for being a more fashionable place to live than others. As the first passages demonstrate, under the emperor Augustus the city was formally organized into fourteen regions and then subdivided into neighborhoods. The division into fourteen served as an administrative division for the responsibility of certain public services, such as protection against fires. In the smaller neighborhoods, there was a crossroads in each where the residents worshipped the neighborhood's protective gods, knows as the *Lares*. These *Lares* were celebrated at an annual festival known as the *Compitalia*, so named for the shrines called *compita* (for more on this topic, see **6.12** in this volume). The festival was an excellent way to create bonds among the people of the lower classes.[10] One inscription is provided below as an example of the evidence of these neighborhood connections, but there exist many others. The final passage by Juvenal mentions that each place had its own feel, so a move from the Esquiline to the Subura region was significant.

Further reading: Lott 2004; Lott 2013; Richardson 1992: 424.

Suetonius, *Augustus* 30.1 (see also **10.12** on this passage)
He divided the area of the city into regions and wards; the former were looked after by magistrates selected each year by lot while he appointed "masters" for the latter chosen from the plebs in each neighborhood.

Dio, *Roman History* 55.8.7
The whole city, which is divided into fourteen pieces …

*Corpus of Latin Inscriptions* 6.452
To the Augustan *Lares* and to the *Lares* of the neighborhood of Jupiter Fagutal and to the protective spirits of the Caesars.

Juvenal, *Satires* 11.50–2
For it is no longer worse to be bankrupt[11] than to move from the burning Subura to the Esquiline.

# Housing in the city of Rome

## 2.9 Multi-story apartment housing: *insulae*

There were multiple types of housing in the ancient city that depended on one's status and wealth. Many people lived in apartment buildings called *insulae* (the Latin word that means islands) paying rent to a landlord. The remains of such a complex, the Insula dell'Ara Coeli, are located at the base of the Capitoline Hill. These apartments had multiple floors, but it is disputed how high they might have gone. Some passages, as is the case with Aulus Gellius below, are straightforward in their mentions of multi-level structures. There are other passages, such as those from Livy, that describe seemingly fantastical events of large animals climbing to the upper floors of an apartment complex. Despite the extreme nature of these passages, they can stand as additional textual evidence of multi-level dwellings.

Further reading: Aldrete 2009: 78–80; Claridge 2010: 263–4; Dyson 2010: 218–20; Stambaugh 1988: 175–8; Storey 2003; Storey 2004; Yavetz 1958.

Cicero, *On the Agrarian Law* 2.96
They will laugh at and mock Rome [for being] placed in mountains and valleys, elevated and suspended with stories of a building, not with the best roads, with the narrowest paths, in comparison to their Capua, spread out in a most even plain and situated most magnificently.

Martial, *Epigrams* 7.20–1
When he has brought these things [large amounts of food and drink] home up two hundred steps, anxiously he has closed himself in his room bolted shut.

Martial, *Epigrams* 1.117.1–7
Lupercus, however often you go to meet me, you say directly, "Do you want me to send a boy to whom you may hand your little book of epigrams? I will send them back to you immediately once I have read them." Don't disturb the boy, Lupercus. It is a long journey if he wants to come to the Pirus [pear tree]. I live up three flights of stairs, but also steep ones.

Suetonius, *Augustus* 89.2
Augustus even read out whole books to the Senate and to the people and made them known often through proclamation, such as the speeches of Quintus Metellus "On Increasing Offspring" and Rutilius's "On the Size of Buildings," so that he might better persuade them that both things were not first considered by him, but that they had been a care even then to their ancestors.

Aulus Gellius, *Attic Nights* 15.1.2 (See also **10.9** in this volume on fires)
Therefore we friends of his [the rhetor Antonius Julianus] surrounding him were following him home. When approaching the Cispian Hill, we caught sight of an apartment house [*insula*], high and with many stories, on fire and everything nearby was now burning in an enormous conflagration. Then someone there from the companions of Julianus said: "The returns on urban properties are large, but the dangers are by far the greatest. If there were some remedy so that the houses at Rome were not burning all the time, I would have put up for sale my country properties and would have purchased city properties."

Aelius Aristides, *Regarding Rome* 26.8
And Rome has not been poured on the surface, but … it reaches to the furthest point of the air, so that the height is not similar to an occupation of snow, but rather to the headlands themselves. And just as some man surpassing the others in size and strength is not content if he does not carry the rest raised above him, so this city is not content,

having been founded on so much land, but in carrying other cities of equal measure above it, one on another.[12]

Livy, *History of Rome* 21.62.3
At Rome or near the city, many omens happened in that winter ... In the Forum Boarium, a cow climbed to the third floor of its own will and then, frightened by the panic of the tenants, threw itself down.

Livy, *History of Rome* 36.37.2
In the beginning of that year ... it was recorded that, in the Carinae,[13] two domesticated cows had reached the roof of the building by the stairs.

## 2.10 Building codes and structural soundness of *insulae*

Apartment living could be unpleasant, with many people in small spaces, the smells of so many people together, and of course the dangers of living on upper floors should a fire occur. These dwellings were not always structurally sound, despite the existence of at least some building codes. The emperor Augustus limited the height of buildings to seventy feet. Vitruvius describes the regulations on the thickness of walls.

Strabo, *Geography* 5.3.7
Augustus Caesar managed such problems [fires and building collapse] of the city by organizing a company of freedmen to assist against conflagrations. Against the collapse of buildings he reduced the height of new buildings and prevented the building of structures on public roads to seventy feet.

Vitruvius, *On Architecture* 2.8.17
The public laws do not allow walls with thickness greater than a foot and a half to be put in a common place. Moreover, the rest of the walls, lest the spaces become rather narrow, are arranged with the same thickness. Walls made of brick, unless they are two or three bricks thick, are not able, with a thickness of a foot and a half, to support more than one story. However in this greatness of the city with an infinite number of citizens, it is necessary to offer a countless number of dwellings. Therefore since the level floors are not able to accept such a great number of people to live in the city, the situation itself compels us to arrive at a remedy with the height of the buildings. And so these high constructions, with stone pillars, with brick structures, with walls of quarried stone, joined together with numerous stories, bring about viewpoints from the upper rooms to the highest benefit. Therefore with

walls increased by the height from various stories, the Roman people have excellent dwellings without obstruction.

Vitruvius, *On Architecture* 2.8.20
Indeed I wish that wattled walls had not been discovered. As much as they are indeed beneficial for speed and the extension of space, by that much are they a greater and common disaster, because they have been prepared as if torches for fires. And therefore it seems to be better to have the expense of bricks than to be in danger with the savings of the wattled walls.

## 2.11 On the closeness of apartments

In the passage below, Martial remarks on the lack of space in urban apartments: neighbors are so close that they can touch each other from their windows. Even given that, in the bustle of urban life, he does not see his neighbor Novius.

Martial, *Epigrams* 1.86
Novius is my neighbor and is able to be touched with a hand from my windows. Who would not envy me and think that I am fortunate at all hours, since it is permitted for me to enjoy a connected companion. He is as far from me as Terentianus, who now rules Syene on the Nile. It is not allowed for us to eat together, not even for me to see him, nor to hear him. In the entire city, there is not anyone so near and so far away from me. I must go further away or he must do so. If anyone does not wish to see Novius, let him be his neighbor or his tenant.

## 2.12 Evidence of specific *insulae* in the city

In addition to the physical remains of apartments in the city, there are numerous inscriptions that mention specific complexes. Tertullian also mentions the height of one complex, the Insula Felicula.

Further reading: Dyson 2010: 218; Richardson 1992: 209–11.

*Corpus of Latin Inscriptions* 6.29791[14]
[Insula Sertoriana]
Among these properties, the Insula Sertoriana is happily for the benefit of my daughter Aurelia Cyriacetis. [The insula consists of] six upper-story apartments, eleven shops, and a storage space under the stairs.

---

*Corpus of Latin Inscriptions* 6.33893
[The Insula Vitaliana was on the Esquiline in Via delle Sette Sale]
Publius Tullius Felus, a workman of the Insula Vitaliana.

---

Tertullian, *Against the Valentinians* 7
You would believe that such floors of the skies are the Insula Felicula.

---

*Corpus of Latin Inscriptions* 6.9383
Diophantus rent collector at the apartments.

---

*Corpus of Latin Inscriptions* 6.6296
Demosthenes building attendant.

---

*Corpus of Latin Inscriptions* 6.6297
Diogenes building attendant.

## 2.13 Renting an apartment

Owning property could be a good investment for a landlord. Of course, there were risks, such as fire and collapse (see Chapter Ten) and tenants who did not pay rent. Ancient sources describe the start of the rental year as July 1, and discuss high and rising rents, and the ways in which a landlord might use the rent received.

Further reading: Frier 1977; Frier 1978; Frier 1980; Lanciani 1896; Yavetz 1958.

---

Diodorus, *The Library of History* 31.18.2
When Ptolemy, king of Egypt, was driven out by his brother, in common pitiable appearance he came to Rome with one eunuch and three slaves. On his journey, he learned about the lodging of the topographer Demetrius and having searched for him, he lodged with him, with whom he had engaged rather frequently in his residency in Alexandria. On account of the greatness of the rents in Rome, he lived in an altogether narrow and cheap attic.

---

Cicero, *Letters to Atticus* 12.32.2
I want you to propose this to my son Marcus, if it does not seem unsuitable to you: he should apply the expenses of his travel abroad to the rents of the Argiletum and Aventine properties, with which he would have easily been happy, if he were at Rome and renting a house, which he was intending to do. When you have proposed

this to him, I myself wish that you manage the rest, in a way that we may give to him from those rents the money he needs. I will maintain that neither Bibulus nor Acidinus nor Messala, who I hear will be in Athens, will make greater expenses than what is received from these rents. And so I wish for you to see first who are the tenants and how much they pay for rent, then that they are the kind who pay on time.

---

Cicero, *In Defense of Caelius* 17

A man who is in the power of his father prepares no accounts. Never at all has he made any loans. The expense of one sort has been brought up, that of his rent. You said that he rented for thirty thousand sesterces. Now I understand that the apartment house of Publius Clodius is for sale, in whose house this man [Caelius] rents, for ten thousand sesterces, I believe. However, since you wish to please that man [Clodius], you have accommodated your lie to his circumstances.

---

Martial, *Epigrams* 12.32.1–4; 23–5

O Vacerra, the shame of the Kalends of July [July 1], I saw your luggage, not taken in place of two-years' rent, being carried by your wife with her seven red hairs[15] and your white-haired mother along with your enormous sister ... Why do you seek a house and mock the property manager, when you are able to live for free? This procession of luggage is suitable for the bridge.[16]

---

Suetonius, *Tiberius* 35.2

He took away from a senator the broad stripe on his garment when he learned that he had moved away to his gardens before the Kalends of July, so that he might rent a house more cheaply in the city after that day.

---

Suetonius, *Nero* 44.2

Nero commanded all the ranks to contribute a part of their wealth, and moreover that tenants of private houses and apartments pay one year's rent to the imperial treasury.

# Elite houses

## 2.14 The houses of Cicero, Pompey, and Marc Antony

In contrast to apartment housing, an elite person lived in a *domus*, a private house. As scholars have shown, the house of a person was their public face. Below are examples of these houses in the city and, in particular, the houses of well-known men. Cicero says that his house overlooked the whole Forum. It was located on the Palatine Hill and was burned by Clodius when Cicero went into exile. Cicero eventually was able to regain the site of his home and rebuild. In the second passage below, Cicero describes the house of Pompey, referred to as *rostrata*, since it was decorated with the *rostra* (beaks) from ships. After Pompey's death, Marc Antony lived there. This passage is a good example of a house representing a man's identity. Cicero links the house to the great deeds of Pompey and cannot imagine how Antony, whom he finds to be disgraceful, is living there.

Further reading: Aldrete 2009: 75–8; Clarke 1991; Hales 2009; Patterson 2000b; Richardson 1992: 123, 133.

Cicero, *On His House* 100

But if my house not only is not returned to me but even offers a memorial to my enemy of my pain, of his crime, of public ruin, who would think this a return rather than an everlasting punishment? My house, priests, is in sight of nearly the whole city. If the house remains not as a memorial of the city, but as a tomb inscribed with an enemy name, I must move to some other place rather than live in this city in which I may see trophies over me and over the state.

Cicero, *Philippics* 2.68–9

Have you even dared to enter that house, to enter that most venerable threshold, to show your most impure face to the household gods of that building? Does it not shame you to lodge in this house for such a long time, this house upon which no one was able to look for so long, no one was able to pass by it without tears? This house in which, although you are not bright, nothing can be pleasant for you. Or when you have looked at these beaks of ships [the trophies of Pompey] at the entrance, do you think that you are entering your house? It cannot be! Although you are without mind and feeling, nevertheless you recognize yourself, your things, and your people ... I feel pity for the walls and the ceilings. What indeed had that house ever seen, except what was chaste, except from the best character and the most venerable military discipline?

## 2.15 Domus Publica (Public House)/House of Julius Caesar

Julius Caesar moved to the Domus Publica from the Subura,[17] a district located between the Viminal and the Esquiline Hills. He lived in the Domus Publica because of his status as *pontifex maximus* (chief priest) of Rome. It was the role of the *pontifex maximus* to oversee the Vestal Virgins, who lived in the attached Atrium Vestae. When Augustus became *pontifex maximus*, he chose to retain his Palatine residence. In order to satisfy the requirement of his office to live in a *domus publica*, he opened part of his own residence to the public and installed a shrine of Vesta there.

Further reading: Beard, North, and Price 1998: 189–91; Richardson 1992: 133–4; Severy 2003: 100.

---

Suetonius, *Julius Caesar* 46
Julius Caesar lived first in the Subura in a small house, however after having been made *pontifex maximus*, he lived on the Sacra Via in the Domus Publica.

---

Dio, *Roman History* 54.27.3
But as to the requirement that the *pontifex maximus* live in a public house, he made public part of his own house and he gave the Domus Publica to the Vestal Virgins, since it shares a wall with their dwelling.

## 2.16 Imperial housing I: House of Augustus and House of Livia

The house of the emperor Augustus was on the Palatine Hill, a fitting location with its connection to the early days of Rome and Romulus and Remus. While his house was a modest one, in keeping with the moral image he tried to portray to the Roman people, it was part of a larger complex of buildings on the Palatine. A temple of Apollo was built near it on the same plot of land after a lightning strike was interpreted as a sign. The rooms of the house had beautiful paintings and the public can see some of them today. The house was excavated in the 1960s and most recently there have been major efforts to conserve the site. There is also a nearby home, the so-called House of Livia, with its own splendid paintings. It is unclear if the house was actually that of Livia, the wife of the emperor Augustus, but attributions have been made in the past, thanks to the proximity of the dwelling and to an inscription on a lead pipe. From the time of Augustus, the Palatine Hill became the location for imperial residences.

Further reading: Coarelli 2014: 138–44; Foubert 2010; Milnor 2005: 47–93.

---

Suetonius, *Augustus* 72.1–2
At first he lived near the Roman Forum, above the Steps of the Ringmakers, in a house that had been of the orator Calvius. After that he lived on the Palatine, but in the no less modest house of Hortensius, which was distinguished neither in spaciousness nor elegance, in which there were short porticoes of Alban columns, and rooms without

any marble or remarkable pavements. For more than forty years, he remained in the same bedroom in the winter and the summer. Although he found the city insufficiently nourishing for his health in the winter, he continually spent winters in the city. If at any time he intended to do something in secret or without interruption, there was a solitary spot for him in the upper part of the house, which he called Syracuse or workshop.

---

*Corpus of Latin Inscriptions* 15.7264
[So-called House of Livia, inscription on a lead pipe]
Julia Augusta.

---

## 2.17 Imperial housing II: the Domus Aurea

The Domus Aurea, the Golden House, was the residence of the emperor Nero. Nero's residence before this one was the Domus Transitoria; it is assumed that the widespread fire in 64 CE destroyed much of it (see **10.3** in this volume). The Golden House was a large and luxurious structure and included not only the residence, but significant grounds with much open space and an artificial lake known as the Stagnum Neronis. One of the significant features of the house mentioned by Suetonius is the dining room with revolving panels. The house was destroyed during the reign of his successors, the Flavians—Vespasian, Titus, and Domitian. Vespasian had the Flavian Amphitheater (now known as the Colosseum) built on the site of the Stagnum Neronis. In recent years, the Domus Aurea site has closed numerous times due to structural instabilities.

Further reading: Ball 2003; Coarelli 2014: 180–6; Richardson 1992: 119–21.

---

Tacitus, *Annals* 15.42.1
But Nero used the downfall of his country and erected a house in which jewels and gold were not as much a marvel, used from a long time ago and made common by luxury, as the fields and pools. On this side were woods, in the manner of wilderness, and on that side open spaces and views. Severus and Celer, the directors and designers, had the disposition and boldness to try through art what nature had refused and to play with the power of an emperor.

---

Suetonius, *Nero* 31
In no other thing, however, was he more wasteful than in building a house. He made it from the Palatine all the way to the Esquiline and at first he called it the Transitoria [Passage-way]. Soon, once it was consumed by fire and rebuilt, he called it the Golden

House, about whose space and elegance it will suffice to have reported these things. There was an entryway in which a colossus stood at 120 feet, in the likeness of the emperor himself. The spaciousness was so great that it had triple porticoes a mile long, likewise a pool like a sea,[18] surrounded with buildings, after the manner of a city. Besides there were country-lands varied with plowed lands and vineyards and pastures and woodlands, with a multitude of every sort of cattle and wild beast. In the rest of the parts, everything was covered with gold, adorned with jewels and shells of pearls. The dining room was paneled with ivory boards that revolved and were furnished with pipes, so that they might sprinkle flowers and perfumes from above. The principal one of the dining rooms was round, and was turned days and nights in the constant change of the heavens. The baths were flowing with sea waters and water from Albula [the Tiber]. When the house was completed in such manner and he dedicated it, only so much did he acknowledge: he said that he had begun at last to inhabit a place like a human being.

# Protecting the city

## 2.18 Setting up firefighting units

When he divided the city into regions, Augustus established the seven barracks of the cohorts (*cohortes vigilum*) of the watchmen of the city, plus fourteen sites called *excubitoria* as watchposts. Remains and inscriptions have helped to determine the locations of some of these structures. One *excubitorium*, the one for the seventh legion, is located at Via della Settima Coorte 9, and was excavated in the 1860s. At an earlier period, firefighting teams consisted of private crews, such as that of Rufus Egnatius in historian Velleius Paterculus's writings.

Further reading: Claridge 2010: 407; Coarelli 2014: 351–2; Daugherty 1992; Rainbird 1986; Reynolds 1926; Stambaugh 1988: 128.

Velleius Paterculus, *Roman History* 2.91.3
Not long after, Rufus Egnatius, who was closer in all things to a gladiator than a senator, gathered the favor of the people in his aedileship. He had increased the favor to such a degree by extinguishing fires daily with his private slave crew that he continued with a praetorship.

Dio, *Roman History* 55.26.4–5
While at this time much of the city was destroyed by fire, Augustus selected free men in seven divisions to aid it and he placed a knight as commander of it and in a short time

he was going to dismiss them. However, he did not do this last thing. For having learned from experience that the aid from them was most useful and absolutely necessary, he kept them. And these night watchmen exist even now in their own manner, enrolled not from freedmen only still, but from others, and they have stations in the city and get a pay from the treasury.

## 2.19 The *vigiles* (firefighters) and their firehouses and watchposts

There are a number of inscriptions that remain regarding the firefighters known as *vigiles* (those who stay awake and are vigilant). The inscriptions frequently point to specific cohorts of the particular regions. In particular, inscriptions 6.2998–3091 of the *Corpus of Latin Inscriptions* are about the seventh cohort. A number of the inscriptions explicitly mention the seventh cohort, while others just note that their duties were completed.

*Corpus of Latin Inscriptions* 6.233
To the *genius* [protective spirit] of the first cohort, Augustus Maximilianus, most renowned man, prefect of the firefighters.

*Corpus of Latin Inscriptions* 6.3003
Lucius Passienus Rogatus performed as a night watchman in the month of June.

*Corpus of Latin Inscriptions* 6.3010
I, Vettius Florentinus, night watchman in the month of June, made this. Let me give thanks to the *genius* [protective spirit] of the fire station and to my comrades in perpetuity.

*Corpus of Latin Inscriptions* 6.3035
Seventh cohort of firefighters.

*Corpus of Latin Inscriptions* 6.2994
To the Spirits of the Dead of Titus Avidius, Roman soldier, of the seventh cohort of the firefighters, *siponarius* [the one who pumps] of Laetorius, Avidia, a Roman mother [dedicates] this to her most pious son.

## 2.20 Firefighting equipment and techniques

Literary sources provide evidence of some of the equipment that was used by firefighters. The first instance from Petronius refers to the imagined death of

Trimalchio, a freedman. This passage refers to the use of water and axes. In the *Digest*, an early sixth-century CE compilation of earlier legal texts and rulings, the jurist Ulpian refers to some additional equipment that was used.

---

Petronius, *Satyricon* 78

One slave in particular, of that undertaker who was the most respectable among them, thundered [with his trumpet] so strongly that he roused the whole neighborhood. And so the firefighters who were guarding the nearby region, having thought that the house of Trimalchio was burning, broke open the door suddenly and with water and axes began to make a disturbance with their duty.

---

Ulpian, *Digest* 33.7.12.18

Pegasus and very many jurists say that vinegar is prepared for the sake of extinguishing a fire. Likewise caps, siphons, poles and ladders, and mats and sponges and waterbuckets and brooms are kept together.

---

## 2.21 The Praetorian Guard at the *Castra Praetoria*

The Praetorian Guard that served as protection for the emperor was housed in a military camp called the Castra Praetoria, constructed in Rome 21–3 CE during the reign of the emperor Tiberius. Sources, such as the historian Tacitus, describe Aelius Sejanus, the prefect of the praetorian cohorts, as having a role in Tiberius's establishment of the camp. It sits between the Via Nomentana and the Via Tiburtina, under the site of the current Biblioteca Nazionale constructed in the 1960s.

Further reading: Bingham 2013; Coarelli 2014: 247–8; Fuhrmann 2012; Nippel 1995; Richardson 1992: 78–9; Stambaugh 1988: 126.

---

*Corpus of Latin Inscriptions* 15.7239b, c

[Inscriptions found on lead pipes for water to the camps]

The Praetorian Camp.

---

Tacitus, *Annals* 4.2

Sejanus extended the power of the prefecture, which was modest before this time, by gathering into one military camp the cohorts that were scattered through the city, so that they might receive orders at the same time and so that by their number, by their strength, and by seeing each other, confidence might arise in themselves and fear among other people. He alleged that a scattered army indulged in license. If anything sudden should happen, they would be assisted as well with greater help and they would act more seriously if the fortification would be stationed at a distance from the enticements of the city.

Suetonius, *Tiberius* 37.1
Tiberius especially had concern for maintaining peace from rioting, robbery, and the lawlessness of insurrections. He set up stations of soldiers through Italy more regularly than customary. He established a military camp at Rome in which the praetorian cohorts were stationed together, who before that time were unsettled and scattered in lodgings.

Dio, *Roman History* 57.19.6
This Sejanus for some time ruled the praetorians with his father. When his father was sent to Egypt, he alone held leadership of them and he firmed it up as follows: he brought together the troops into one fortification, the ones who were by themselves and apart from one another, like those of the night watchmen, so that their orders could be found out altogether and with speed and for everyone to be fearful of them.

# Grain and the city

## 2.22 Distribution of grain and the Porticus Minucia

There were distributions of grain to the plebs. While the number of recipients remains unclear, it is likely that it reached the hundreds of thousands. As can be seen from the inscriptions below, the Porticus Minucia served as one place for the distribution of the grain dole. According to the inscriptions, there was a specific entrance number and door number to which the recipient went each month on a certain day. There is also evidence of a commissioner of the Porticus Minucia. The porticus was located near the Theater of Balbus. In his *Achievements*, Augustus notes that he gave grain to the people at his own expense. Pliny the Younger describes grain distribution as a perpetual gift under Trajan. It is clear that when there was a grain shortage in the city, there was panic among the people.

Further reading: Coarelli 2014: 279; Dyson 2010: 245; Erdkamp 2013; Mattingly and Aldrete 2000; Richardson 1992: 315–16.

*Corpus of Latin Inscriptions* 6.10223
Tiberius Claudius Augustus Ianuarius, freedman, curator, from the Minucia, on the fourteenth day, from door forty-two.

*Corpus of Latin Inscriptions* 6.10224b
Gaius Sergius Alcimus, son of Gaius, lived three years, three months, and three days, received grain on the tenth day from door thirty-nine.

*Corpus of Latin Inscriptions* 6.1532
The commissioner of waters and the Porticus Minucia.

Augustus, *Achievements* 15.1–2; 4
To the Roman plebs, I paid out, man by man, 300 sesterces, according to the will of my father and in my name. When I was consul for the fifth time, I gave 400 sesterces to each man from the spoils of war. Likewise, moreover, in my tenth consulship, from my estate I paid out to each man 400 sesterces as a subsidy. And as consul for the eleventh time, I bought, as an individual, grain and I made twelve distributions of it. With tribunician power for the twelfth time, I gave each man for the third time 400 sesterces. My subsidies never reached less than 250,000 men. During my eighteenth year of tribunician power and consul for the twelfth time, I gave sixty denarii to each of the 320,000 of the urban plebs … As consul for the thirteenth time, I gave sixty denarii to the plebs who were receiving public grain. These were a bit more than 200,000.

Dio, *Roman History* 54.1.3–4
They went to Augustus, begging him to be nominated dictator and at the same time commissioner of the grain, just as Pompey was once. And this second request he accepted out of necessity, and he ordered two men of those who had been generals for five years before to be chosen each year for the distribution of the grain. He did not accept the dictatorship.

Pliny the Younger, *Panegyric* 29
I think that the abundance of grain is like a perpetual subsidy. Care of the grain once gave glory to Pompey, no less than when he expelled bribery from the field, drove out the enemies from the sea, and traversed East and West in triumph. Pompey was not more civil than our father [emperor Trajan], who with wisdom, with determination, with faithfulness, opened roads and harbors, returned paths to the lands, seas to the shores and shores to the sea.

Tacitus, *Annals* 6.13
In the same consulship, the seriousness of the price of grain was nearly approaching insurrection. For a number of days, in the theater, more boldly than was customary toward the emperor, many things were demanded urgently.

# The City at Work and Play:
# Commerce and Leisure

In many ways, Rome was characterized by two opposing concepts that largely align with our modern ideas of commerce and leisure: *negotium* and *otium*. The first term, *negotium*, literally means absence of leisure (*nec/otium*), but might also be translated as business, occupation, or employment. The second, *otium*, in addition to meaning leisure, also encompasses the idea of free time as well as peace, quietness, and even ease. In essence, *otium* was everything *negotium* was not: relaxing, effortless, and enjoyable. Yet even though the amount of time at work or leisure varied considerably depending on socio-economic status, juridical status, gender, and age, it seems most Romans spent their days busy with both. Rome was very much a city that worked and worked hard. Slaves, former slaves, and the urban poor were involved in the production, manufacturing, and commercial transactions that supported the city's economy (**3.1**) as well as its leisure (**3.6**), while members of the upper classes helped the city run through their public service by holding government offices and keeping their hands free from direct participation in trade and commerce (**3.5**). Certain districts in the city were associated with particular types of commerce (**3.1**): the sale of goods from the mundane to the exotic, some brought to the capital via the Tiber (**3.3**) and sold on the street, in markets, or special venues (**3.2, 3.4, 3.19**), and the provision of services largely by slaves or former slaves. Some business transactions blurred the lines between *negotium* and *otium* such as prostitution, for what was one person's means of earning a living was another's leisure (**3.7, 3.8**). Several pastimes such as visiting the baths, attending dinner parties, and browsing for books (**3.9–10, 3.13–18**) also show how *negotium* and *otium* were often just different sides of the same coin depending on one's perspective, since the pleasures of these leisure activities were not possible without the efforts of others from masseurs to cooks to librarians. Yet other ways of enjoying spare time in the city such as gambling (**3.12**) or strolling through gardens and art-filled temples (**3.21–3**) were truly about relaxation alone without relying on the labor of others. And there was something to satisfy everyone's tastes from entertainments open to all during public holidays (**3.11**, and see Chapter Five as well) to literary readings reserved for the select few (**3.20**).

# The city that works

## 3.1 Professions and occupations

This selection of funerary inscriptions reflects the city's commercial character with certain districts linked to the sale of particular products, types of trade, or kinds of services. These short commemorative notices suggest that tradespeople, vendors, and artisans, who were predominantly former slaves, took pride in their job titles and the specific locations within the city where they worked, such as the Sacra Via (see also **8.17** in this volume). They also attest to both the diversity and specificity of occupations, and the wide range of commodities available in Rome from staples such as olive oil to luxury goods like gold or purple-dyed clothing. Although more occupational inscriptions for men survive overall, it is worth highlighting the significant presence of women in the commercial life of the city reflected in the examples here which showcase women working as sellers of foodstuffs, dealers in luxury items, seamstresses, and midwives. When visiting the city today, one finds plenty of individual vendors on the streets and in outdoor and indoor markets selling fruit, flowers, souvenirs, and other merchandise. Some of the modern markets are associated with major sites and topographical features of the ancient city such as the Campagna Amica Market near the Circus Maximus or the Piazza Vittorio Market, which is also known as the Esquilino Market for its original location on the Esquiline Hill.

Further reading: Holleran 2012: 51–61; Joshel 1992: 62–91.

*Corpus of Latin Inscriptions* 6.9718
The bones of Lucius Cluvus, olive oil dealer in the Carinae district and freedman of Lucius Cerdo.

*Corpus of Latin Inscriptions* 6.9822
Gaius Iulius Epaphra, fruit seller in the Circus Maximus, in front of the *pulvinar*,[1] [made this dedication] for himself and his wife Venuleia Helena, freedwoman of Gnaeus, son of Gnaeus.

*Corpus of Latin Inscriptions* 6.9801

Aurelia Nais, freedwoman of Gaius, fishmonger from the Galban warehouse district. Gaius Aurelius Phileros, freedman of Gaius, her patron. Lucius Valerius Secundus, freedman of Lucius.

*Corpus of Latin Inscriptions* 6.9179

Gaius Cacius Heracla, freedman of Gaius, banker in the Esquiline Forum, [made this] for himself and his freedmen and freedwomen.

*Corpus of Latin Inscriptions* 6.9662

Caedicia Syntyche [set this up] for her fellow freed slave Marcus Caedicius Faustus, a banker on the Sacra Via.

*Corpus of Latin Inscriptions* 6.33886

Gaius Tullius Crescens, marble dealer from the Galban warehouse district, made this for himself while still living, and for Tullia Primilla, his dearest fellow freed slave, and for their freedmen and freedwomen and their descendants.

*Corpus of Latin Inscriptions* 6.33914[2]

To the spirits of the dead. Gaius Julius Helius, shoemaker from the Porta Fontinalis, made this for himself; Julia Flaccila, his daughter; and for Gaius Julius Onesimus, his freedman, and his freedwomen and their descendants. He made this while alive.

*Corpus of Latin Inscriptions* 6.9284

Quintus Gavius Primus, freedman of Quintus, sandal-maker from the Subura, lived twenty-five years.

*Corpus of Latin Inscriptions* 14.2433

To Lucius Plutius Eros, freedman of Lucius Plutius, a purple dyer from the Tuscan quarter. Plutia Auge, freedwoman of Lucius, set this up for herself and for Veturia Attica, freedwoman of Gaius and Gaius.

*Corpus of Latin Inscriptions* 6.9673

To the spirits of the dead. For Quintus Fabius Theogonus, seller of paints and unguents who did business on the Esquiline near the statue of Plancus.[3] Fabia Nobilis made this for her excellent patron [who was] incredibly kind towards her, most deserving and devoted, and for herself.

*Corpus of Latin Inscriptions* 6.9214
Sellia Epyre, dressmaker of gold [clothing] on the Sacra Via, [wife of] Quintus Futus Olympicus.

*Corpus of Latin Inscriptions* 6.9221
Lucius Furius Diomedes, freedman of Lucius, stone-engraver from the Sacra Via, [made this] for Cornelia Tertulla, daughter of Lucius, his wife.

*Corpus of Latin Inscriptions* 6.4226
Sacred to the spirits of the dead. Calamus Pamphilianus, slave of Tiberius Claudius Caesar Augustus Germanicus, steward of the Lollian warehouses,[4] gave this gift from his own funds by decree of the town council.

*Corpus of Latin Inscriptions* 6.9664
To the spirits of the dead. Lucius Lepidius Hermes, freedman of Lucius, bronze and iron salesman near the Temple of Fortune at the basin of Ares, and Obellia Threpte made [this dedication] for Lucius Lepidius Hermeros, son of Lucius, of the Palatina tribe, who lived eight years, one month, twenty-two days, and to Lepidia Lucilla, daughter of Lucius, who lived five years, nine days, the sweetest and most dutiful children toward them [i.e., their parents], and to their freedmen and freedwomen and their descendants.

*Corpus of Latin Inscriptions* 6.9671
Gaius Clodius Euphemus, freedman of Gaius, dealer in foodstuffs and wines at the fountain of the Four Scauri in the Velabrum, set up this altar for himself and consecrated and dedicated it to his children and their descendants.

*Corpus of Latin Inscriptions* 6.9683
To the spirits of the dead. Marcus Abudius Luminaris, patron and also husband, made [this tomb] for Abudia Megiste, freedwoman of Marcus, a most pious and well deserving seller of grains and vegetables from the Middle Staircase, and for himself and his freedmen and freedwomen and their descendants, and for his son Marcus Abudius Saturninus, of the senior body of the Esquiline voting tribe, who lived eight years.

*Corpus of Latin Inscriptions* 6.9721
Gaius Grattius Plocamus, freedman of the midwife Hilara from the Esquiline Hill.

---

*Corpus of Latin Inscriptions* 6.9884

Titus Thoranius Salvius, freedman of Titus, [made this tomb] for himself and for his wife Matia Prima, freedwoman of Gaia [and] a seamstress from Six Altars who lived forty-six years.

---

*Corpus of Latin Inscriptions* 6.9891

To the spirits of the dead. To Claudius Bacchylus, [who] lived forty-nine years. Data, dealer in silk, [made this] for her well-deserving husband and fellow slave, and for herself.

---

## 3.2 Taking back the street: an emperor curbs the spread of commerce

The poet Martial reports that in 92 CE, the emperor Domitian (here referred to as Germanicus, an honorific title he took in 84 CE after campaigning against the Chatti in Germany) issued an edict to limit shopkeepers' stalls from protruding too far into the street. He also sought to keep vendors and others, such as barbers, from plying their trades in the middle of the street, which would disrupt the flow of traffic, especially pedestrian traffic, and could be dangerous in the case of barbers in particular. Some "street barbers" were based in *tabernae* (shops) but also used the space in front of their units as additional workspace while others worked from a stool in the street so long as there was a fountain or basin nearby for water.

Further reading: Holleran 2011; Laurence 2011.

---

Martial, *Epigrams* 7.61

The bold peddler had appropriated the entire city and no threshold kept within its own limits. Germanicus, you ordered unimportant quarters of the city to expand and what had just been a footpath has become a road. No pillar is wrapped around with flagons chained together; the praetor is not forced to walk in the midst of mud. A razor is not drawn at random in the middle of a dense crowd, nor does a grimy low-class tavern take over the whole street. The barber, shopkeeper, cook, and butcher stick to their own thresholds. Now it is Rome: recently it was one big shop.

---

## 3.3 The Tiber and commerce at Rome

The Tiber played a critical role in bringing goods to the city of Rome, especially grain to feed the populace, which mainly arrived during the summer months given the Mediterranean's relatively short prime sailing season (see also **1.6** in this volume). A tremendous amount of merchandise came into Rome— products from all over the world, as Pliny the Elder boasts—that had to be brought up the Tiber for storage and sale. Goods were unloaded into the huge warehouses built along the left bank of the Tiber, downstream from the Aventine Hill. This was known as the Emporium district from the wholesale market (*emporium*) that was established in 193 BCE and enhanced in 174 BCE, as Livy records. Eventually the *emporium* extended over 1,000 m along the river with the enormous warehouses of the Porticus Aemilia and Horrea Galbae situated behind in the region southwest of the Aventine. These warehouses (generally called *horrea*) were vast in size, sometimes multi-storied such as the Galban *horrea* (see also mention of this in **3.1** in this volume), which had more than 140 separate storage rooms on the ground floor alone, covering a total area of more than 20,000 m².

Further reading: Aldrete 2007: 134–6; Claridge 2010: 403–4; Coarelli 2014: 345–6; Dyson 2010: 310–13; Holleran 2012: 64–80; Richardson 1992: 143–4, 193.

---

Pliny the Elder, *Natural History* 3.5.53–4

Over 150 miles it [the Tiber] divides Etruria from the Umbrians and Sabines, passing not far from Tifernum, Perugia, and Ocriculum. Then, less than sixteen [Roman] miles from the city, it separates the territory of Veii from that of Crustuminium, then that of Fidenae and Latinum from Vaticanum. But below where the Chiana from Arezzo flows into the Tiber, the latter is increased by forty-two tributaries (the chief ones, moreover, being the Nera and the Severone which itself is navigable and encloses Latium in the rear), yet it is increased no less by the aqueducts and such a great number of springs carried through into the city. For that reason, it is fit for ships from the Mediterranean as large as you please, and is the most peaceful trafficker of products in the whole world—nearly it alone is inhabited and overlooked by more villas than the rest of the rivers in all the lands.

---

Livy, *History of Rome* 35.10.12

That year [193 BCE], the aedileship of Marcus Aemilius Lepidus and Lucius Aemilius Paulus was notable. They condemned many people grazing their cattle on public lands which they had not leased; from that money, they set up gilded shields on the roof of the Temple of Jupiter, built a porticus outside the Porta Trigemina, added an emporium near the Tiber, and constructed another porticus from the Porta Fontinalis to the altar of Mars where the road led into the Campus Martius.

---

Livy, *History of Rome* 41.27.8
And outside the Porta Trigemina, they [Quintus Fulvius Flaccus and Aulus Postumius Albinus, the censors of 174 BCE] paved the emporium with stone and enclosed it with a fence, and they arranged for the porticus of Aemilius to be repaired, and they built a staircase from the Tiber to the emporium.

## 3.4 Rome's many markets

Rome boasted many commercial markets where a variety of commodities could be bought and sold. In his discussion of the etymology of locations within the city, Varro claims that originally each market was designated a *forum* along with an adjective that specified the particular items available there. The establishment in 179 BCE of a central *macellum* (the city's very large food market during the Republican period) absorbed many of these specialized markets, bringing them together into one place. Rome is still a city of many markets and has both bustling open-air and covered markets today, small and large, such as the one in Campo dei Fiori, which has been in existence since the late 1860s. Here you can buy the fixings for dinner including fresh fish, vegetables, and spices, as well as kitchen utensils and a tablecloth for cooking and serving the meal!

Further reading: Dyson 2010: 249–52; Holleran 2012: 93–8, 160–72; Richardson 1992: 162–5, 240–1.

Varro, *On the Latin Language* 5.146
The place to which they would bring their disputes, and where they would bring the things they wished to sell, they called a *forum*. Where things of one type were brought, an epithet was added from that type, as in the *Forum Boarium* [Cattle Market], the *Forum Holitorium* [Vegetable Market]: this was the old *macellum* where masses of vegetables [were brought] … Along the Tiber, near the Temple of Portunus, they call it the *Forum Piscarium* [Fish Market]; thus Plautus says, "At the *Forum Piscarium*."[5] Where things of various kinds are sold at the Cornelian cherry grove is the *Forum Cuppedinis* [Market of Delicacies], from the Latin *cuppedium*, delicacy, that is from *fastidium*, excessive nicety, which many call the *Forum Cupidinis* [Market of Greed] from *cupiditas*, greed.

## 3.5 Elite attitudes about working to make a living

Tradespeople and artisans appear to have taken pride in their professional identities, yet some elite thinkers disparaged the services these individuals provided, which literally made the city work, because they believed paid employment, especially manual labor, was sordid. Members of the elite, such as Cicero, prized landowning and public service as honorable ways for noble Romans to spend their time and contribute to society. Some could live off the income from their estates (some of which were productive agricultural estates) and other investments in real estate such as the immensely wealthy Marcus Crassus who shrewdly bought up buildings destroyed by fire cheaply then presumably redeveloped the land and sold for considerable profit (see **10.9** in this volume). Cicero, too, made money from real estate in the city of Rome and elsewhere, and seems not to have had great concern for the wellbeing of his tenants or properties, some of which he reports (*Letters to Atticus* 14.9) were structurally unsound or had already collapsed (cf. **2.13** and **10.8** in this volume).

Further reading: Balsdon 1969: 130–5; Frier 1980: 21–34; Joshel 1992: 62–91.

Cicero, *On Duties* 1.50–1

Now concerning occupations and means of earning a livelihood, which should be considered suitable for a gentleman and which are lowly, we have generally accepted these. First, those means of earning a livelihood are rejected which incur people's hatred: those of harbor-tax collectors and moneylenders. Moreover, not becoming to a gentleman and lowly are the means of earning a livelihood of all hired workmen whose labor, not skill, is what is paid for: indeed, for these men their very wage is a contract of servitude. Men who buy from merchants to sell the goods immediately must also be considered lowly, for they would not profit at all unless they completely lied [about prices] and indeed there is nothing more vile than misrepresentation. All mechanics are involved in vulgar trades, for a workshop cannot possess anything gentlemanly. These trades that should be least approved of are those that provide for pleasures: "Fishmongers, butchers, cooks, poulterers, and fishermen," as Terence says.[6] Add to these, if you please, perfumers, dancers, and the entire variety show troupe. However, in those occupations in which either greater intelligence resides or for which a considerable societal benefit is sought, such as medicine, architecture, and the teaching of noble pursuits, these are respectable for those whose ranks they suit. Moreover, trade, if it is on a small scale, ought to be considered lowly; but if it is on a large scale and well-funded, importing many things from all parts of the world and distributing to many without misrepresentation, then it should not altogether be reproached.

## 3.6 Labor for leisure

Considerable labor was required to enable and facilitate the leisure others enjoyed both at home and in public, so *otium* was never entirely divorced from *negotium*. This sample of epitaphs, dating mainly from the first and second centuries CE, reflects some of the workers who made leisure activities outside the home possible such as actors, charioteers and others involved in the theater and the games (cf. **3.10** and **3.15** in this volume, and see Chapter Five generally on entertainment at the circuses, theaters, and amphitheaters). It is worth noting the young age of some of these individuals who most likely would have begun working in childhood whether they were slaves or freed persons, a situation that is paralleled in domestic contexts where we find many slave children at work.

Further reading: Bradley 1991: 103–24; Dalby 2000: 209–42; Joshel 1992: 73–6.

---

*Corpus of Latin Inscriptions* 6.9935
Publius Curius Euporus, flute-maker from the Sacra Via.

---

*Corpus of Latin Inscriptions* 6.10078
I, Florus, lie here, a child driver of a two-horse chariot, who, while I longed [to race] my chariot quickly, quickly fell to the shades [of the dead]. Ianuarius [made this] for his sweetest foster child.

---

*Corpus of Latin Inscriptions* 6.8583
To the spirits of the dead. To Tiberius Claudius Speclator, imperial freedman, procurator at Formi, Fundi, and Caieta, procurator at Laurentum[7] of the [emperor's] elephants. Cornelia Bellica [dedicated this] to her well-deserving husband.

---

*Corpus of Latin Inscriptions* 6.9794
Publius Cornelius Philomusus, freedman of Lucius, scene painter and also contractor, made this monument placed here for Cornelia Lycce, freedwoman of Publius, a chaste freedwoman eighteen years old buried here, and for himself and his family and their descendants.

---

*Corpus of Latin Inscriptions* 6.10106
Sleep! To Claudia Hermiona, chief mime actress of her time. Her heirs [made this monument].

---

---

*Corpus of Latin Inscriptions* 6.10111
Luria Privata, mime actress, lived nineteen years. Bleptus made [this].

---

*Corpus of Latin Inscriptions* 6.10114[8]
Marcus Ulpius Apolaustus, freedman of the emperor, the greatest of pantomimes, crowned twelve times [in competitions] against pantomimes and all [other] theater actors.

---

# Sex and the city

## 3.7 Accusations of an empress's double-life

Prostitution was legal in Rome both for the women and men who sold their bodies for money and for customers who paid for sex, though there were stigmas associated with working in the sex trade and likewise visiting brothels, especially if with regularity. In public, female prostitutes were readily identifiable by their prescribed attire: the man's toga, which advertised their transgression of traditional gender roles and status as quasi-masculine, and their bleached or dyed hair. Neither their appearance nor the places they worked were glamorous, including the brothel or *lupanar* (related to *lupa*, "she-wolf"). A brothel that survives at Pompeii had several small rooms or cubicles side by side, each equipped with a bed and decorated with small frescoes depicting scenes of heterosexual sex. In his well-known sixth satire condemning marriage and vilifying wives, Juvenal portrays the empress Messalina nightly forsaking her noble status as wife of the emperor Claudius and mother of the prince Britannicus to satisfy her lust in a common brothel. Though there may be little historical truth regarding Messalina's actions, Juvenal's description of the brothel as dank and dirty is probably accurate.

Further reading: Knapp 2011: 236–64; McGinn 1998: 169–70; McGinn 2013: 369–88; Toner 1995: 102–16.

---

Juvenal, *Satires* 6.115–32
Do you worry what happened in a private household, what Eppia did? Look at the rivals of the gods,[9] hear what Claudius endured. When his wife sensed that her husband was asleep, she used to leave with no more than a single maid as her companion. The whore-empress dared to put on a nighttime hood and prefer a mat to her bedroom

in the imperial palace. With a blond wig concealing her black hair so, she entered the warm brothel with its old curtain and an empty cubicle—her very own. Then, naked, with her nipples gilded, she prostituted herself under the pseudonym She-Wolf and showed off your belly, noble-born Britannicus. She greeted men enticingly as they entered and asked for her fee. Then, when the pimp was already dismissing his girls, she left sad, and yet she was the last to close up her cubicle, the best she could do, still burning, her hard genitals excessively swollen. Exhausted by the men but not yet satisfied, she departed. Filthy, with cheeks blackened from the smoke of the lamp, and befouled, she brought the stench of the brothel to the emperor's couch.

## 3.8 The state and the sex trade in the third century CE

In 40 CE, the emperor Caligula instituted a tax on prostitutes which was innovative at the time for Rome, though a similar tax had long existed in Egypt and several Greek cities including Athens, Cos, and Syracuse. The tax remained in effect for over four centuries, even under Christian emperors who were embarrassed by it because the state had become dependent on the revenue it generated. Some scholars question whether later pagan emperors genuinely felt unease about the tax, as is suggested in the second passage, which comes from the biography of the early third-century CE emperor Severus Alexander. Since the specific authors of such biographies of later emperors are not certain, the collective name *Scriptores Historiae Augustae* (SHA) or writers of the *Augustan History* is used. The biographies contain a mixture of historical facts and colorful but dubious anecdotes that often highlight the emperors' fondness for luxury and debauchery, and illustrate their poor administration of the state. In these two excerpts, the contrast is startling between Elagabalus's unorthodox and seemingly outrageous treatment of prostitutes and the approach of his successor, Severus Alexander. It is worth noting that many important buildings in the cityscape were the usual haunts of prostitutes who did not work only in brothels.

Further reading: McGinn 1998: 248–87; Toner 1995: 102–16.

SHA, *Life of Elagabalus* 26.3–5
He gathered together into a public building all the female prostitutes from the Circus, the theater, the stadium, all [other] places, and from the baths, and delivered a speech to them, as if he were a military man, calling them fellow soldiers, and he argued his point of view about kinds of positions and pleasures. Afterwards, he invited to a similar meeting pimps, male prostitutes collected from everywhere, and the most dissolute slave boys and youths. And although he had come out to meet the female prostitutes

dressed in women's clothes, baring his breasts, to meet the male prostitutes he dressed in the garb of boys who sell themselves for sex. After his speech, he announced an imperial largesse of three *aurei* each, just as is given to soldiers, and asked that they pray to the gods so that they might find others to commend to him.

---

SHA, *Life of Alexander* 24.3
He forbade the taxes imposed on pimps, female prostitutes, and male prostitutes from being deposited into the sacred state treasury, but assigned them to the public expenditures for the restoration of the theater [of Marcellus], the Circus, the Amphitheater, and the Stadium.[10]

---

# The pleasures and perils of the baths

## 3.9 Differing opinions on the baths: pleasures we love—and hate

Visiting the baths was an integral part of daily life as this funerary inscription for a former slave of the imperial household, dated to the Julio-Claudian period, shows. In the age of Augustus, Rome had 170 bathhouses, a combination of large, public complexes (*thermae*) and numerous small, private establishments (*balneae*) that charged modest entrance fees; by the fourth century CE, the city boasted nearly nine hundred facilities. The baths were for relaxing, exercising, socializing, and much more as Seneca's vivid portrait conveys. Given his wealth, it is highly unlikely that he actually lived above a bathing establishment as he claims, but he nevertheless provides a valuable account of the typical activities that took place there. Despite his complaints, he no doubt frequented the baths himself, as they were a central institution in Roman society.

Further reading: Balsdon 1969: 26–32; Fagan 2011a; Yegül 2010.

---

*Corpus of Latin Inscriptions* 6.15258
He lived fifty-two years. To the sacred spirits of Tiberius Claudius Secundus. Here he has everything with him. Baths, wine, and sex ruin our bodies, but baths, wine, and sex make life. Merope, the freedwoman of Caesar, set up [this tomb] for her dear companion, and also for herself, her household, and their descendants.

---

Seneca, *Letters* 56.1–2
May I die if silence is as much a necessity as it seems for a man who has retreated into his studies. Look, all sorts of noises surround me on all sides: I am living above

a very bathhouse! Now, imagine for yourself all the types of sounds that can make the ears the object of hatred. When the strongmen are exercising and toss about their arms heavy with lead weights, when they either are exerting themselves or pretending to, I hear their grunts, and whenever they have let out the breath they've been holding in, I hear their wheezing and harsh exhalations. When I run into some lazy guy who is satisfied with a cheap rubdown, I hear the clap of the hand hitting his shoulders; the sound changes as the hand comes down flat or cupped. But if the scorekeeper for the ballgame comes along and begins to count the balls, it's all over. Now, add in the guy who picks fights and the thief caught red-handed and the man who likes to hear his own voice in the baths. Then add those guys who jump into the pool with a huge splash as they hit the water. Besides those whose voices are, if nothing else, proper, think about the armpit hair plucker with his shrill, high-pitched voice (so that he'll be better noticed) repeatedly testing his lungs and he's never silent except when he's plucking armpits and forcing someone else to cry out instead of him! Then you hear the various calls of the drink vendor and the sausage seller and the confectioner and all the hawkers from the pubs, each selling his wares with his own distinctive intonation.

## 3.10 Severus Alexander's public works: bath complexes

Following Marcus Agrippa's sponsorship of the first of Rome's great bath complexes (*thermae*) on the Campus Martius in the 20s BCE, several emperors built lavish establishments in various parts of the city including Nero, also on the Campus near the Pantheon, and Titus and Trajan, who located their facilities near the Colosseum. In 227 CE, Severus Alexander rebuilt and expanded Nero's baths (*thermae Neronianae*), after which they were renamed in his honor. The new complex, which measured approximately 190 m by 120 m, included a large swimming pool, various bathing rooms ranging from a cold room to a hot, sauna-like room, and exercise yards (*palaestrae*). The monumental remains of the Baths of Caracalla, which Severus Alexander likely also completed, are situated beyond the Porta Capena near the Via Appia and can still be visited today (see Fig. 3.1). The changing room attendant commemorated in this brief epitaph, who was employed at the Baths of Caracalla, would have overseen the room where bathers left their clothes, though sometimes at their own peril since theft of bathers' clothing was apparently a perennial problem at bathhouses.

Further reading: Claridge 2010: 357–65; Coarelli 2014: 327–31; Richardson 1992: 387–9; Yegül 2010.

**Figure 3.1** Remains of the Baths of Caracalla. Photo credit: Manuel Cohen/Art Resource, NY.

---

SHA, *Life of Alexander* 25.3–7

He restored the works of earlier emperors, and he himself founded many new ones. Among these were the baths named after him (Thermae Alexandrianae), which were adjacent to what had been the Neronian Baths (Thermae Neronianae), and the aqueduct, which even now is called Alexandriana. Once his baths were built, he planted a grove of trees nearby where private houses had been which he had purchased then demolished. He was the first of the emperors to call one bathtub "the Ocean" since Trajan had not done this, but had assigned his bathtubs names for the days of the week. He completed and decorated the Baths of Antoninus Caracalla, adding colonnades to it.

---

*Corpus of Latin Inscriptions* 6.9232

Cucumio and Victoria made this for themselves while living; he was the changing room attendant at the Baths of Caracalla.

---

# Holidays and popular pastimes

## 3.11 Public holidays

Numerous days in the Roman calendar were holidays that featured *ludi* (games or shows) consisting of chariot racing, theatrical performances, gladiatorial contests, and wild animal hunts (see Chapter Five generally). The number of days devoted to *ludi* steadily grew from fifty-seven at the beginning of the first century BCE to seventy-seven in the age of Augustus, then as many as 177 by the mid-third century CE. Ovid's poem titled *Fasti*, which proceeds day-by-day through the first six months of the year, describes many religious festivals which had *ludi*, some lasting for several days such as those in honor of the goddess Magna Mater (see **6.13** in this volume). While some holidays were for the whole populace, others were for specific groups of people. Here he mentions lesser-known games held on June 7 called the *Ludi Piscatorii* or Fishermen's Games, which were celebrated by men who worked in the Tiber as divers and fishermen. The references in the opening lines to the constellations Boötes and Ursa Major reflect the poet's interest in astrological lore.

Further reading: Balsdon 1969: 244–329.

Ovid, *Fasti* 6.235–40
The third Phoebe after the Nones[11] is said to remove Lycaon, and Ursa does not fear from behind. At that time I remember watching *ludi* on the grass of the Campus and they were said to be yours, flowing Tiber. They are the feast days for the men who drag dripping nets and cover their bronze fishing hooks with bits of food.

## 3.12 Augustus's penchant for gambling

For relaxation, Romans of all ages and classes enjoyed a variety of games of skill and chance. Gambling was technically illegal except during the Saturnalia festival in December, which Suetonius refers to in his description of the emperor Augustus's fondness for dice games. There appears to have been little enforcement of the law, however, and gambling was ubiquitous and remained popular across the social spectrum. Gaming tables have been found scratched into the pavement of several central locations including the Forum, Basilica Julia, Colosseum, the entrance to the Temple of Venus and Rome, even in the house of the Vestal Virgins on the Palatine—and some of these, though faded over time, can still be seen today. Not surprisingly, taverns were regular spots for gaming and gambling, while many also played in the privacy of their houses, especially after or even during meals, as Suetonius also records Augustus doing. The most common items used were dice (*tesserae*) thrown in threes, and knucklebones (*tali*) thrown in fours. Knucklebones, the small bones found in the leg of most four-legged animals between the shin and the ankle, were oblong with four sides, two wider and two narrower, and rounded at the two ends. The Romans identified each of the four flat sides on a knucklebone as plain, convex, concave, or twisted, and assigned it a corresponding number (1, 3, 4, 6 respectively). The top throw was a Venus, which meant that each of the four knucklebones showed a different face, while the lowest was the "dog" in which all ones were thrown.

Further reading: Balsdon 1969: 154–9; Toner 1995: 89–101; Trifilò 2011.

Suetonius, *Augustus* 71.2–4

He was in no way disturbed by the rumor that he gambled, and he played openly and publicly for amusement, even when he was an old man and outside of the month of December, on other holidays and ordinary working days too. There is no doubt about this, for in a letter in his own handwriting he says, "I dined, my dear Tiberius, with the same men; Vinicius and the elder Silius were also dinner guests. During dinner, both yesterday and today, we played like old men; for when the dice were thrown, whoever had thrown a 'dog' or a six, put a denarius into the middle for each of the dice, and whoever had thrown a Venus collected the whole pot." And again in another letter he wrote, "My dear Tiberius, we spent the Quinquatria festival[12] pleasantly enough, for we played all day long and kept the gaming-board warm. Your brother made a big fuss about his success, though in the end he didn't lose much, but from substantial losses and beyond hope, little by little he won back. For my part, I lost 2,000 sesterces since I had been extravagantly generous in my play, as I'm generally accustomed to be. For if I had exacted from each the stakes, which I let go, or if I had kept what I had given to each, I should have won 50,000. But I prefer it this way, for my generosity will carry me to heavenly glory." To his daughter he writes, "I sent you 250 denarii, which is the amount I had given to each of my dinner guests if they wished to play amongst themselves either at dice or 'odd and even' during dinner."

## 3.13 Dinners

A staple of Roman social life was dining with others, either for a simple dinner (*cena*) or a more elaborate dinner party (*convivium*). At the parties of the wealthy, poetry readings, theatrical performances, and live musicians such as flute players and dancers could entertain the guests, but the food was a major focus. The Romans were passionate about their food and drink, and some wealthy hosts spared no expense in order to serve expensive and exotic delicacies aimed at impressing their guests. Lower on the social scale, dinners and dinner invitations were common themes for some Roman poets who, given their socio-economic circumstances, were probably in a better position generally to accept offers for dinner than to extend them themselves. Catullus presents himself as lacking the means to host a proper dinner so asks his friend to come with not just the meal itself, but the whole party. Martial, paying homage to Catullus in the opening line of his poem, draws on similar ideas. He invites his guest to a dinner that consists of the sorts of foods one could typically buy as snacks at a bathhouse followed by fare he cannot afford to serve but will mention to convince his friend to come. Among these items some are local such as the cheese purchased in the Velabrum, a commercial district southwest of the Roman Forum, while others are from elsewhere in Italy and perhaps beyond. As any modern visitor to Rome knows, the city is a great place for eating whether for a slice of pizza or a gelato while standing around on the street or a multi-course dinner that lasts long into the night.

Further reading: Balsdon 1969: 32–53; Dunbabin and Slater 2011; Gowers 1993.

---

Catullus, *Poem* 13

You will dine well, dear Fabullus, at my place in a few days, if the gods favor you, if you've brought with you a good and large dinner, not forgetting a dazzling girl and wine and wit and all kinds of laughter. If, I say, you've brought these things, my charming friend, you will dine well: for the moneybag of your Catullus is full of cobwebs! But in return you'll get pure love, or something sweeter and more refined: for I'll offer perfume, which the goddesses and gods of love have bestowed upon my girl. When you smell it, you'll ask the gods, Fabullus, to make you all nose.

---

Martial, *Epigrams* 11.52

You will dine nicely at my place, Julius Cerialis: if you have no better offer, come. You will be able to keep the eighth hour; we will bathe together—you know how close Stephanus's baths are to me. First, you'll be given lettuce (useful for moving the bowels), and leek shoots, then an aged tuna that is larger than a small Spanish mackerel but garnished with eggs and rue leaves. Other eggs, roasted over a low flame, won't be lacking, and a lump of smoked cheese from the Velabrum district, and olives that have felt the frost at Picenum. These are enough for appetizers. Do you want to know the rest? I'll lie so that you'll come: fish, shellfish, sow's udder, and fattened birds from the poultry yard and the marsh, which not even Stella normally serves except for a very special dinner. I promise you more: I won't recite anything to you, although you yourself may read your *Giants* right through, or your poems on the countryside, second to immortal Vergil's.

---

## Literate leisure: Rome's libraries and bookshops

### 3.14 Rome's intellectual legacy and the city's first public library

According to Suetonius (*Julius Caesar* 44.2), Julius Caesar had plans to build a public library in Rome and to commission Marcus Varro, a leading scholar of the time (and the author of **3.4** above), to collect and classify Greek and Latin works for the new building. The assassination of Caesar in 44 BCE ended these plans, but some time after 39 BCE, Asinius Pollio, one of Caesar's supporters and a respected author in his own right, undertook a similar project and established Rome's first public library. Built from the spoils of his successful military campaigns against the Illyrians, Pollio's library was located just off the Forum and featured sections for Greek and Latin works. Statues of famous authors adorned the building, including one of Marcus Varro, a living author, which was an unusual gesture as Pliny the Elder reports amid his discussion of different ways eminent Roman authors such as Ennius and Vergil were honored.

Further reading: Casson 2001: 79–81; Marshall 1976: 261–3; Richardson 1992: 59.

---

Pliny the Elder, *Natural History* 7.30.115

In the library at Rome founded for public use by Asinius Pollio, which was the first in the world built from the spoils of war, a statue was set up of one living man alone: Marcus Varro. That this was done by a leading orator and citizen, bringing glory to one individual from the well-known multitude of men of intellectual renown at that time, was no less an honor, I truly believe, than when Pompey the Great gave a naval crown to the same Varro for his achievements in the war with the pirates.

## 3.15 Latin and Greek libraries in the Temple of Apollo

Among Augustus's many building projects were libraries for Greek and Latin works built in conjunction with the Temple of Apollo on the Palatine. The books were originally housed in a single chamber that may have been preceded by a colonnade; remodeling completed under Domitian resulted in two identical, adjacent apsidal halls. Although some have suggested one hall housed works in Latin and the other in Greek, there is no conclusive evidence for organization by language in this fashion. Like Pollio's library, the Palatine Library also had images of distinguished authors. Gaius Julius Hyginus, Augustus's freedman, was the library's first librarian. Subsequent librarians took pride in holding these posts as the inscription below for a freedman of the emperor Caligula suggests.

Further reading: Casson 2001: 81–4; Nicholls 2010; Richardson 1992: 59.

Suetonius, *Augustus* 29.1, 29.3

He built many public works from which these are notable: his Forum with the Temple of Mars Ultor; the Temple of Apollo on the Palatine; and the Temple of Jupiter Tonans (Jupiter the Thunderer) on the Capitol … He erected the Temple of Apollo in that part of his house on the Palatine which the diviners declared the god had desired because it had been struck by lightning. He added a porticus to it with Latin and Greek libraries, and when he was growing older, he often also held Senate meetings there and reviewed the lists of jurors.

*Corpus of Latin Inscriptions* 6.5188

Alexander Pylaemenianus, slave of Gaius Caesar Augustus Germanicus, in charge of the Greek library in the Temple of Apollo. He lived thirty years.

## 3.16 Reading for pleasure from Rome's lending libraries on the Palatine

Members of the upper classes enjoyed reading literature of various sorts during their leisure but did not or could not always own works of interest themselves. In this letter from the future emperor Marcus Aurelius to Marcus Fronto, his teacher of rhetoric and very close friend, he reports to Fronto on how he spent part of a day while outside the city of Rome lounging and reading items he had borrowed from one of Rome's public libraries. He imagines Fronto at Rome wishing to read exactly the same things and so dispatching a slave to acquire them first in the Library of Apollo on the Palatine, then to the library housed in the Domus Tiberiana, the palace where Marcus lived, which was also on the Palatine.

Further reading: Marshall 1976: 261–3; Richardson 1992: 136–7.

Marcus Cornelius Fronto, *To Marcus, Caesar* 4.5.2

We set out for the hunt, we did brave deeds—we heard a report that the boars had been captured for indeed there was no opportunity for seeing them. Yet we climbed a steep enough hill; then in the afternoon we retreated home. I took myself back to my little books. So with boots dragged off, clothes put aside, I lingered on the couch for about two hours. I read the elder Cato's speech *On the Property of Pulchra*, and another in which he accused a tribune. "Hey," you are saying to your slave boy, "Go as fast as you can! Bring me back these speeches from the Library of Apollo." You send him in vain, for those books have also followed me. You have to work on the librarian at the Tiberian Library; something's going to have to be spent on this, which he can share with me—equal parts for each—when I come back to Rome.

## 3.17 Chance discoveries in Rome's libraries

Libraries in Rome could be places for both learning and socializing for the intellectually and socially elite as this passage from Aulus Gellius suggests. The library he refers to was in the Forum Ulpium (also known as the Forum of Trajan), dedicated in 112/113 CE, and consisted of a pair of small rectangular buildings located on either side of the Column of Trajan. As was standard for Rome's libraries, Trajan's library contained works by both Greek and Latin authors, and apparently non-literary materials as well in the form of government records such as the old praetorian edicts Gellius and his friend examined (for problems with flooding and efforts to maintain Rome's waterways, see **10.6** and **10.12** in this volume).

Further reading: Casson 2001: 84–8, 98–101; Claridge 2010: 186; Marshall 1976: 263; Richardson 1992: 177–8.

---

Aulus Gellius, *Attic Nights* 11.17.1

By chance I was sitting in the library in the Temple of Trajan and looking for something when the edicts of the praetors of olden days fell into my hands, so I gladly read and got to know them. Then, in a certain earlier edict, I found it written thus: "If anyone of those who have taken public contracts for clearing the rivers of nets [*flumina retanda*] will be brought to me, he will be accused because he had not done what his contract stipulated he ought to do." Accordingly, we wanted to know what "clearing of nets" was. A friend of mine sitting with us said that he had read in the seventh books of Gavius's *On the Origin of Words* that the trees which either projected from the river banks or stood out in the beds of the rivers were called *retae*, and were named from the word for "nets" [*retes*], because they impeded boats passing by and almost netted them [*inretirent*]. For that reason he thought that it was customary to contract out for the rivers "to be cleared of nets," that is cleaned out, so that there was neither any delay nor danger for boats unexpectedly encountering such branches.

---

## 3.18 Bookshops

Books were part of the world of luxury in Rome, a commodity primarily destined for the hands of the elite, although some, like Cicero (*Letters to Quintus* 3.4.5), disdained commercial booksellers and preferred to rely on their own educated slaves and freedmen instead to acquire desired texts. Books do not seem to have been sold with other items but instead were available in indoor shops dedicated to the sale of books alone. Many bookshops were located in the city center off the Roman Forum, which was also in close proximity to four of the most important libraries in Rome: the library of Pollio across from the Forum (see **3.14** in this volume); the library in the Temple of Apollo on the Palatine Hill; the library in the Temple of Peace situated at the northeast corner of the Forum, which Martial mentions below; and Trajan's library in the Forum of Trajan (see **3.17** in this volume). The Vicus Sandaliarius, where Galen notes bookshops were concentrated, was northeast of the Temple of Peace. There appears to have been a regular demand among the elite for books for personal use and to stock both private and public libraries. Not unlike today, Roman bookshops were also places that encouraged customers to browse and linger, even socialize.

Further reading: Casson 2001: 104–6; Marshall 1976: 253–4; White 2009.

---

Martial, *Epigrams* 1.2
You who long for my little books to be with you wherever you are and wish to have them as companions on a long journey, buy these which the parchment confines in short pages. Give your book boxes to the large volumes: a single hand holds me. Yet, so you're not unaware of where I'm on sale and wander the whole city aimlessly, look for Secundus, the freedman of the learned Lucensis, behind the entrance to the Temple of Peace and the Forum of Pallas.[13]

---

Galen, *preface to My Own Books* (Kühn 19.8)
In the Vicus Sandaliarius, where the greatest number of bookshops in Rome is located, I spotted some men arguing whether a book being sold was mine or someone else's, for it was inscribed, "Galen the doctor." One declared it mine, but one of the scholars, disturbed by the unusualness of the inscription, wanted to see the introduction. After reading the first two lines, he immediately threw the text aside and announced, "This is not Galen's style, and this book has been falsely inscribed."

---

# Different tastes

## 3.19 High-end shopping in the Saepta Iulia

In the early empire, one of the main areas for buying and trading in luxury goods such as jewelry, gemstones, fine furniture, and special domestic slaves, was the Saepta Iulia located on the Campus Martius just east of the Pantheon and the Baths of Agrippa. This very large rectangular enclosure (310 m long and 120 m wide), with colonnades on its two long sides, was planned by Julius Caesar but finished and dedicated by Marcus Agrippa in 26 BCE. The Saepta was originally intended as the voting place for two of the assemblies (see **7.3** in this volume), but under the Julio-Claudian emperors it was used for staging gladiatorial shows and gymnastic competitions. By Martial's day, it was *the* place to go for purchasing, or at least perusing, high-end items. He offers a vivid description of one character who spends the entire day strolling the Saepta: he ogles attractive slave boys and expensive works of art all the while assuming the air of a connoisseur, but at the end of the day he only buys two cheap wine cups and does not even have a slave attending him to carry the purchases home!

Further reading: Holleran 2012: 249–52; Richardson 1992: 340–1.

---

Martial, *Epigrams* 9.59

Mamurra, often wandering in the Saepta and for a long time, here where golden Rome wastes her wealth, inspected pretty boys and devoured them with his eyes—not those whom the outer stalls exposed publicly for sale, but those whom the floor of a secret sales platform reserves and neither the people see nor a crowd of one—me—sees. Then, satisfied, he uncovered square tables and round tabletops which had been covered up, and demanded the oily ivory table legs displayed on a high shelf; and, after measuring four times a dinner-couch for six inlaid with tortoise-shell, he sighed that it was not sufficient for his citrus-wood table. He relied on his nose to determine whether the bronzes smelled of Corinth,[14] and condemned even your statues, Polyclitus. Complaining that the crystal was marred by a tiny bit of ordinary glass, he put his mark on ten murrine vessels and set them aside. He weighed antique wine goblets and if any were cups made famous by Mentor's craftsmanship, and he counted the emeralds set in the embossed gold and every rather large pearl jingling from a snowy-white earlobe. He sought out genuine sardonyxes on every table and made an offer on large pieces of jasper. When, at the end of the day, he was now departing exhausted, he bought two cups for an *as* and carried them off himself!

## 3.20 Poetry readings

Readings or recitations of poetry, as well as prose works, written in Latin or Greek, were a common part of upper-class culture in the late Republic and throughout the Empire. Readings took place in a variety of settings such as auditoriums and temples, and frequently in the homes of the wealthy, including in their gardens, as Juvenal envisages. Sometimes these were large, public gatherings, other times more intimate affairs with the guests primarily friends of the author. Both Juvenal and Pliny the Younger suggest there was an expectation, perhaps even an obligation, to attend recitations and so a number of reluctant listeners could be found in any audience. Each author takes a different approach, however, to the theme of attending recitations. Where Pliny is critical of the behavior of others invited and seems to feel not merely attending but being attentive is necessary, Juvenal is hostile to the entire endeavor and deeply critical of the poets themselves. In the opening lines of his poem, the satirist is setting up his later justification for choosing to write satire rather than other genres of poetry; he dismisses epic, drama, and elegy in turn, and complains particularly about mythological epic with several references to the story of Jason and the Argonauts, which Valerius Flaccus had retold not long before in his *Argonautica,* probably composed in the 70s CE.

Further reading: Fantham 1996; White 1993.

---

Juvenal, *Satire* 1.1–14

Will I always be only a listener? Will I never get my revenge after being tortured so often by hoarse Cordus's epic *Theseus*? Just let it go, then, while that one is reciting for me his Roman comedies and this one his elegies? Just let it go, when an enormous *Telephus* has wasted the day, or an *Orestes* written on the back when the margin at the end of the roll is already full and not yet finished? His own house is not better known to anyone than the grove of Mars and the cave of Vulcan neighboring the Aeolian cliffs are to me. What the winds are doing, which ghosts Aeacus is tormenting, where the other guy is carrying off that stolen golden mini-fleece, what size the mountain ash trees are that Monychus hurled: Fronto's plane trees and his battered marble constantly cry out, and his columns shattered by the unceasing reciter. You're in store for precisely the same thing from the most distinguished poet—and the least.

---

Pliny the Younger, *Letters* 1.13

Gaius Plinius sends greetings to Sosius Senecio. This year has brought forth a large crop of poets: in the entire month of April there was hardly a day when someone was not giving a recitation. I am glad that literary studies are flourishing, that people's talents are coming to light and showing themselves, although people are slow to assemble for an audience. Most of them sit around in the public spaces in the house and while away the time for listening with stories; from time to time they demand that they be told whether the reader has already come in, whether he has read the introduction, whether he has unrolled the scroll quite far.[15] Now at last they arrive—and even then slowly and with hesitation, and yet they don't stay but disappear before the end, some discretely and stealthily, others openly and boldly. Well, people say that, in our parents' recollection, the emperor Claudius Caesar was taking a stroll on the Palatine when he heard a shout and asked what the cause was: when he was told that Nonianus was giving a recitation, he arrived suddenly and unexpectedly during the reading. Nowadays, anyone with a lot of spare time on his hands, though he was asked long before and reminded again and again, either does not come or, if he does come, complains that he has lost the whole day (because he has not lost it). But they must be praised and commended so much more, those whose enthusiasm for writing and giving recitations is not slowed down either by the apathy or the arrogance of the listeners. Truly I have failed almost no one. To be sure, those giving recitations were generally friends; for there is hardly anyone who is fond of literature and not fond of me at the same time. For these reasons, I have spent longer in the city than I had intended. Now I can return to my place of retirement and write something; I won't recite it so that I don't seem to those whose recitations I attended that I was there not as a listener but a lender, for as in other matters, so in the obligation of being a listener, the favor is wasted if it is demanded in return. Farewell.

## 3.21 Temples as galleries of artistic treasures

Roman temples had many functions, including providing space for the display of art. Some served as ancient equivalents to modern art galleries or museums and became tourist attractions for visitors to Rome just as today many come to the city to see art from antiquity to the present day on display in museums and other venues. It was not uncommon for conquering generals to dedicate the artistic plunder they acquired on campaign to temples in Rome, as Livy describes Marcus Marcellus doing, and even to construct a new building for these and other purposes, as Josephus tells us Vespasian did with his Temple of Peace, dedicated in 75 CE. On the aftermath of Marcellus's capture of Syracuse in 212 BCE, Livy reports that Marcellus transported great artworks to Rome to be set up in the Temples of *Honos* and *Virtus* (Honor and Virtue) located on the Appian Way; but he is critical of Marcellus, suggesting that his transfer of Sicily's artistic treasures to Rome paved the way for stripping temples of their art in the future such that by the time Livy was writing at the end of the first century, few of Marcellus's acquisitions could still be seen. Much later, Josephus lauds the emperor Vespasian's new Temple of Peace which concentrated masterpieces previously scattered about in a single place, and housed fine ornaments from the Jewish temple in Jerusalem following its capture by Vespasian in 71 CE. The Temple of Peace, which also contained a public library, was considered by some ancient Romans to be one of the most beautiful buildings in Rome (see **10.4** in this volume).

Further reading: Edwards and Woolf 2003; Miles 2008; Richardson 1992: 190, 286–7; Rutledge 2012.

Livy, *History of Rome* 25.40.1–3

But while these things were being accomplished in Spain, once Syracuse had been captured, Marcellus had settled remaining affairs in Sicily with such great honesty and decency that he increased not only his own fame but also the dignity of the Roman people. He carried back to Rome the ornaments of the city—the statues and paintings that were so numerous in Syracuse; certainly those were spoils of the enemy and acquired by the right of war. From that, however, arose the true beginning of admiration for works of Greek art and this general license for despoiling all things sacred and profane, which finally turned against the Roman gods but first against the very temple that had been so exceptionally adorned by Marcellus. For temples dedicated by Marcus Marcellus near the Porta Capena used to be visited by foreigners on account of their remarkable ornaments of that kind of which a mere fraction now remains.

Josephus, *Jewish War* 7.158–62

Following the triumphal ceremonies and the very firm establishment of the Romans' empire [*imperium*], Vespasian decided to build a Temple of Peace. It was very quickly completed and exceeded all human imagination. He made use of an abundance of wealth sent from the gods for it. In addition, he adorned it with ancient masterpieces of both painting and sculpture; in fact, into that shrine were brought and placed all things, the sight of which men had formerly wandered around the whole earth for, longing to see them while they lay in different lands. Here, too, he set up the golden embellishments from the temple of the Jews of which he was quite proud; but their Torah and purple furnishings of the sanctuary he ordered to be deposited and kept in the palace.

## 3.22 Gardens: diversions and dangers

In the middle Republic, Rome's political elite began buying up vegetable gardens originally for household consumption and transforming these into large urban oases for enjoying *otium* (leisure). Some of these gardens or *horti* were huge, highly desirable pieces of property—often prime real estate that was coveted by the super-rich and politically powerful. Horace refers below to the Gardens of Maecenas, one of Augustus's closest friends, which he designed in the 30s BCE on the Esquiline Hill over the Republican city wall and burial pits for slaves and poor citizens that had lain just beyond (see also **11.6** in this volume). Maecenas also built a residence in his *horti* where he lived in semi-retirement until his death in 8 BCE when he bequeathed the entire property to Augustus. The future emperor Tiberius moved there in 2 CE, as Suetonius reports, and they were later owned by Fronto, the tutor and confidante of the emperor Marcus Aurelius, in the mid-second century CE. Though *horti* were intended as places for relaxation and pleasant encounters, some mixed business and pleasure in them, as Dio records of Vespasian. Gardens could also be settings for transgressions of various sorts including plots, scandals, and murders as well as burials, as Suetonius documents in the case of Caligula's death. Gardens were so prized that they were sometimes brought indoors, as it were, and made eternal by artistic representation as the paintings in the dining room of the House of Livia illustrate well (see Fig. 3.2).

Further reading: Claridge 2010: 305, 330–2; Dyson 2010: 103–4, 148–9; von Stackelberg 2009.

---

Horace, *Satires* 1.8.1–11, 14–16

Once I was the trunk of a fig-wood tree, a useless log, when the carpenter, unsure whether to carve a stool or Priapus, chose that I be a god. From that time on I was a god, a great terror for thieves and birds.[16] For my right hand keeps thieves in check and the red staff extending obscenely from my groin, while a reed fastened on my head frightens the pesky birds and prevents them from settling in [Maecenas's] new gardens. In earlier days, a slave used to pay to have the bodies of fellow slaves, cast

**Figure 3.2** Late first-century BCE fresco of an illusionistic garden with fruit-bearing trees and birds from the House of Livia, now at the Palazzo Massimo alle Terme of the Museo Nazionale Romano in Rome. © Vanni Archive/Art Resource, NY.

out from their narrow cells, carried here in a cheap box: this was a common burial place for the poor masses, for Pantolabus the joker and Nomentanus the wastrel … Now one can live on a wholesome Esquiline Hill and take a walk on the sunny Rampart [*Agger*] where sad folks just used to look upon the ground hideous with whitened bones.

---

Suetonius, *Tiberius* 15.1
Once he had returned to Rome, after bringing his son Drusus down to the Forum,[17] he immediately moved from the Carinae and the former house of Pompey[18] to the Gardens of Maecenas on the Esquiline and devoted himself completely to a life of retirement, only engaging in personal affairs and taking no part in public duties.

---

Suetonius, *Caligula* 59
He lived twenty-nine years and ruled for three years, ten months and eight days. His body was secretly transported to the Lamian Gardens and, partially burned on a hastily erected pyre there, it was buried with a light covering of earth. Later, once his sisters returned from exile, it was dug up, cremated, and buried in a tomb. Before this happened, it is generally agreed that the caretakers of the gardens were disturbed by ghosts, and in that house where he was killed, not a single night passed without some dreadful apparition until the house itself was consumed by fire.

---

Dio, *Roman History* 65.10.4
Vespasian lived in the palace very little, spending most of his time in the gardens named after Sallust and there he received anyone wishing [to see him]—not only senators but other people too.

## 3.23 Spare time in the city

The late republican and imperial city was filled with places for recreation and the Campus Martius, often simply called the Campus, encompassed many. This large flood plain of the Tiber extended for over a mile north and south from the Capitoline Hill beyond the Porta Flaminia, and the same extent east and west from the Quirinal to the Pons Neronianus. It was divided into smaller units, some of which were also designated by the term *campus* (field), such as the Campus Agrippae. Some of this large tract of land remained open green space pleasant for strolling, exercising, or practicing military maneuvers, as Strabo notes enthusiastically. Much was built up, though, with considerable development taking place under Augustus and under the direction of Agrippa in particular whose new bath complex and other facilities were fed by an innovative aqueduct, the Aqua Virgo, completed in 19 BCE (see **8.3** and **8.7** in this volume). Martial's poem, addressed to his senatorial friend Julius Martialis, conjures up many of the simple pleasures afforded by the Campus if only he and his friend could divest themselves of their responsibilities to enjoy them.

Further reading: Dyson 2010: 140–5; Richardson 1992: 65–7.

---

Strabo, *Geography* 5.3.8

The size of the Campus is astounding, for it accommodates chariot races and other equestrian exercises at the same time and unhindered, and allows for such a great crowd of people exercising by playing ball, with hoops, and wrestling. The works of art set up all around, and the ground covered in grass throughout the year, and the crowns of the hills that are above the river up to its bed: these offer the appearance of a scene from a painting and present a sight that is hard to drag oneself away from. Near this campus there is also another campus with a great multitude of colonnades round about, as well as groves, also three theaters and an amphitheater, and lavish temples one right after another, so this locale would seem to declare the rest of the city second-best.

---

Martial, *Epigrams* 5.20

If, dear Martialis, I were allowed to enjoy careless days with you, if permitted to arrange time free from duties and together to have leisure for genuine living, we should not know either the halls or mansions of men of power, neither sour lawsuits nor the sad Forum nor haughty ancestral busts; but riding about, conversations, books, the Campus, the colonnades, the shade, the Aqua Virgo, the baths: these should always be our haunts, these our tasks. At the moment, neither of us lives for himself, and we feel the good days slipping away and passing by, our days lost and entered into the account books. Does anyone, when he knows how to live, put it off?

## 3.24 A critique of leisure

Many of the places in the city where ordinary Romans enjoyed relaxation and leisure were looked down upon by the elite. In this passage from one of Seneca's moral essays, he disparages places frequented by average citizens such as brothels, baths, and eating-houses called *popinae*, which were popular spots to purchase hot, prepared food and where drinking, gambling, and prostitution were often available as well. In contrast, he associates places where the elite conducted the business of the state and their own daily affairs with the quality of virtue or excellence.

Further reading: Toner 1995; Toner 2009.

Seneca, *On the Happy Life* 7.3–4

Why do you compare things that are very dissimilar, on the contrary, opposites? Virtue is something lofty, distinguished and regal, unconquerable, unwavering; pleasure is something lowly, servile, weak, fleeting, whose haunt and residence are brothels and eating-houses. Virtue you will find in the temple, in the Forum, in the Senate House, standing in front of the city walls, dusty and sun-burned, with calloused hands; pleasure you will more often find lying hidden, seeking the darkness around the baths and sweating rooms and places that fear the aedile—soft, weak, drenched in wine and perfume, pale or painted with cosmetics and laid out for a funeral like a corpse. The highest good is immortal, does not know to come to an end, has neither satiety nor regret; for an upright mind is never altered, neither hates itself nor has it changed anything from a life that is the best. But then pleasure is extinguished once it has especially been enjoyed; it does not have much space so fills it quickly and both grows weary and withers after its first assault.

4

# The City by Day and Night

Cities and neighborhoods generally look and feel differently depending on the time of day as the activities that take place within them and lend them their character change with the hours. The complexion of the urban landscape is never the same from one point of the day or night to the next. Those who live in or visit urban spaces during daylight hours usually experience these spaces very differently after dark. In ancient Rome, perhaps even more so than today, this was the case because the presence or absence of natural light dramatically affected how and when buildings, streets, and open areas were used and by whom. Romans fitted their activities mainly into the hours when there was good natural light, usually beginning work or other commitments soon after dawn (**4.3**, **4.5**) and retiring for the day shortly after sunset. Some especially productive individuals, though, appear to have followed their own schedules, as Pliny the Younger reports of his highly industrious uncle (**4.4**). Using a device called a sundial (**4.1**), which determines the hour of the day at a given latitude by the position of the sun, the Romans divided the day from sunrise to sunset into twelve equal parts, which they called "hours" (**4.2**). The first hour was immediately after sunrise, the sixth fell at midday, and the twelfth was the "hour" directly before sunset. Roman hours also varied in length depending on the season with the twelve "hours" being shorter in the winter (about forty-five minutes each instead of seventy-five). Artificial lighting was limited, especially at night. Lamps might be set up for special occasions (**4.7**), and affluent Romans would travel with an entourage of slaves carrying torches to light their way while poorer Romans struggled by candle- or moonlight because there were no street lights in Rome (**4.9**). At night, the streets were not only challenging to navigate because it was difficult to see where one was going and to avoid obstacles such as stone benches, uneven pavement, and carts and other vehicles that were banned during the day, but also because the streets were apparently filled with dangers from above, such as falling potsherds or slop buckets, and below with thugs and drunks lurking who were eager to pick fights (**4.8**, **4.9**). Darkness was thought to invite and conceal illicit behavior, including criminal activity (**4.8–4.11**). The night was generally disapproved of as an inappropriate time for conducting religious rituals, particularly those involving women, but there were some exceptions including ceremonies for Bona Dea (the Good Goddess) and the many sacrifices and festivities that comprised the Saecular Games in 17 BCE (**4.12**, **4.13**). Not only the appearance of neighborhoods changed with time of day or night, but even their entire atmosphere of which sounds and smells were significant components. The sensory experiences of being in any one part of Rome could vary considerably over the course of a day and night. One constant, though, if Martial can be trusted, is that the city was never completely quiet (**4.5**, **4.6**; cf. **3.11** in this volume).

## Daytime in the city

### 4.1 Rome's first sundials

The seventh book of Pliny the Elder's *Natural History* concludes with a discussion of the Romans' time-keeping methods, including debate concerning when and where the city's first sundial was erected and the problems of accuracy involved in relying on sundials. After dismissing one report, Pliny takes Marcus Varro as authoritative who places the first public sundial near the Republican Rostra in the Roman Forum (see **7.1** in this volume). Private sundials also existed and many have been found at Pompeii and Herculaneum.

Further reading: Balsdon 1969: 17–18.

---

Pliny the Elder, *Natural History* 7.60.212–15
In the Twelve Tables,[1] only sunrise and sunset are indicated by name; some years later, noon was also added, with the consuls' assistant announcing it from the Senate House when he had seen the sun between the Rostra and the Graecostasis.[2] When the sun sloped from the Maenian Column toward the Carcer, he announced the last hour, but he only did this on clear days down to the First Punic War [264–241 BCE]. It is reported by Fabius Vestalis that the Romans' first sundial was erected eleven years before the war with Pyrrhus [begun in 281 BCE] by Lucius Papirius Cursor at the Temple of Quirinus when he was dedicating the temple which had been vowed by his father; but Vestalis does not specify either the method for making the sundial or its craftsman, where it was brought from or in which text he found this information. Marcus Varro

records that the first public sundial was set up on a column along the Rostra during the First Punic War after Catina in Sicily had been captured by the consul Marcus Valerius Messala, and that it was brought from Sicily thirty years later than 264 BCE, the year of Papirius's sundial. The lines of this sundial did not agree with the hours, yet they followed it for ninety-nine years until Quintus Marcius Philippus, who was censor together with Lucius Paullus, placed a more accurate one next to it; among the censors' projects, this gift was very well received. However, even then the hours were uncertain when it was cloudy up to the next *lustrum*[3]; then Scipio Nasica, the colleague of Laenas, was the first to divide the hours of the nights and days equally using a water-clock, and he dedicated this time-piece under a protective roof in 159 BCE.

## 4.2 Hour by hour

Although Romans of all social classes normally rose at dawn to start their days, status and rank could greatly affect the way the hours of the day were spent. Two contemporaries illustrate this well—the poet Martial and the senator Pliny the Younger—and offer rather different perspectives on a typical day in Rome. Though Martial lacks the means to be a man of leisure, he focuses on both the work and recreation that occupied ordinary people during the day. In contrast, Pliny emphasizes the social and professional obligations that consume his time and appears to resent these commitments, which he later explains prevent him from being able to write freely without interruption or criticism, not beholden to anyone, as he can only do once he leaves Rome and retires to one of his villas (see **2.7** in this volume).

Further reading: Balsdon 1969: 16–55.

Martial, *Epigrams* 4.8
The first hour and the second tire out clients at the *salutatio*. The third hour keeps the hoarse barristers at work. Into the fifth Rome stretches her various tasks. The sixth hour offers rest to the weary; the seventh will be the end to the siesta. The eighth until the ninth hour is enough for the gleaming wrestling floors. The ninth orders us to rumple the dining couches heaped up with cushions. The tenth is the hour for my little poetry books, Euphemus, when your concern moderates the divine banquets and goodly Caesar [Domitian] is relaxed by the heavenly nectar and holds in his huge hand meager cups. Then let in the jokes: my Thalia[4] is afraid to approach a morning Jove with unrestrained steps.

Pliny the Younger, *Letters* 1.9.1–3
It is astonishing how one accounts or seems to account for individual days in Rome, but not for several days in a row. For if you were to ask someone, "What did you do

today?" he would reply, "I attended a boy's coming of age ceremony, I celebrated a betrothal or wedding rites; one man asked me to witness his will, another for legal assistance in court, a third summoned me to act as an assessor." These things that you did on that day seem vitally important, but if you reconsider that you have done these same things every day, they seem pointless and much more so once you have left the city. In fact, then the realization comes to you: "How many days I have wasted on tedious things!"

## 4.3 Ritual obligations at dawn

The *salutatio* was a morning reception held in the atrium (reception room) of the home of a wealthy, powerful man known as a patron. Beginning at daybreak, his clients (*clientes*) would come to pay their respects, thereby acknowledging publicly his social superiority and their deference and dependence. Clients might ask patrons for favors or pass on information or instructions, and generally received a modest handout of food or money at that time. Upper-class men not at the top of the social hierarchy might have a small group of clients but also be clients themselves, having patrons who were more established and influential. After the formal greetings, clients were sometimes expected to accompany their patrons to the Forum and elsewhere in the city so the throng of followers would serve as a visible demonstration of patrons' power and influence. In an excerpt from one of Cicero's letters to his close friend Atticus, he attests to his morning routine as a patron but suggests that the experience was not entirely satisfying. Offering the perspective of a client, Martial makes it clear in several of his poems that despite the benefits a client might receive, the *salutatio* was a social obligation not all were happy to undertake: it could be a significant imposition on a client's time and energy due to its early hour and the distance to reach a patron's residence—and the efforts might not even be appreciated.

Further reading: Balsdon 1969: 21–4; Saller 1982: 128–9.

Cicero, *Letters to Atticus* 1.18.1
My house is nicely filled up early in the morning and I go down to the Forum accompanied by droves of friends. But from a great crowd, I cannot find anyone with whom I can either joke freely or enjoy a private sigh. This is why I am waiting for you, longing for you, and now even summoning you, for there are many things which are distressing and troubling me which, once I have your ear, it seems to me I can pour out during conversation on a single stroll.

Martial, *Epigrams* 1.108
You have (and I pray that it remains and increases in size for many years!) a house, beautiful indeed, but across the Tiber. Yet my attic rental faces the Vipsanian laurels[5] and I have already become an old man in this district. I must move so that I can pay my respects to you at your house in the morning, Gallus. It's worth my while, even if that house of yours were farther away. But to you it is not much if I present a single toga-clad client: it is much to me, Gallus, if I deny this one man.[6] I will pay my respects to you at the tenth hour rather often:[7] in the morning, my book will bid you "good day" on my behalf.

Martial, *Epigrams* 3.36
What one who has recently become a new friend does for you, Fabianus, you order me to do for you: that, shivering at the break of day, I always pay my respects to you and let your sedan-chair drag me through the midst of mud; that, worn out, I follow you at the tenth hour—or later—to the Baths of Agrippa though I myself bathe at the Baths of Titus. Have I deserved this, Fabianus, for my thirty Decembers of loyalty, that I should forever be a newbie in terms of your friendship? Have I deserved this, Fabianus, that, with my own toga threadbare, you think I have not yet earned my discharge?

Martial, *Epigrams* 5.22
If I did not wish and deserve to see you at home in the morning, Paulus, may your Esquiline residence be even farther away from me. But I live right next-door to the Tiburtine column[8] where rustic Flora[9] looks at ancient Jupiter[10]: I must surmount the steep footpath uphill from the Subura and the dirty paving stones with steps that are never dry, and I can hardly break through the lengthy herds of mules and the loads of marble which you see being dragged on many ropes. More burdensome, still, is the fact that after a thousand exertions, Paulus, when I'm exhausted, your doorman tells me you're not at home! This is the result of my pointless labor and poor soaked toga: it was scarcely worth my while to see Paulus in the morning. A dutiful client always has discourteous friends: you cannot be my patron unless you stay in bed.[11]

## 4.4 Making the most of the day—and night

Some extraordinary Romans apparently followed their own schedules and made very productive use of the hours before dawn, as Pliny the Younger details in a lengthy letter about his uncle's unique habits. According to his nephew, Pliny the Elder was an extremely accomplished and industrious individual who never wasted an opportunity to engage in study and was never idle. Here the younger Pliny explains how his uncle, though a busy man who had important official duties, was able to write so many volumes on diverse topics from javelin throwing to oratory to natural history, which is the only one of his works to survive from antiquity (see **4.1** in this volume).

Further reading: Gibson and Morello 2011.

---

Pliny the Younger, *Letters* 3.5.8–11

From the time of the Vulcanalia[12] he used to begin to work by lamplight not for the sake of taking the auspices but for working on his studies as soon as it was fully dark—in winter from the seventh hour or eighth at the latest, and often from the sixth. Admittedly, he very readily fell asleep, and sometimes sleep came over him and left him in the midst of his very studies. Before dawn, he used to go to the emperor Vespasian (for that man also made use of nighttime hours) and from there to the posts assigned to him. Once he had returned home, he would put whatever time remained to his studies. After a meal (which was light and easy during the day in the custom of men of old), often in the summer if he had some spare time he would lie in the sun; a book would be read aloud, he would make notes and take excerpts, for he read nothing that he did not excerpt and was even accustomed to say that no book was so bad that it was not beneficial in some part. After the sun, he generally bathed in cold water then would have a little food and sleep for a very short time. Then he would work until dinnertime as if it were another day.

## 4.5 An early start to the school day

Rome lacked schools that were separate buildings with dedicated classrooms. Children of the elite were regularly educated at home with private tutors, but ordinary children whose parents could afford some schooling sent them outside the home to attend school. Teachers rented space where it was available including rooms in private and public buildings, and many gave lessons outdoors in spaces off the forum, in colonnades, even on the side of a street. The noise of passers-by and traffic, as well as the possibility of bad weather, must have posed considerable distractions for teachers and especially for students. Yet as Martial complains, teachers themselves could be terrible distractions not for students but for those who lived near their outdoor classrooms. Their lessons, begun before daybreak, stereotypically featured yelling at the students and punishing them by whippings. Martial claims the noise on an average morning when school was in session was louder than what a blacksmith produced while crafting an equestrian statue or a crowd cheering a favorite at the Colosseum (here called the grand Amphitheater: see **5.17** in this volume).

Further reading: Balsdon 1969: 94–106; Dolansky 2014.

---

Martial, *Epigrams* 9.68

What have you to do with us, wicked schoolteacher, hateful creature to boys and girls? The crested roosters have not broken the silence yet and already you're thundering with your savage growl and whips. So harsh do bronzes ring after they've been struck by anvils when a blacksmith is fitting a lawyer on the middle of his horse; a gentler uproar rages in the grand Amphitheater when the winning Thracian gladiator is cheered by his own crowd of supporters. We neighbors aren't asking for sleep the whole night, for it's a small thing to be awake, but a big deal to be awake all night long. Dismiss your students! Would you be willing, loudmouth, to accept as much to keep quiet as you do for shouting?

---

# Non-stop activity

## 4.6 The city that's never silent

As is the case in a modern metropolis, Rome was busy with activity at almost all hours of the day and sometimes into the night as well. Several authors including Cicero, Pliny the Younger, and Martial write about the need from time to time to escape the noise and pressures of the city with its constant hustle and bustle by temporarily retiring to properties located outside the city (see **2.7** in this volume). Many owned suburban villas for this purpose that were not far from Rome so they had both easy access to their country retreats and proximity to the capital if they needed to return quickly. It was, however, not unusual for wealthy Romans to own several villas with certain properties farther away on the sea or in the hills. Martial, who had a small farm north of Rome in Nomentum, provides a vivid portrait of a city that barely sleeps and so, he claims, prevents him from doing the same. He enumerates the sounds that disrupt his sleep and disturb his peace on a typical day as Rome's ordinary citizens went about their business, and he levels some familiar complaints against schoolteachers. The poet also reveals some of his prejudices in his charges against worshippers of Bellona, a goddess of war, and Jews.

Further reading: Balsdon 1969: 196–204.

---

Martial, *Epigrams* 12.57

You ask why I often retreat to my little country place in dry Nomentum and my villa's humble hearth? There is no place in the city for a man of modest means either for thinking or resting, Sparsus. Schoolteachers ruin your quality of life in the morning, bakers at night, and all day long there are the hammers of the coppersmiths. On this side, the moneychanger, with all the time in the world, rattles a pile of Neronian coins on his dirty table; on that side, the hammerer of tiny nuggets of Spanish gold beats his worn rock with a glimmering mallet. Bellona's frenzied mob does not quit, nor the talkative shipwreck survivor with his bandaged body, nor the Jew taught by his mother to beg, nor the half-blind hawker of sulfur matches. He who can count the losses of lazy sleep will say how many bronze implements urban hands clash when the eclipsed moon is being beaten about by the Colchian magician's wheel.[13] You, Sparsus, don't know such things and can't know them, pampered as you are in Petilius's palatial estate whose ground floor looks down on the hill tops, where there is "country in the city" and a Roman vine dresser (and there isn't a larger harvest on Falernian hills). Within your boundary there is a wide track for your chariot, the sleep of the deep and quiet disrupted by no tongues, and there is no daylight unless it's let in. Me? The laughter of the passing throng wakes me up and Rome is at my bedside. Whenever I'm exhausted and disillusioned and want to sleep, I go to my villa.

## 4.7 Entertainment at all hours of the day

With few exceptions, most activities in Rome took place during daylight hours, including public entertainments such as gladiatorial fights and theatrical performances. According to Suetonius, the emperor Caligula was innovative by having some theatrical shows staged at night, and perhaps also by presenting contests in the Circus that lasted the entire day. The amphitheater where he held some games was located in the southern part of the Campus Martius. Dedicated in 29 BCE, it was the first stone amphitheater built at Rome and remained in use until it was destroyed by fire in 64 CE. The Saepta Iulia, which was completed by Agrippa in 26 BCE (see **7.3** in this volume), had been used for gladiatorial combats since Augustus, so Caligula was simply following past practice in staging games there.

Further reading: Dodge 1999; Richardson 1992: 11, 340–1.

Suetonius, *Caligula* 18.1–2

He put on several gladiatorial games, some in the amphitheater of Statilius Taurus, some in the Saepta, and included bands of the choicest African and Campanian boxers from both regions. He himself did not always preside over the contests, but sometimes imposed the task of doing so either on magistrates or friends. He offered theatrical shows of different kinds both continuously and in many places; he sometimes held them at night and the entire city was lit up with lamps. He also distributed donatives of various things and disbursed baskets of food to individuals. During the feasting, he sent his own portion to a Roman knight who was cheerfully and passionately eating across from him, but to a senator, on account of the same behavior, he sent a communiqué in which he appointed him praetor outside the usual order. He also provided numerous circus shows from morning until evening, sometimes with a hunt of panthers and leopards intervening, and sometimes the equestrian exercises of the Troy game.

# Under the cover of darkness

## 4.8 Nero's nighttime escapades

Ancient biographers such as Suetonius and Plutarch were keen to describe the character and habits of great men, especially if these were unusual or particularly shameful. In this passage, Suetonius focuses first on Nero's recklessness and then on his indulgence. Despite the many dangers lurking in the city after dark, the biographer claims that when Nero was in his late teens and early twenties, he enjoyed going out at night looking for mischief by instigating assaults on passers-by and breaking into taverns, which nearly cost him his life. His behavior during the day was less risky, but also problematic in its extravagance and rejection of social conventions as illustrated by his endless banquets, which spanned hours and began at midday though banquets normally only began in the early evening, and featured the company of prostitutes and dancing girls.

Further reading: Balsdon 1969: 153–4; Champlin 2003.

Suetonius, *Nero* 26–7

At first he even displayed his irresponsibility, lust, extravagance, greed, and cruelty gradually, in secret, and as though an error of his youth, but even then there was no doubt for anyone that those vices were in his nature, not his age. Immediately after dusk, once he had grabbed a freedman's cap and a wig, he would go into cook-houses and wander around neighborhoods looking for fun, yet not without personal danger since he was accustomed to beat up those returning from dinner, to wound them when they fought back and throw them into sewer drains. He also used to burst into taverns and plunder them, then set up a market in his home where, after the booty was divided up for auction, he squandered the profits. In brawls of this kind he often risked his eyes and his life, and was nearly killed by a certain senator whose wife he had touched inappropriately. For this reason, he never ventured out in public thereafter at that hour without tribunes secretly following behind him at a distance … He dragged out banquets from midday until midnight, quite often having refreshed himself by warm pools or in summertime with icy-cold ones. Sometimes he used to dine in public where his naval battle had formerly been held, or in the Campus Martius or Circus Maximus, enjoying the attention of prostitutes and Syrian dancing girls from across the city.

## 4.9 The hazards of the night

Rome could be a dangerous place once night fell with little light to illuminate the streets and the places where trouble lurked. Satirists like Martial and Juvenal found much to critique about the city both in daylight hours and after dark from their perspectives as poets and clients (see also **2.2** and **4.3** in this volume). The narrator of Juvenal's third satire, a man named Umbricius, is fed up with urban life and what he sees as Rome's numerous flaws and injustices for a man of his station, so he is preparing to leave the city behind. The present section follows a harangue about the disruptions that routinely prevent him from sleeping, especially the noise from the constant traffic of wheeled vehicles that were not allowed in the city during the day (cf. **4.6** in this volume). He then moves on to what one can expect if going out in the city at night, beginning with the dangers of things falling from open windows before concentrating on inevitable encounters with a drunk itching for a fight who avoids tussling with wealthy men accompanied by attendants and lamps, but gladly picks on lowly and solitary clients.

Further reading: Braund 1996: 230–6; Holleran 2011.

Juvenal, *Satires* 3.268–301

Now consider other varied dangers of the night: what a distance it is from the lofty roofs from which a potsherd strikes your head; how often cracked and broken pots fall from windows, and with how much weight their crash marks and damages the pavement. You might be regarded as careless and ill prepared for sudden mishaps if you go out to dinner without having made a will. For as you pass by on that night, there are as many opportunities to die as there are watchful windows standing open. Therefore, you should pray and bring a pitiful offering with you so the windows are satisfied with pouring down [the contents of] their shallow basins on you. The belligerent drunk, who by chance has not killed anyone, pays the price. He endures a night like Achilles when he was grieving for his friend: he lies on his face, then soon on his back, and so he won't be able to sleep otherwise; a brawl with somebody makes him sleep. But however reckless he is, seething with youth and unmixed wine, he is cautious about the man whose scarlet cloak and very long line of attendants recommends that he be avoided, besides the many torches and bronze lamps. As for me, whom the moon is accustomed to escort or the fleeting light of a candle whose wick I regulate sparingly, me he despises. Learn the lead-up to a pathetic brawl, if a brawl is when *you* do the beating and only *I* get beaten up. He stands opposite me and tells me to stop. I have to obey; for what can you do when a madman forces you and he's also stronger? "Where are you coming from?" he shouts. "With whose sour wine and boiled beans are you swollen up? Which shoemaker has been eating young leeks and a boiled sheep's tongue with you? Nothing to say to me? Tell me or take a kicking! Say where you stake your claim: in which synagogue am I to look for you?" If you try to say something or silently retreat, it's all the same: in both cases they hit you, then, still angry, they secure a guarantee that *you'll* have to appear in court. This is a poor man's freedom: after he's been beaten up and struck down from the blows, he begs and pleads to be allowed to go home with a few teeth.

## 4.10 Plotting murder and mayhem under the cover of night

In 63 BCE, a nobleman named Lucius Sergius Catilina, commonly known today as Catiline, plotted a violent overthrow of the government after he was defeated in that year's consular elections and had no legitimate means of achieving power in Rome. During the second half of the year, he began to organize his supporters in Italy to bring about revolution. He sent Gaius Manlius, a former officer in Sulla's army, north of Rome to Etruria to recruit an army, while in Rome, along with a number of senators and high-ranking officials, he crafted plans to assassinate Cicero, one of the year's two consuls. The historian Sallust, who may have observed the events at Rome firsthand, provides a detailed account from the conspiracy's beginnings to its suppression by Cicero and Catiline's eventual death in battle in January 62 BCE (see also **11.17** in this volume on execution of several co-conspirators at the Carcer, Rome's prison). In this excerpt, Sallust documents a crucial meeting held in the middle of the night on November 7, which led to an assassination attempt on Cicero later that same day in the early morning hours when patrons typically received visitors for the *salutatio* (see **4.3** in this volume).

Further reading: Odahl 2010: 45–69; Pagán 2004: 27–49.

Sallust, *Conspiracy of Catiline* 27.2–28.3
Meanwhile, Catiline contrived many things at Rome: laying plots for the consuls, preparing fires, occupying strategic locations with armed men. He himself was armed and ordered the others to do likewise. He encouraged them to be vigilant always and continuously ready. He rushed about day and night, staying awake yet not getting exhausted either by sleeplessness or effort. Finally, when he achieved nothing by pursuing many courses of action, he once again called together the ringleaders of the conspiracy through Marcus Porcius Laeca in the dead of night. At that meeting, he

complained considerably about their faint-heartedness. He informed them that he had
sent Manlius ahead to the crowd of men he had assembled for taking up arms, and that
there were similarly other men in other strategic locations to initiate the war. He himself
wished to set out to his army, if they first crushed Cicero who stood in the way of his
plans. With other men frightened and hesitating, Gaius Cornelius, a Roman knight,
thereupon promised his own services and with him Lucius Vargunteius, a senator. They
resolved to go to Cicero's house a little later that night, along with armed men, as if to
pay him an early morning greeting, and to stab him by surprise, not expecting it in his
own home. When Curius learned how much danger threatened the consul, he hastened
through Fulvia to disclose to Cicero the treachery that was being prepared. And so
those men were denied admission and had undertaken such a great crime in vain.

## 4.11 Secret nocturnal rites for Bacchus

Although religious rites for the Greek god Bacchus (Dionysus) had been practiced
in Italy for some time and apparently without issue prior to their suppression
early in the second century, the Senate decided to take action against the cult's
adherents in 186 BCE. Livy offers a lengthy and dramatic account of the event
known as the Bacchanalia (which he refers to as a conspiracy). He details the
initial spread of Bacchic worship in Italy, the consuls' and Senate's supposed
discovery of the cult that year, and their stern reaction against the several
thousand men and women allegedly involved in the city of Rome alone. Among
the Senate's concerns was that the rites were now being held at night and darkness
concealed behavior the cult seemed to encourage such as both homosexual and
heterosexual promiscuity. The initiation of minors was also an issue. Moreover,
Bacchic worship and the cult's structure posed significant challenges to gender
and status norms since prominent roles were available to women and individuals
of all classes were mingling together. In this excerpt from Livy's long narrative, he
reports much of the testimony of a key informant, a freedwoman named Hispala
Faecenia who had initially witnessed troubling aspects of the cult when she was a
slave; then, more recently, she had learned about additional scandalous practices
from her young lover, Aebutius, whose parents were pressing him to get initiated.

Further reading: Beard, North, and Price 1998: 91–8; Pagán 2004: 50–67.

Livy, *History of Rome* 39.13.8–13
Then Hispala disclosed the origin of the rites. At first, it was a ritual for women, and
it was customary that no man be admitted. They had three days set each year during
which people were initiated into the Bacchic rites in the daytime, and matrons were
usually made priestesses in turn. Paculla Annia, from Campania, changed everything

when she was a priestess, as though on the advice of the gods. For she had been the first to initiate men, her sons Minius and Herennius Cerrinius; and she held the rites at night rather than by day, and instead of three days in the year, she had established five days of initiation in every month. Since the rites were performed in common and men mingled with women, and there was the addition of the license darkness afforded, no crime or disgrace was omitted there. There were more illicit sexual acts among men with one another than among women. If any were less tolerant of vice and rather unwilling to commit an offense, they were sacrificed as victims. To consider nothing a sin: this was the highest religious devotion among them. Men, as if their minds had been seized, would speak prophesies with a frenzied shaking of their bodies. Matrons, in the dress of Bacchantes, their hair strewn about, would run down to the Tiber with burning torches, then, because the torches had live sulfur in them along with calcium, after the torches had been plunged into the water, they would bring them out with their flames renewed.

## 4.12 Nocturnal sacrifices by women

Roman men had grave concerns about women performing nighttime sacrifices and seem primarily to have been afraid that women's chastity could be compromised since they associated darkness with licentiousness. The prominent involvement of women in the Bacchanalia of 186 BCE, in which there were accusations of sexual debauchery among both men and women (see **4.11** in this volume), seems to have increased these reservations. This is certainly evident in Cicero's text that takes the form of a dialogue in which the interlocutors expound on the laws that ought to be in effect in the ideal Roman state. Cicero indicates that nighttime sacrifices performed on behalf of the populace were acceptable. One such ceremony was the December sacrifices for the Bona Dea or Good Goddess, conducted exclusively by women in the home of a leading official, usually a praetor or consul. Sometimes these women's rites apparently turned into extraordinary occasions as Plutarch records. In his biography of Cicero, Plutarch relates that in the midst of the Catilinarian conspiracy, when the rites for Bona Dea were being observed in Cicero's home, his wife received a clear sign from the gods that Cicero should support the proposal to execute the conspiracy's leaders (see **4.10** in this volume). Equally dramatic is the lengthy account in Plutarch's *Life of Caesar* that follows his initial explanation of the Bona Dea and her unique rituals that is included here. For the biographer goes on to detail the scandal that surrounded the rites in Caesar's house in 62 BCE when the young noble Clodius Pulcher, who was allegedly having an affair with Caesar's wife, snuck into the house disguised in women's clothes but was caught and put the integrity of the ritual at risk.

Further reading: Beard, North, and Price 1998: 129–30; Takács 2008: 98–101.

---

Cicero, *On the Laws* 2.9.21, 2.14.37

"There shall be no sacrifices by women at night except those which are performed with proper ceremony on behalf of the people; nor shall anyone be initiated into mystery cults except into the Greek rites of Ceres, as is customary." Indeed, these laws must be enacted most carefully so that the bright light of day guards the reputation of women when they are in view of many people, and so that "initiations into the mysteries of Ceres take place by rituals used for initiations already existing at Rome." In this type of matter, the ancient resolution of the Senate concerning the Bacchanalia and the investigation and punishment meted out by the consuls and soldiers make the sternness of our ancestors clear. And so that we do not by chance seem too harsh, in the very center of Greece, Diagondas of Thebes legally abolished all nocturnal rites forever.

---

Plutarch, *Life of Caesar* 9.3–4

The Romans have a goddess that they call Bona [Good], just as the Greeks call her Gynaeceia [Women's (Goddess)]. The Phrygians claim this goddess as their own and say she was the mother of King Midas, while the Romans say that she was a Dryad nymph who was wedded to Faunus, but the Greeks believe she was one of the mothers of Dionysus whose name is not to be spoken. That is why when they are celebrating her festival, the women cover over the roofs of their houses with vine-branches and, in accordance with the myth, a sacred serpent is enthroned near the goddess. It is forbidden for a man to come to the sacred rites or even to be present in the house where they are taking place; but the women on their own are said to perform many rites that are considered Orphic with respect to the nature of the worship. So when the time of the festival occurs, the man who is consul or praetor [at whose house the ceremony has to be held] retires from his house, along with every male, while his wife takes control of it and sets it in order for the celebration. The most important rituals are celebrated by night when lightheartedness mingled with nighttime festivities is evident, and plenty of music.

## 4.13 Three days and nights of ceremonies to mark a new age

At least twice during the Republican period (in 249 and 146 BCE), the Romans celebrated a festival called the *Ludi Saeculares* or Saecular Games, which marked approximately a century in Roman history (called a *saeculum*). In 17 BCE, Augustus revived the practice and subsequent emperors followed his lead: Claudius in 47 CE, Domitian in 88 CE, and Septimius Severus in 204 CE. Reflecting themes of fertility, prosperity, and rebirth, which were used to define Augustus's rule, his *Ludi Saeculares* featured prominent roles for matrons and children: the former prepared sacred banquets for the goddesses Juno and Diana while the latter sang in choirs at the Temple of Apollo on the Palatine and then on the Capitoline Hill on the final of the three initial days (see **6.9** in this volume). Traditionally these games spanned three days and nights at the beginning of June, but under Augustus seven days of festivities were added starting on June 5 that included additional performances of Latin and Greek plays, sacrifices, an animal hunt, and circus shows. The official records of the Board of Fifteen for Performing Sacrifices (*quindecemviri sacris faciundis*), which Augustus and his son-in-law Agrippa headed, detail the many ceremonies the *ludi* encompassed. As this excerpt demonstrates, sacrifices were performed both during the daytime and at night on each of the first three days with a variety of deities as the recipients. The records of the *ludi* are preserved in a large marble inscription of which the beginning is lost and other parts are fragmentary as indicated below in brackets. The inscription was set up in the northwest Campus Martius at the Tarentum, an altar where many of the ceremonies took place.

Further reading: Beard, North, and Price 1998: 201–6; Rawson 2003: 317–23; Severy 2003: 57–9.

---

*Corpus of Latin Inscriptions* 6.32323, lines 90–1, 100–4, 108–10, 115–16, 119–20, 133–4, 138–40, 153–4

On the following night [i.e., May 31] in the Campus Martius next to the Tiber [the emperor Caesar Augustus sacrificed nine female lambs to the divine Moirai[14]] as whole burnt offerings according to the Greek rite and by the same [rite he sacrificed nine female goats and prayed in this manner ...] Once the sacrifice was complete, shows were presented at night on a stage to which no theater was added nor was any seating set up, and 110 matrons, for whom it had been decreed by the Board of Fifteen for Performing Sacrifices in an edict, held *sellesternia*[15] with two chairs placed for Juno and Diana. On the Kalends of June, the emperor Augustus Caesar sacrificed a perfect bull to Jupiter Best and Greatest on the Capitol and Marcus Agrippa sacrificed another at the same place ... Then the Latin Games were held in a wooden theater which had been erected on the Campus Martius next to the Tiber, and in the same manner mothers of households held *sellesternia* and the shows, which had been begun at night, were not interrupted ... Moreover, at night, next to the Tiber, the emperor Caesar Augustus made a sacrifice to the divine Illithyiae[16] of nine cakes, nine *popana*, nine *phthoes* ...[17] Four days before the Nones of June [i.e., June 2], [the emperor Augustus Caesar] sacrificed a heifer to Juno Regina on the Capitol and Marcus Agrippa [sacrificed another in the same place] ... Games were held as on the previous day [...]. At night, moreover, next to the Tiber, [the emperor] Caesar Augustus [sacrificed a pregnant sow ... to Mother

Earth] ... Matrons held *sellesternia* [on this day in the same manner which they had on the previous day]. Three days before the Nones of June [i.e., June 3], on the Palatine, the emperor Caesar Augustus and Marcus Agrippa made a sacrifice [to Apollo and Diana] of nine cakes, nine *popana*, nine *phthoes* ... After the theatrical games ended at the [...] hour, near that place where sacrifice had been made on the previous nights and a theater had been erected and a stage, the turning posts were set up and chariot races were presented, and Potitus Messalla presented trick riders.

# Spectacle in the City

The venues of spectacle from the ancient city loom large over the modern cityscape of Rome, from the imposing remains of the Colosseum (called the Flavian amphitheater in antiquity, as explained below) to the still majestic Theater of Marcellus, and even to the large open, park-like space of the Circus Maximus. No matter one's interest in the ancient world, the remains of large-scale entertainment venues from ancient Rome are difficult to overlook in the city today. It is likely that it is, in part, on account of these monumental ruins that many people continue to be fascinated by Rome. Thanks to popular culture, there may exist the misperception that all the Romans did was attend daily gladiatorial contests and chariot races. In fact, spectacles were not daily events. There were varying ancient reactions to attending the different forms of spectacle, from fanatic enthusiasm to severe criticisms of spectacle as a waste of time (**5.1**). The types of entertainment below include the circus (**5.2–8**), the theater (**5.9–15**), walking in porticoes (**5.16**), the arena (**5.17–19**), and the stadium (**5.20**). While there are some overall ideas from ancient writers on the viewing of spectacles, many of the passages quoted concern particular types of events and places.

Further reading: Aldrete 2009: 121–40; Aldrete 2014; Beacham 1999; Bergmann and Kondoleon 1999; Coleman 2000; Dodge 2011; Dunkle 2014; Futrell 2006; Humphrey 1986; Kyle 2006: 251–338; Lim 1999; Purcell 2013.

## General thoughts on Roman spectacle

### 5.1 Criticisms of spectacle

Modern popular culture, in particular film, presents images of the Romans that leave the viewer with only one idea in mind: that of Romans who enjoyed the blood and gore of the killings of men and beasts before large crowds of screaming spectators. One often finds chariot races and gladiatorial matches on the small screens of TV and the large screens of the movie theater, but not often images of the Roman theater. While these modern receptions of the ancient world shed much light on the values of our own societies, the viewpoints of the ancient Romans on their own spectacles were complicated. In this section, there are only negative opinions on the gladiatorial contests and chariot races, provided by the historians Tacitus and, later in the fourth century CE, Ammianus Marcellinus. As you will see in later sections, other authors offered more positive viewpoints on some events and on their participants.

Tacitus, *A Dialogue on Oratory* 28.2–3; 29.3

Whatever evils are born first in the city of Rome, soon spread through Italy, and now they trickle into the provinces. Although your affairs are better known to you, I will speak about the city [of Rome] and its particular and native vices ... Now indeed the particular and peculiar vices of this city almost seem to me to be conceived in the womb of the mother: an inclination for actors and eagerness for gladiators and horses. If the mind has been seized and besieged by these things, how little a space remains for good arts?

Ammianus Marcellinus, *Roman History* 14.6.25

But in fact, among the crowd of the lowest and poorest class, some of them pass the night in wine shops, some hide under the awnings in the shades of theaters, which Catulus, in his aedileship, was the first to hang, in imitation of lascivious Campania. Or they fight during contests with dice, making ugly noises by drawing their breath into their broken noses. Or what is the greatest of all inclinations, from dawn to the evening, sun or rain, they become exhausted, searching for, into the minutest detail, the excellent aspects and the faults of the charioteers and their horses. And it is quite wondrous to see so many plebeians with a certain passion infused into their minds when they are hanging on the results of chariot contests. These and similar things allow nothing memorable or serious to be accomplished at Rome.

Ammianus Marcellinus, *Roman History* 28.4.28–30

Now let us come to the idle and lazy people ... These people spend all their time with wine and dice and debauchery and pleasures and spectacles. For them the temple and dwelling and meeting place and all the hope of their desires is the Circus Maximus. One can see many of them gathered throughout the fora and the crossroads and the streets and assemblies, having quarrelsome disputes amongst themselves with, as usually happens, some defending this thing and others that. Among them are those who have lived to abundance: more important from the authority of their age, by their white hair and wrinkles, they shout that the state is not able to remain standing, if in the future race, the charioteer whom each person favors, does not jump out of the gates first and does not go around the turning post closely enough with his inauspicious horses.[1]

# Circus

## 5.2 The building and transformations of the Circus Maximus

The Circus Maximus, the Greatest Circus, had space for 250,000 spectators at its high point of development. Its location is between the Palatine and Aventine Hills. It was an oval, elongated arena suitable for chariot races, but at various points in Rome's history, other sorts of spectacles were also held there. Over the years in antiquity, important people enhanced and changed the Circus, as they did with many other monuments in Rome. The structural elements of the Circus included (1) starting gates for the horses; (2) turning posts around which the charioteers would have been expected to maneuver; (3) a trench added by Julius Caesar to separate the racetrack from the spectators' seats; (4) lap markers (in the shapes of eggs and dolphins); (5) the barrier in the middle of the racing track; (6) and the general seating and the imperial box.

There is evidence of not only the Circus Maximus itself, but how Romans fervently supported different teams (or as we get from the Latin *factio*, different factions).

Parts of the seating areas have been excavated and still stand. Although modern tourists may imagine that it was the Colosseum that had the biggest crowds, the Circus was in fact the largest spectacle in the ancient city, as we can see from its seating capacity.[2]

Today the Circus is a grassy area that is used as a public space. While the daily use now may draw limited numbers of people, there have been large events held there, including a large-scale viewing party for the final of the World Cup in July 2006, a Rolling Stones concert in June 2014, and a Bruce Springsteen concert in July 2016. Of course, there have been concerns as to the preservation of the site with so many people using it at once for an event.

Further reading: Claridge 2010: 299–300; Coarelli 2014: 323–6; Coleman 2000: 210–17; Humphrey 1986; Meijer 2010; Richardson 1992: 84–7.

---

Dionysius of Halicarnassus, *Roman Antiquities* 3.68.1
Tarquinius built the largest of hippodromes [Circus Maximus], lying between the Aventine and Palatine Hills. He was the first to make covered seats around it. Up to this time, spectators stood on benches, with beams supporting the wooden stands.

---

Dio, *Roman History* 49.43.2
Since Agrippa saw that the men in the Circus were getting tripped up by the number of laps, he established the dolphins and the egg-shaped pieces so that the rotations of the track could be shown.

Suetonius, *Julius Caesar* 39.2
For the games at the Circus, a space of the Circus was extended from either side and a trench was added to the circuit. The noblest young men drove four-horse and two-horse chariots and horses for vaulting.

Suetonius, *Claudius* 21.3
Claudius improved the Circus Maximus with marble barriers and golden turning posts, which before were of tufa[3] and wood. He established particular seats for the senators who had been accustomed to watch the games with the general public.

Pliny the Elder, *Natural History* 36.24.102
Among our great works, should we not mention the Circus Maximus, constructed by the dictator Caesar with a length of three stades and a width of one, with buildings of four acres, and with seating for 250,000?

*Corpus of Latin Inscriptions* 6.955
To the *imperator* Nerva Trajan Augustus Germanicus Dacicus ... from the thirty-five tribes because, by the generosity of the best emperor, their privileges have been increased by the addition of seats.

## 5.3 The experience of people watching spectacles at the Circus Maximus

Some ancient writers depict the spectators of the chariot races at the Circus Maximus as very devoted to their favorite faction (on this see **5.5**). Other writers focus on the dynamics of people in the audience. For example, in Ovid's love poetry, we get the experience, even if exaggerated, of a man at the races who tries to get close to a woman while being in the midst of the excitement of the race and of the crowd itself. Juvenal describes a similar situation, as he mentions a young man watching the races with a young woman, in the middle of a shouting and excited crowd, rooting for their favorite team and placing bets.

Further reading: Henderson 2002.

Ovid, *The Loves* 3.2.1–7; 9–24

I do not sit eager for the noble horses. I pray that he wins, the one you yourself favor. I have come to speak with you and to sit with you, lest the love you inspire not be known to you. You watch the races, I will watch you. Let us both look upon what is pleasing and let each of us nourish our own eyes. O, he is the lucky driver of horses, the man you favor ... Why do you flee in vain? The line compels us to be joined. The Circus holds these opportunities in the seating of the place. You, however, whoever you are on her right, be careful with my girl. She is annoyed by the touch of your side. You, also, who watch behind us, draw together your legs. If you have any shame, do not press her back with your hard knee.

Juvenal, *Satires* 10.78–81

For the people who were once giving power, offices, legions, everything, now limit themselves, and with anxiety wish for only two things: bread and circuses.

Juvenal, *Satires* 11.197–204

Today the Circus possesses all of Rome and the noise strikes the ear, by which I deduce the win of the green team. For if it loses, you will see this city sad and stunned, as when the consuls were conquered in the dust of Cannae. Let the young men watch, for whom shouting and bold bets are fitting, and with an elegant girl sitting nearby. Let our wrinkled skin drink in the spring sun and flee from the toga.

Suetonius, *Caligula* 26.4–5

Caligula handled the rest of the orders with similar arrogance and violence. Having been disturbed by the loud noise of the people occupying the free seats in the Circus in the middle of the night, he drove them all away with sticks. In this tumult, more than twenty knights were crushed to death, the same number of matrons, and above this a countless number of the rest of the crowd. At the stage plays, sowing a reason for discord between the plebs and the knights, he was giving the free seats rather early, so that the equestrian seats might be taken by the lowest people. At a gladiatorial contest, sometimes when the awnings were drawn back when the sun was burning the most, he was forbidding that anyone be let out.

## 5.4 The emperor at the Circus

Suetonius presents a more privileged experience for watching the races, as the emperor Augustus watches the spectacles from the nearby upper-floors of friends' houses or from his own imperial box called the *pulvinar*. Martial describes Domitian at the Circus, and Pliny the Younger likewise presents the experience of the emperor Trajan watching the games, emphasizing that it is a good place for the emperor to be seen by his people.

<u>Further reading</u>: Roche 2011: 58; Van den Berg 2008.

---

Suetonius, *Augustus* 45.1
Augustus himself was watching the circus games nearby from the upper rooms of friends and freedmen, sometimes from the imperial box sitting with his wife and children. At times he was away from the spectacle for very many hours, at times for whole days. He sought pardon and entrusted things to men who would preside in his place. But whenever he was present, he was doing nothing else, either for the sake of avoiding rumor, because he recalled that his father Caesar was rebuked commonly for reading books and letters and replying during the spectacle, or because of a zeal and pleasure of watching which he never disguised and often openly confessed.

---

Augustus, *Achievements* 19
I made ... the imperial box at the Circus Maximus.

---

Martial, *Epigrams* 8.11
The Rhine knows that you have arrived now into your city. For it even hears the voices of your people. The shouting itself of new happiness frightened the Sarmatic peoples and the people of Istria and the Getae. While long expressions of joy were worshipping you in the sacred Circus, no one perceived that the horses had been sent out four times and were running. Rome has loved no leader in this way, nor has she loved you in this way, Caesar. Now Rome is not able to love you more, even if she herself wishes.

---

Pliny the Younger, *Panegyric* 51.3–5
Here the immense side of the Circus rivals the beauty of temples, a building worthy of a people that is the conqueror of nations, nor less worthy of being seen than the spectacles that will be watched there. Moreover it is both worthy to be seen not only because of its appearance but also because the place makes equal the emperor and the people ... It will be allowed to your citizens to look upon you in turn. It will be permitted to see not only the seat of the emperor but the emperor himself in public, sitting with the people, for whom you added 5,000 seats.

## 5.5 The four factions, their stables, charioteers, and their (over)zealous fans

Many Romans, including some emperors, were fans of one particular team of charioteers and their horses. The factions were referred to by four colors: *albata* (white), *prasina* (green), *russata* (red), and *veneta* (blue), and included not only well-known charioteers, but also well-known horses for which the crowd could cheer (and on whom they could bet). Tensions ran so high that some people chose to place curses on the opposing factions. Pliny the Elder tells the story of a fan going so far as to throw himself on the funeral pyre of a beloved charioteer. Domitian established two new factions, the gold and the purple, but it seems that these did not endure.

Besides the literary sources, thanks to epigraphic evidence we have additional information concerning the various factions. In the *Corpus of Latin Inscriptions* (6.10044–82), one can find inscriptions pertaining to the Circus. According to these inscriptions, we know that charioteers moved between factions over the course of their careers. Some of the inscriptions note the number of victories a charioteer won as a member of each faction.

Each faction would have had stables that were used not only for the horses, but also as a gathering place for the charioteers. These stables were not next to the Circus Maximus, but rather located in the lower Campus Martius (Richardson 1992: 366).

Further reading: Bell 2014; Cameron 1976; Carter and Edmondson 2014: 540–1.

---

*Corpus of Latin Inscriptions* 6.10044
Let the victory of the Blues always last happily.

---

*Corpus of Latin Inscriptions* 6.10048
Gaius Appuleius Diocles, driver for the red faction, born in Lusitania, Spain, he lived forty-two years, seven months, and twenty-three days. He first drove for the white faction in the consulship of Acilius Aviola and Corellius Pansa. He had his first win in that same faction in the consulship of Manius Acilius Glabrio and Gaius Bellicius Torquatus. He first drove for the green faction in the consulship of Torquatus Asprenas and Annius Libo. He first won in the red faction in the consulship of Laenas Pontianus and Antonius Rufinus. [The inscription continues with a summary of his numerous victories and monetary prizes.]

---

*Corpus of Latin Inscriptions* 6.10049a
Marcus Aurelius Polynices, a slave born in his master's house, who lived twenty-nine years, nine months, and five days, won 739 palms[4]: 655 in the red faction, fifty-five in the green faction, twelve in the blue faction, and seventeen in the white faction.

---

Pliny the Elder, *Natural History* 7.53.186
It is found in the register of public acts that at the funeral procession of Felix, charioteer of the red faction, one of his fans threw himself onto the funeral pyre.

---

Martial, *Epigrams* 10.53
I am that Scorpus, the glory of the clamoring Circus, your applause, Rome, and briefly your sweetheart. Envious Lachesis [one of the Fates] snatched me in my twenty-seventh year, believing that I was old since she counts my palms of victory.

---

Martial, *Epigrams* 11.1.13–16
In that place, there are two or three who are the sort to unroll the bookworms of my silliness, but only when the betting and stories about Scorpus the charioteer and the horse Incitatus have been exhausted.

---

Pliny the Younger, *Letters* 9.6
To Calvisius
I have spent all this time with my writing tablets and books in the most pleasant quiet. You ask: How were you able to do so in the city? There were races at the Circus, the sort of spectacle by which I am not even slightly attracted. Nothing new, nothing different, nothing that is not enough to have seen once. For this reason, I am more in amazement that so many thousands of men so childishly want to see horses running and men standing in chariots again and again. If, however, they were attracted either by the speed of the horses or the skill of the men, there would be some reason. But they favor and love the clothing, and if in the middle of the course itself and the race, this color there would be changed for that color here, the zeal and favor will transfer and they will abandon suddenly the driver and the horses whom they recognize at a distance and whose names they shout. So great is the esteem, so great is the significance in one very cheap tunic. Not only among the crowd which is cheaper than the tunic, but among certain serious men. When I think about them sitting idle, insatiable, in this empty, trivial, incessant business, I take some pleasure because I am not captivated by this pleasure. And I spend my leisure during these days most agreeably in literature, days that others waste in the idlest occupations.

---

Suetonius, *Caligula* 55.2
Caligula was so devoted and dedicated to the green faction that he constantly dined and passed the time in their stables. At a certain revel, he gave two million sesterces in presents to the driver Eutychus. He was accustomed to have his soldiers proclaim silence in the neighborhood, so that the horse Incitatus would not be disturbed the day before a race. In addition to a marble stable for horses, an ivory pen, purple coverings, collars made with jewels, he also gave the horse a house, a household, and furniture, so

that those invited in the horse's name would be received more elegantly; it is also said that he intended a consulship for it.

---

Suetonius, *Domitian* 7.1

Domitian added two factions to the games in the Circus: the gold and purple colors were added to the four earlier ones.

---

Tacitus, *Annals* 14.14.1

Nero had an old desire for driving in the racing car of a four-horse chariot, and a no less foul fondness of singing with the cithara in the theater. He was reminding people that to race with horses was a royal thing and that it was done habitually by ancient leaders and that it was frequently praised by poets and given for the glory of the gods.

---

Tacitus, *Histories* 2.94.3

[The emperor] Vitellius, caring only about squandering money, constructed stables for the charioteers. He was filling the Circus with spectacles of gladiators and wild beasts and was wasting his money as if he had it in the highest abundance.

## 5.6 Elephants, protests, and other events of interest at the Circus

While the main spectacle discussed by ancient authors regarding the Circus was chariot racing, there are other instances of note. Pliny the Elder describes a spectacle that involved elephants, such as for the dedication of the Temple of Venus Victrix attached to the Theater of Pompey. Suetonius tells of Augustus placing extra protection on the streets for the people not attending the spectacles. Thanks to the openness of the seating, the Circus was supposedly a place where the emperor could be petitioned more easily. However, this was not always a positive experience. Josephus describes an example of people protesting taxes to the emperor Caligula and being put to death as a result.

---

Pliny the Elder, *Natural History* 8.7.20–1

Also in the second consulship of Pompey, at the dedication of the Temple of Venus Victrix [Venus the Bringer of Victory], twenty elephants fought in the Circus, or as some relate, seventeen, with the Gaetulians throwing javelins against them. There was the wondrous struggle of one elephant, who, with its feet stabbed, crawled against the band of men on its knees. It snatched their shields, throwing them high up, which when they were falling down, were a pleasure to the spectators, since they were collected into an orb, as if they were thrown by skill, not by the anger of a beast. There was a great marvel another time, when one elephant was killed by a single blow, since

101

a javelin driven under the eye had reached the vital areas of the head. The elephants altogether tried to break out, although iron barriers surrounded them, but not without the distress of the people. For which reason, Caesar, as dictator, afterwards when he was about to give a similar spectacle, surrounded the arena with channels.

---

Suetonius, *Augustus* 43.1
On the days of spectacles, Augustus placed guards in the city so that there would not be danger from robbers for the small number of people remaining away [from the spectacles].

---

Josephus, *Antiquities of the Jews* 19.24–7
In this time, there were the horse races. The Romans were very eager for this spectacle and they came together zealously into the Circus. Having come together as a mass, they asked their rulers for what they needed. The rulers, deciding that their needs were incontestable, did not in any way disoblige them. They entreated Gaius [Caligula] with ardent supplication to relax their taxes and to lighten some of their heavy payments. He refused to lift them. When they shouted more, he sent men in different directions and ordered them to seize the ones shouting and to lead them forward and kill them.

## 5.7 Active life around the Circus Maximus

There was an animated life that occurred around the venues of spectacle. Around the Circus Maximus, there were a number of shops, vendors, and even astrologers. There were also a number of residential spaces.

---

Dionysius of Halicarnassus, *Roman Antiquities* 3.68.4
Outside, around the hippodrome [the Circus], there is another colonnade of one story that has shops in it and houses over it. There are entrances and ways up located at each shop for the spectators, so that it will not trouble the vast number of people as they enter and depart.

---

Cicero, *On Divination* 1.132
Finally, I do not value the Marsian augur, the village diviners, or the astrologers from the Circus.

## 5.8 The Circus Maximus was not the only circus

There are excavated remains of another significant circus, that of Maxentius, but it is located on the Via Appia outside the city. There are also mentions of other circuses in Rome. For example, there was the Circus Flaminius in the Campus Martius. This circus was not a traditional circus, likely lacked the shape of the typical circus and did not have seats. It was instead a public square, which was said to be a location for spectacles, assemblies, and market days, as well as a possible point in the triumphal procession. There was also the Circus of Gaius and Nero, introduced by Caligula and enhanced by Nero, located under the area of St. Peter's Basilica and Square (see **9.17** for the obelisk that was located in this spot).

Further reading: Claridge 2010: 250–1, 426–8; Coleman 2000: 217–19.

---

Varro, *On the Latin Language* 5.154
It is called the Circus Flaminius since it was built around (*circum*) the Flaminian Field and also because there the horses run around (*circum*) the turning posts in the Taurian Games.

---

Cicero, *Letters to Atticus* 1.14.1
Then at the incitement of the consul Piso, the most unreliable tribune of the plebs Fufius leads forth Pompey into the assembly. This business was happening in the Circus Flaminius where a gathering for the market day was taking place on that day.

---

Suetonius, *Claudius* 21
Claudius frequently arranged races in the Vatican circus [the Circus of Gaius and Nero].

---

Tacitus, *Annals* 14.14.4
A space was closed in the Vatican valley where Nero might guide his horses without a public spectacle.

---

# Theaters

## 5.9 The construction of a theater

This section covers only the permanent theaters in the city of Rome. Prior to the building of the Theater of Pompey in 55 BCE, theaters were temporary structures built from wood and taken down after performances over concerns about the corrupting influence of theaters. Authors such as Vitruvius describe the ideal conditions for the building of a theater, from the placement of the theater to the number of entrances to the acoustics of the space. There were three major theaters in the city of Rome: that of Pompey, followed by the Theater of Balbus and the Theater of Marcellus.

Further reading: Sear 1990; Sear 2006.

Vitruvius, *On Architecture* 5.3.1–2; 5.3.5

Once the forum has been established, then a place as healthful as possible must be chosen for the watching of plays on the festival days of the immortal gods, as was written in the first book about health in the placement of the city walls. For during the plays, people, along with their spouses and children, remain seated, held by their delights. Their bodies, unmoved on account of the pleasure, have their skin exposed, onto which the breaths of the breezes settle. If the winds come from marshy or other corrupt regions, they will infuse the bodies with harmful spirits. And so, if a place for the theater is chosen more carefully, then defects will be avoided ... It is necessary to arrange very many and spacious entrances, ones that do not connect the upper seats with the lower, but a path should be made straight and direct from all seats, so that when people leave the spectacles, they are not pressed together, but have separate exits from all seats without obstruction.

## 5.10 Experience of the theater

According to Suetonius, Julius Caesar offered plays in multiple languages for the multicultural audiences of Rome. But for some ancient writers, the spectacle is not on the stage, but in the theater itself, as is the case with Ovid who describes it as an ideal place for finding a partner in love. The spectators themselves become part of the spectacle.

Suetonius, *Julius Caesar* 39.1

Julius Caesar put forth spectacles of varied types: contests of gladiators, also plays given in districts in the whole city by actors of all languages.

Ovid, *Art of Love* 1.89–92; 99–100

But you should especially hunt at the curved theaters, these places are richer than your desire. There you will find a girl to love, a girl to play with, a girl to touch once, a girl you wish to keep ... They come to see, they come so that they themselves may be seen. That place holds the injury of chaste modesty.

## 5.11 Seating at the theater

Although not the first person in ancient Rome to provide hierarchical seating at the theater, under the emperor Augustus there was a tightening of the seating organization, giving defined rows to senators, to married men, women, and so on. Suetonius describes the elaborate setup of the theater, which was likely part of the *lex Iulia theatralis*, the Julian theater law.

Further reading: Rawson 1987.

---

Suetonius, *Augustus* 44

Augustus brought into order and regulated the very disorderly and very loose habit of watching the games. He was moved by the insult to a senator, whom, in Puteoli[5] at very crowded games, no one had received in a full house. Therefore a decree of the senators was made that whenever any spectacle was offered anywhere publicly, the first row of seats would be free for senators. At Rome he forbade ambassadors of free and allied peoples to sit in the orchestra when he had discovered that some of the freedmen were being sent. He separated the soldiers from the people. He appointed their own rows to married men of the plebeians, to young men their own section and their tutors next to them, and he decreed that no one clothed in black should sit in the middle section. He did not allow the women to watch the gladiators unless from the upper seats, when it had been customary in the past for them to watch in mixed company. To the Vestal Virgins alone he gave separate seats in the theater, facing the tribunal of the praetor. But for the spectacle of the wrestlers he removed the whole female sex to such an extent that in the games for his entrance to the office of *pontifex maximus* [chief priest], he put off a requested pair of boxers to the morning of the following day and he proclaimed that he did not want women to come to the theater before the fifth hour.

---

Tacitus, *Annals* 2.83

The equestrian order named the seating section, which was called "of the younger ones," Germanicus.

---

## 5.12 Dedication of the Theater of Balbus

The Theater of Balbus was the smallest of the permanent theaters in Rome and was located in the Campus Martius. It was built by Lucius Cornelius Balbus, a member of the emperor Augustus's circle and dedicated in 13 BCE. Suetonius tells us that this theater was one of the buildings erected with the encouragement of Augustus. It was located under the present Palazzo Mattei and Palazzo Caetani. Its location is confirmed by fragments of the Marble Plan with the inscription *Theatrum Balbi*.[6] The Crypta Balbi, a porticus, was attached to the theater. A museum focusing on urban archaeology now stands on the Via delle Botteghe Oscure on top of the ruins. Archaeologists have referred to the excavation of the site as "one of the most important urban excavations in modern Rome" (Dyson 2010: 146). The site preserves layers of the city from different periods. The passages that follow describe the building, dedication, and decoration of the theater.

Further reading: Claridge 2010: 247–9; Coleman 2000: 223; Dyson 2010: 146; Richardson 1992: 381–2.

---

Suetonius, *Augustus* 29.4–5

Augustus often urged distinguished men, each one according to his means, to adorn the city with monuments, either new ones or ones restored and improved. Many monuments were built by many men at that time, such as the Temple of Hercules and the Muses by Marcius Philippus, the Temple of Diana by Lucius Cornificius, the Hall of Liberty by Asinius Pollio, the Temple of Saturn by Munatius Plancus, the theater by Cornelius Balbus, the amphitheater by Statilius Taurus, and many excellent sites by Marcus Agrippa.

---

Dio, *Roman History* 54.25.2–3

It happened that message of Augustus's arrival to the city came in those days when Cornelius Balbus was putting on spectacles to dedicate the theater that is named for him even now. He was proud as if he himself were bringing back Augustus and yet he was unable to enter his theater except by boat because of the Tiber overflowing.

## 5.13 The building, dedication, and use of the Theater of Pompey

The Theater of Pompey was Rome's first stone theater built by Gnaeus Pompeius Magnus (Pompey the Great) and dedicated in 55 BCE. As the passages below illustrate, the theater was dedicated with great fanfare. As Coarelli notes (2014: 285), the theater is a good example of "urban continuity," since the "internal curve is perfectly reflected in the buildings that surround Piazza di Grotta Pinta." One can see remains of the theater inside certain neighborhood restaurants.

---

Cicero, *Letters to Friends* 7.1.2–3 [to his friend M. Marius who missed the show]

If you are asking, the games were altogether most magnificent, but not to your liking. I make that conclusion from my own taste ... Why should I tell you other things? Indeed you know the rest of the spectacles, which had not even the charm that average spectacles are accustomed to have. The sight of the splendor was removing all merriment ... Why should I think that you missed the wrestlers, you who despised the gladiators in which Pompey himself confesses that he lost both time and trouble. Remaining are the beast hunts, two each day over five days, magnificent, no one denies it, but what delight can it be to a cultivated man when either a weak man is torn to pieces by the strongest beast or a remarkable beast is pierced by a hunting spear. If these things must be seen, you have seen them often. Nor I who watched these spectacles, did I see anything new. The final day was of the elephants in which there was great admiration of the crowd, but no delight remained. There was even a certain pity that attended it, a belief that there is an association between mankind and that beast.

Plutarch, *Life of Pompey* 52.4
Once Crassus finished his consulship, he went to govern his province, while Pompey opened his theater and held gymnastic and musical contests in it at its dedication. He gave contests of wild animals in which five hundred lions were killed, as well as an elephant fight, the most astounding spectacle.

Dio, *Roman History* 39.38.1
In these days Pompey dedicated the theater of which we are now proud. In it he gave spectacles, including musical and gymnastic contests. In the hippodrome [Circus] he gave horse races and the slaughter of animals of all sorts. They killed five hundred lions in five days and eighteen elephants fought armed men.

## 5.14 The death of Julius Caesar at the Curia of the Theater of Pompey

The Curia of Pompey was part of the complex at the Theater of Pompey and was a meeting spot for the Senate. It was also the location of the assassination of Julius Caesar in 44 BCE.

Further reading: Coleman 2000: 221–2; Richardson 1992: 383–5.

Livy, *Summaries* 116.3
For these reasons, a conspiracy was formed against Caesar. The leaders of the conspiracy were Marcus Brutus, Gaius Cassius, and from Caesar's own side, Decimus Brutus and Gaius Trebonius. Caesar was killed in the Curia of Pompey with twenty-three wounds and the Capitol was occupied by his killers.

Suetonius, *Augustus* 31.5
Augustus also moved the statue of Pompey from the hall in which Gaius Caesar had been killed and he set it opposite the main door[7] of the theater on a marble arcade.

Plutarch, *Life of Caesar* 66
These things I suppose were of their own will. But the place of that murder and the gathering, in which the Senate was assembled at that time, contained a statue of

Pompey. It had been an ornament of Pompey as embellishment for this theater and so it was altogether apparent to be the work of a spirit guiding and calling the deed to that place. It is also said that Cassius, looking upon the statue of Pompey before the undertaking, in silence summoned him ... Brutus Albinus deceitfully detained Antony outside with a long discussion, since Antony was loyal to Caesar and strong. But Caesar entered and the Senate rose in respect. Brutus's men placed themselves around the back of Caesar's chair, other men moved to meet him as if to join in the request of Tillius Cimber concerning the exile of his brother and they followed him up to his chair. Once Caesar took his seat, he rejected their requests and he was feeling irritated at the things placed before him. They joined in entreating him, following him up to his chair. When he sat down and broke away from their requests, they pressed more forcibly and he was irritated at each of them. Tillius seized his toga with both hands and pulled it down from his neck. This was the agreed-upon signal for the attack. First Casca struck him with a dagger in the neck. The blow was neither fatal nor deep, for he was agitated, as is likely at the beginning of a great daring act and Caesar turned around, seized the dagger with his hands and held onto it. Both cried out at the same time. Caesar, thus stabbed, said in Latin, "Most vile Casca, What are you doing?" Casca, his attacker, cried out in Greek, "Brother, help me!" Such was the beginning of the attack. Consternation and fear held those who did not know of the attack before. They neither fled nor helped Caesar, not even daring to make a sound. Those ready for the murder displayed their daggers and surrounded Caesar in a circle. Whichever way he turned, he was struck, receiving blows to the face and eyes, as if a wild animal trapped by everyone's hands. For it was necessary for all of them to engage in the sacrifice and taste the murder. For this reason, Brutus added one blow to the groin. It is said by some that Caesar fought the others, struggled this way and that, and cried out, but when he saw Brutus had drawn his dagger, he pulled his toga over his head and fell, either by chance or pushed by his killers, at the pedestal on which stood the statue of Pompey. The murder stained the pedestal with much blood so that it seemed that Pompey, in vengeance, stood over his enemy, who lay at his feet, gasping from his wounds. It is said that Caesar received twenty-three wounds and many of the attackers were wounded by each other in placing so many blows on one body.

## 5.15 The building, dedication, and use of the Theater of Marcellus

Of the three stone theaters in the city, the Theater of Marcellus was the largest and could hold the most spectators (see Fig. 5.1). The project was started by Julius Caesar, but was not finished at the time of his death. Augustus completed the site and dedicated it to his nephew Marcellus, who died in 23 BCE. The theater, even after it was no longer used in its original function, took on new roles as a fortress and a palazzo in later centuries. The Temple of Apollo Sosianus and the Porticus of Octavia were nearby the theater.

**Figure 5.1** Theater of Marcellus. Photo credit: Scala/Art Resource, NY.

There are significant remains of this theater still visible. During the summer, spectacular events are held outdoors at this site, including a concert series, with the monuments illuminated by floodlights. The Palazzo Orsini, a luxurious property sitting atop the theater, was put up for sale in 2012.

Further reading: Claridge 2010: 275–7; Dyson 2010: 145; Richardson 1992: 382–3.

---

Augustus, *Achievements* 21
I built a theater in the name of my nephew Marcus Marcellus, near the Temple of Apollo, in great part on land purchased from private owners.

---

Dio, *Roman History* 43.49.2
Caesar, wanting to build a theater like Pompey, laid the foundations of one but did not complete it. Augustus finished it and named it after his nephew Marcus Marcellus.

---

Dio, *Roman History* 53.30.5–6
Augustus gave Marcellus a public funeral, eulogizing him as was customary. He placed him in the tomb he was building and he honored his memory by naming the theater, whose foundations were laid down earlier by Caesar, Marcellus.

Suetonius, *Augustus* 29.4

Augustus built some works in the names of others, of course of his grandsons and his wife and his sister, such as the Porticus and Basilica of Gaius and Lucius, likewise, the Porticus of Livia and the Porticus of Octavia and the Theater of Marcellus.

Suetonius, *Augustus* 43.5

Again at the beginning of the games at which he was dedicating the Theater of Marcellus, it happened that the joints of his curule chair[8] became loose and he fell backwards.

Pliny, *Natural History* 8.25.65

Augustus, at the dedication of the Theater of Marcellus, was the first in all of Rome to display a tamed tiger in a cage.

## 5.16 Porticus of Livia, Porticus of Octavia, and Porticus of Pompey

Porticoes were covered colonnades and there are some ancient authors who refer to porticoes as good locations for romantic rendezvous or simply as places to walk. Other authors, such as Vitruvius, mention the utilitarian function of the porticus, considered to be an ideal spot for shielding spectators from inclement weather. Vitruvius also discusses its possible implications for healthfulness.

A porticus was part of Pompey's theater complex. There were other porticoes in the city, including but not limited to that of Livia (the wife of the emperor Augustus) and of Octavia (sister of the emperor Augustus). The significant remains of the Porticus of Octavia, near the Theater of Marcellus, are still visible and located only steps from the numerous restaurants and cafes that line the modern Via del Portico d'Ottavia. The Porticus was eventually used as part of the church Sant'Angelo in Pescheria and used as a fish market (there is an inscription that survives as a testament to this use).

Further reading: Claridge 2010: 239–41, 253–6, 339–40; Coarelli 2014: 283–5; O'Sullivan 2011: 80; Richardson 1992: 318–19; von Stackelberg 2009: 81–2; Woodhull 2003.

Vitruvius, *On Architecture* 5.9.1

Behind the stage, a porticus should be established so that when sudden rains interrupt the spectacle, the audience may have a place to go from the theater, and there may also be a place for preparing the stage equipment. For example, there is the Porticus of Pompey.

Vitruvius, *On Architecture* 5.9.5
The spaces in the middle, open to the sky and between the porticoes, should be adorned with green plants and trees because walks that are open to the sky are very good for health.

Cicero, *On Fate* 8
Is the nature of the place [Rome] able to make it that we walk in the Porticus of Pompey rather than in the Campus?

Propertius, *Elegies* 4.8.75–7
And don't walk around all dressed up in the Pompeian shade, nor when sand covers the lascivious Forum. Beware of turning your neck sideways towards the highest point of the theater or letting an open litter permit your delay.

Propertius, *Elegies* 2.32.11–16
Of course the Pompeian Porticus is too base for you with its shady columns, noble with its brilliant ceilings and the rows crowded with plane-trees rising equally and the rivers which fall from the calm Maro and the sound that falls in the whole circle from the murmuring waters, when Triton suddenly pours water from his mouth.[9]

Ovid, *The Art of Love* 1.67–70
Only walk lingering under the Pompeian shade,[10] when the sun approaches the back of the lion of Hercules. Or where the mother has added her own gifts to the gifts of the son, a work rich with foreign marble. You should not avoid the Porticus of Livia, sprinkled with old paintings and holding the name of its founder.

Pliny the Elder, *Natural History* 14.3.11
What Valerianus Cornelius thought worthy of memory above all was that one vine at Rome in the Porticus of Livia covers the open-air promenades with its shady branches and the same one is fertile with twelve amphorae of new wine.

Pliny the Younger, *Letters* 1.5.9
We met at the Porticus of Livia, when we were each traveling one to the other.

*Corpus of Latin Inscriptions* 6.1034
[On the Porticus of Octavia]
*Imperator* Caesar Lucius Septimius Severus Pertinax Augustus Arabicus Adiabenicus Parthicus Maximus with tribunician power eleven times, *imperator* eleven times, consul three times, father of the country, and *imperator* Caesar Marcus Aurelius

Antoninus Pius Felix Augustus with tribunician power six times, consul, proconsul, restored [this porticus] that was ruined by fire.

# Amphitheaters

## 5.17 The building and magnificence of the Flavian Amphitheater

One can continue to find today the remains of Roman amphitheaters across the former Roman world, from France to Libya to Switzerland to Tunisia to the United Kingdom, not to mention all of the ones in Italy (see Fig. 5.2). Despite the numerous remains in various places, there is one amphitheater that tends to be on top of the list of monuments to visit for all tourists: the Colosseum. In ancient Rome, the Colosseum was known as the Flavian Amphitheater, named for the imperial family responsible for its construction (started by Vespasian in 70 CE and completed in 80 CE by his son Titus). It was only in the Middle Ages that it came to be known by the name we often call it today, the Colosseum. It took this name from the Colossus of Nero, the large statue of Nero that stood near the amphitheater. The emperors built the structure on the site of the lake

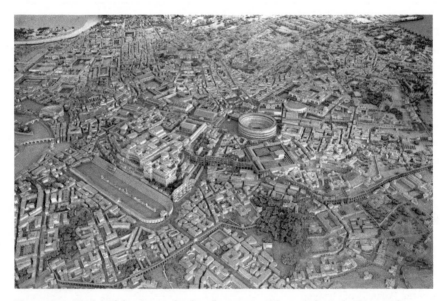

**Figure 5.2** Model of the city in the fourth century CE, made by Italo Gismondi (twentieth century CE). On display at the Museum of Roman Civilization. The Colosseum is in the center and on the left is the Circus Maximus. © Vanni Archive/ Art Resource, NY.

that was part of Nero's Domus Aurea (Golden House) (for more on this house, see **2.17** in this volume).

Even in the city of Rome itself, the Flavian amphitheater was not the first nor the only amphitheater. The first stone amphitheater in the city was that of Statilius Taurus. We know where it stood in the city, but nothing remains of it. There are remains visible of another, much smaller amphitheater: the Amphitheatrum Castrense, located near the church of S. Croce in Gerusalemme.

The Flavian Amphitheater is certainly the most well-known monument from ancient Rome, at least to the modern tourist. This is likely in great part due to its monumental remains and its glorification in film and popular culture. There has been recent controversy over having its maintenance sponsored by corporations. At present, the Colosseum remains open to the public and there are numerous exhibits held there.

As part of the work to recreate the lived experience of the Romans and to better understand the monuments themselves, recent digital work has tried to repopulate the Colosseum. Such work helps us to think about, in a concrete way, the issues crowds would have faced in the Colosseum. Furthermore, there has been scholarly work not only on the placement of people within the Colosseum and other entertainment venues, but also on their comfort.

Further reading: Claridge 2010: 312–19; Coarelli 2014: 164–70; Coleman 2000: 227–35, 239–40; Dodge 2013; Dodge 2014; Fagan 2011b; Futrell 1997; Gallia 2016; Gutierrez et al. 2007; Hopkins and Beard 2011; Lovatt 2016: 361–8; Richardson 1992: 7–11; Rose 2005; Scobie 1988; Welch 2009.

---

Suetonius, *Vespasian* 9.1
Vespasian made new works: a Temple of Peace very near to the Forum and a temple of the Divine Claudius on the Caelian Hill that was begun by Agrippina, but almost completely destroyed by Nero, also an amphitheater in the middle of the city as he learned Augustus had intended.

---

Suetonius, *Titus* 7.3
When the amphitheater was dedicated and the nearby baths quickly constructed, Titus gave a most splendid and plentiful gladiatorial display, as well as a naval battle in the old *naumachia*,[11] and in the same place a gladiatorial exhibition, and in one day there were five thousand beasts of every sort.

---

Martial, *On Spectacles* 1

Let barbarous Memphis be silent about the wonders of the pyramids, let Assyrian work not mention Babylon, nor let the soft Ionians be praised for the temple of Trivia. Let the altar crowded with horns leave Delos unnoticed, nor let the Carians carry to the stars with immoderate praises the Mausoleum hanging in empty air. All work yields to Caesar's amphitheater. Fame will speak of one work before all.

---

Martial, *On Spectacles* 2

Here, where the starry Colossus sees the constellations nearby and tall scaffolding rises in the middle of the Sacra Via,[12] where the hateful halls of the fierce king were shining and one house was standing in the whole city, here, where the venerable mass of the remarkable Amphitheater is erected, was the lake of Nero. Here where we marvel at the baths,[13] speedy gifts and an arrogant field had taken houses from the poor. Where the Claudian Porticus spreads out its wide shade was the farthest part of the end of the palace. Rome has been returned to herself and with you as guardian, Caesar, the delights that were of the master are of the people.

---

## 5.18 Spectators at the amphitheater

Ancient writers themselves have what may seem to be conflicting viewpoints within their own works on the experience of being at the amphitheater for gladiatorial games. Seneca, for instance, found the spectacles problematic but praised the virtues of the contenders. Augustine, writing near the end of the fourth century CE, describes how the arena entices his student Alypius and shows that the pull of the arena existed even for Christians. Some inscriptions in the *Corpus of Latin Inscriptions* identify names and/or locations of seat holders.

---

*Corpus of Latin Inscriptions* 6.2059

Seats designated in the Amphitheater in the consulship of Lucius Aelius Plautius Lamia and Quintus Pactumeius Fronto, received from Laberius Maximus, procurator, superintendent of grain … in the first terrace, twelfth wedge.

---

Seneca, *Letters* 7.2–5

Nothing is so destructive to good character as to sit idly at a spectacle. Then indeed through pleasure, the vices creep in more easily. What do you think I am saying? I return more greedy, more ambitious, more wanton, yes even crueler and more inhuman, since I was among men. By chance I fell upon a midday spectacle, expecting games and wit and something relaxing, by which the eyes of men may take a rest from the human bloodshed. It was the opposite. Whatever was fought before, that was mercy. Now, once the nonsense was over, there were the true murders. The men have nothing with which to cover themselves. They expose their whole bodies to the blows and they never launch their hands in vain. Many prefer this to the usual pairs and requested gladiators. Why not? There is no helmet, the sword is not driven back by a shield. Where are the protections? Where are the skills? All these things are the delays of death. In the morning, men are thrown to lions and bears. At midday, they are thrown to the spectators. They demand that the killers be thrown to those about to kill them and they hold back the victor for another slaughter. The result of the fights is death. The matter is settled by sword and fire. These things happen while the sand of the arena is empty. "But he committed robbery!" someone says. "He killed a man!" So what? Since he killed someone, he deserves to suffer this. What do you deserve, wretched one, that you are watching this? "Kill, lash, burn! Why does he run into the sword so fearfully? Why does he kill without boldness? Why does he die with little pleasure? Let him be driven to his wounds with lashes. Let them receive mutual strikes on bare and open chests." The spectacle is at intermission. Meanwhile let men be slaughtered, lest there is nothing happening.

---

Martial, *On Spectacles* 3.1–2
Caesar, what race is so distant, so barbarous, that a spectator from it is not in your city?

---

Pliny the Younger, *Panegyric* 33
Then a spectacle was seen that was neither weak nor loose nor what might soften and break the spirits of men, but one that kindles them to honorable wounds and contempt of death, when they perceive a love of praise and desire for victory even in the bodies of slaves and criminals.

---

Augustine, *Confessions* 6.8.13
Alypius had gone to Rome to learn law and there he was taken incredibly by the extraordinary longing for gladiatorial displays. Although indeed he was opposed to and detested such things, when he met certain friends and schoolmates of his in the road, by chance while returning from lunch, with friendly force they led him, who was refusing vehemently and resisting, into the amphitheater on days of cruel and fatal games. He was saying these things: "If you drag my body into that place and you deposit it there, are you able to direct my mind and my eyes to those sights? And so I will be present and absent and I will overcome you and them." Once they heard these things, they led him forth with them nonetheless, perhaps because they wanted to discover whether he was able to accomplish that very thing. When they arrived there and they were fixed in the seats they were able to get, everything was boiling with savage pleasures. He, with his eyes closed, forbade his mind to proceed into such evils. If only he had closed up his ears! For at a certain fall of a fight, when a huge shout of the whole mob had struck him violently, he was overcome by

curiosity and as if prepared to despise and overcome the sight, whatever it was, he opened his eyes. And he was struck through and through by a wound in his soul greater than that man, whom he desired to watch, received in his body. And he fell more miserably than that man for whom the shout was made ... Indeed when he saw that blood, he drank in the cruelty and did not turn himself away, but fixed his gaze. And he was drinking up the madness and was not knowing it and he was pleased by the evil of the contest and was made drunk by the bloody pleasure. And he was not now that same man who had come but one from the crowd to which he had come and a true companion of those by whom he had first been led. What more? He watched, he shouted, he burned, then he took away with him the insanity by which he was incited to return, not only with those by whom he was first dragged, but even before those men and dragging others.

## Training gladiators at the city's schools

### 5.19 Training at the Ludus Magnus and the Ludus Matutinus

The Ludus Magnus, the Great School, was a training school for gladiators situated close to the Flavian Amphitheater and it was the largest of the four schools in the city established under the emperor Domitian. The modern tourist can still see the remains of the school across the street from the Flavian Amphitheater between Via Labicana and Via S. Giovanni in Laterano. The Ludus Matutinus was another training school for gladiators. It would have trained those fighting in the beast hunts (called the *venationes*) in the morning exhibitions.

Further reading: Coarelli 2014: 170–2; Coleman 2000: 235–7; Richardson 1992: 236–8.

*Corpus of Latin Inscriptions* 6.10164
To the spirits of the dead of Cornelia Frontina. She lived sixteen years and seven months. Her father Marcus Ulpius Callistus, freedman of Augustus, overseer of the armory of the Ludus Magnus and his most venerable wife Flavia Nice, made this for themselves and their freedmen and freedwomen and their descendants.

*Corpus of Latin Inscriptions* 6.10172a, b
Eutychus Neronianus, freedman of Augustus, doctor of the Ludus Matutinus, made this for himself and his well deserving wife, freedwoman Irene, and their freedmen and women and their descendants.

# Stadium

## 5.20 The building of the Stadium of Domitian

The stadium stood where the modern tourist now finds the Piazza Navona, which retains the shape of the original track. The modern buildings are constructed on the former site of the seating. It was constructed under the emperor Domitian. The modern piazza is now the site of two fountains by Giacomo della Porta and of the well-known Fountain of the Four Rivers by Bernini. As the location likely had a lively street life in antiquity, so it does still now, with numerous restaurants and shops lining the former shape of the seats.

Further reading: Claridge 2010: 234–7; Coleman 2000: 241–2; Richardson 1992: 366–7.

---

Suetonius, *Domitian* 5
He erected … a stadium.

---

SHA, *Life of Elagabalus* 26.3
He gathered all the prostitutes from the Circus, the theater, the Stadium, and all other places, and baths.

---

# Religion in the City: Structures, Spaces, and Experiences

From Rome's earliest days, religion profoundly shaped the landscape of the city and the rhythms of its inhabitants' daily lives. Religion was not a separate sphere of activity, confined only to certain spaces or evident only at particular times of the year, but was ever-present, embedded in nearly all aspects of Roman life from politics to military affairs to social interactions. Religion was always visible to the ancient eye whether in imposing structures such as the Temple of Capitoline Jupiter that were part of the built environment (**6.2**), more subtle forms like the boundary stones of the *pomerium* (**6.1**), or natural features on the outskirts of the city including wooded groves sacred to agricultural deities (**6.7, 6.8**). As Rome grew from a small city to the capital of an extensive empire, the number of religious spaces in the city continually increased and its religious complexion changed dramatically. Some eras were more transformative than others, though, in particular the reign of Augustus, which saw the addition of important new temples (**6.10**), religious structures (**6.11**), and rituals (**6.9, 6.12**). Yet the prominence of religion in the everyday life of the city had always been apparent in the many festivals and celebrations that occurred throughout the year and literally filled the streets: the special circuit run by priests during the Lupercalia festival in mid-February (**6.5**); the raucous musical procession and ritual begging of adherents of the Great Mother Goddess in early April (**6.13**); and the ceremonial dancing of the twenty-four priests of Mars to mark the opening and closing of the campaigning seasons in March and October respectively (**6.6**). It is easy to associate the ancient city with traditional gods, temples, rites, and religious personnel (**6.3, 6.4, 6.9**), but Rome was actually home to a wide range of imported customs and beliefs that contributed richly to create a diverse religious landscape. Some originally foreign cults were gradually accepted and incorporated into Roman religious practices, such as the worship of the Phrygian Great Mother and the Egyptian goddess Isis whose temples stood in central locations within the city (**6.13, 6.14**), while others, such as Mithraism, Judaism, and Christianity, remained distinct geographically and otherwise (**6.15–17**).

# Sacred spaces and customary rites

## 6.1 The *pomerium*: Rome's sacred boundary

The city was defined by a sacred boundary called the *pomerium* and certain activities (namely military affairs) could not take place within the area it enclosed. The *pomerium* was not a wall but essentially a virtual boundary, though by the imperial period it was represented physically by large stone blocks (2 m by 1 m) called *cippi*, as Tacitus reports, that marked its route whenever it changed direction and indicated the distance to the next marker. Establishment of the *pomerium* was attributed to Romulus who plowed a furrow to mark out the extent of the city as key buildings were being built. Yet the boundary's origins actually date to his earlier conflict with his brother Remus to determine who would found Rome (see **1.8** in this volume). Romulus, observing twelve vultures from the Palatine Hill, won out over Remus who saw only six from the Aventine. This resulted in the exclusion of the Aventine from the city's sacred enclosure until the emperor Claudius expanded the *pomerium* to include it. More than one hundred boundary stones set up by Claudius to mark his extension of the *pomerium* have been found, including several north of the Piazza del Popolo.

Further reading: Beard, North, and Price 1998: 177–81; Richardson 1992: 293–6.

Tacitus, *Annals* 12.23–4

Claudius expanded the *pomerium* of the city by an ancient custom by which those who have enlarged the empire are permitted to extend the limits of the city as well. However, Roman leaders had not made use of this custom, except Lucius Sulla and the divine Augustus, although they had subdued many nations. The aspirations of the kings or their glory have been variously reported in this regard, but I think the original foundation of the city, and the *pomerium* that Romulus established, merit some attention. The furrow to mark out the town, therefore, began from the Forum Boarium (where we see a bronze statue of a bull because that type of animal is yoked to the plow) so that it would enclose the Great Altar of Hercules. From there stones were placed at fixed intervals along the base of the Palatine Hill to the altar of Consus, the old Senate House, then to the shrine of the Lares and from there to the Roman Forum. They believed the Forum and the Capitol were added to the city not by Romulus, but by Titus Tatius. Subsequently, the *pomerium* increased in accordance with fortune. The limits Claudius established are easy to recognize and have been entered in the public records.

## 6.2 The Temple of Capitoline Jupiter: one temple for three gods

At the end of the sixth century BCE, Tarquinius Superbus (Tarquin the Proud), Rome's last king, completed the massive temple to Jupiter, Juno, and Minerva, known as the Capitoline triad, which his father had earlier vowed and begun. Located on the Capitoline Hill, the temple is often referred to as the Temple of Capitoline Jupiter or the Temple of Jupiter Optimus Maximus (Jupiter the Best and Greatest) even though he shared it with the two goddesses conceived of as his wife and daughter respectively. The temple was grand in terms of its size and decoration, featuring numerous statues and a roof made of gilded bronze tiles. During the middle Republic, the original structure was repaired and expanded, and after it burned to the ground in 83 BCE, it was rebuilt the following decade such that late in the first century BCE Dionysius of Halicarnassus could see it first-hand to describe its magnificence. Very little of the structure remains today, though excavations in the 1990s uncovered more of the temple's huge podium made of grey tufa blocks, some of which are on display inside the Palazzo dei Conservatori museum, which is part of the Capitoline Museums.

Further reading: Claridge 2010: 268–70; Richardson 1992: 221–4.

---

Dionysius of Halicarnassus, *Roman Antiquities* 4.61.3–4

The temple was set upon a high base that had a perimeter of 800 feet, and each side was nearly 200 feet (one would find a small difference between the length which exceeds the width but not by a full fifteen feet). For the temple was erected on the same foundations as the temple built in our fathers' day after the fire [83 BCE], and differs from the original one only in the costliness of the materials. Facing south, the front of the temple has three rows of columns; each side has a single row of columns. There are three parallel shrines inside the temple sharing common walls; the middle one is for Jupiter, on one side is a shrine for Juno and on the other for Minerva, all covered by one pediment and one roof.

---

## 6.3 The Temple of Vesta and the House of the Vestal Virgins: guarding Rome's sacred flame

Rome's only known Temple of Vesta, a goddess primarily of the hearth, was located in the Roman Forum at the foot of the Palatine Hill where ruins of the temple can be seen today. Inside this small round structure, which Ovid attributes to the reign of Numa, six priestesses called Vestal Virgins tended Vesta's sacred fire. Both the fire and the priestesses' virginity were connected to the city's welfare: failure to maintain either meant that the city was in danger and the priestesses at fault had to be punished to restore the gods' favor (see also **11.16** in this volume). Ironically, the temple itself was not immune to fire's destructive powers, as Pliny the Elder records in his account of heroic efforts to save the Palladium; this was a statue of Pallas Athena believed to have been rescued from Troy by Aeneas then placed in the inner sanctuary of Vesta's temple (see **10.4** in this volume). Just southeast of the temple was the Atrium Vestae (Hall of Vesta) where the Vestal Virgins lived. Rome's most prominent civic priestesses, their privileged status is evident not only in the location of their residence, but also in their ritual duties, such as preparation of materials used in all state sacrifices and participation in important festivals such as the Parilia and Lupercalia (see **6.4** and **6.5** in this volume), and in the special rights they had that ordinary Roman women did not, including the right to give testimony in court and to write a will. They were highly respected by society at large and also within their own families, as the inscriptions from statue bases of Vestals found in and around the Atrium Vestae, the Temple of Vesta, and the Forum suggest.

Further reading: Beard, North, and Price 1998: 51–8; Richardson 1992: 42–4, 412–13; Staples 1998; Wildfang 2006.

---

Ovid, *Fasti* 6.257–68, 295–8

They recall that Rome had held its fortieth Parilia when the guardian goddess of the flame was received in her temple. It was the work of the peaceful king; the Sabine land has not produced a temperament more god-fearing than his. What you now see covered in bronze at that time you would see as a roof of straw and the wall was woven from pliant twigs. This little spot, which now supports the Hall of Vesta, was then the great palace of unshorn Numa. Nevertheless, the shape of the temple that now remains is said to have existed before, and there is a reason worthy of approval for the shape. Vesta and the earth are the same: undying fire exists for both. Earth and the hearth indicate their own place ... I foolishly thought for a long time that there were images of Vesta; I soon learned there are none under her curved dome. The inextinguishable fire is hidden in that temple: neither Vesta nor fire has an effigy.

---

Pliny the Elder, *Natural History* 7.43.141

Metellus lived out his old age in blindness, having lost his sight in a fire [in 241 BCE] when he snatched the Palladium from the Temple of Vesta—his motive was remarkable but the consequence pitiable. So it follows, indeed, that he should not be called unfortunate, though he cannot be called fortunate. To no one else in history but him did the Roman people grant that he be driven in a chariot to the Curia whenever he was going to meetings of the Senate, a great and lofty honor given to him for his eyes.

---

*Corpus of Latin Inscriptions* 6.32414

To Flavia Publicia, daughter of Lucius, chief Vestal Virgin, most holy and pious. The divinity of the most holy mother Vesta has fully approved her most holy and scrupulous care of the sacred rites to which she was devoted through all the grades of her priesthood with praiseworthy management. Aemilia Rogatilla, daughter of Gaius, daughter of [Flavia's] sister, together with Minucius Honoratus Marcellus Aemilianus, of a senatorial family, her [i.e., Aemilia's] son, [dedicated this statue base] on account of [Flavia's] outstanding piety and devotion towards her. Placed five days before the Ides of July in the consulship of our lords [Philippus] Augustus, for the second time, and [Philippus] Caesar.[1]

---

*Corpus of Latin Inscriptions* 6.2139

To Coelia Claudiana, chief Vestal Virgin, chosen by the gods, the divinity of Vesta rightly wished to preserve so great a presiding priestess for herself. Coelia Nerviana, her sister, together with her husband Pierius and their children pray that the gods allow [her] to perform [her duties] for so many generations.

---

## 6.4 The Parilia/Romaia festival: celebrating the founding of the city

The Romans observed an annual festival on April 21, which developed different associations over time reflecting the dynamic nature of Roman ritual. The holiday originally focused on purifying and protecting the flocks and herds, but by the late Republic, the day, which was then called the Parilia festival, was also seen as the anniversary of Rome's founding and both rural and urban ceremonies were celebrated. Plutarch, writing late in the first century CE or early in the second, tries to make sense of the festival's changing aspects and overall significance. In his dialogue set at a dinner party in Rome, Athenaeus, writing in the second century CE, indicates that under Hadrian the festival assumed a new name, the Romaia or Festival of Rome, which more obviously connected it to Rome's birthday and with the emperor's massive new Temple of Venus and Rome which he may have dedicated on the Parilia/Romaia in 121 CE.

Further reading: Beard, North, and Price 1998: 174–6, 257–9; Scullard 1981: 103–5.

---

Plutarch, *Life of Romulus* 12.1

It is generally agreed that the founding of the city happened on the eleventh day before the Kalends of May [i.e., April 21], and the Romans celebrate this day as a festival, calling it the birthday of their country. In the beginning, so it is said, they did not sacrifice any living thing, since they thought they ought to keep pure and unstained with blood the festival named for their country's birthday. In fact, before the founding of the city, they had a herdsmen's festival on this day and called it the Parilia.

---

Athenaeus, *The Learned Banqueters* 8.361e–f

And so while many conversations of this nature were still going on, throughout the entire city sounds became audible: both the humming of pipes and the clash of cymbals, the booming of drums along with singing. It happened to be the festival called the Parilia long ago, but now called the Romaia to mark the dedication of the Temple of the Fortune of the City by the wholly excellent and most cultured emperor Hadrian. All the inhabitants of Rome and those staying in the city celebrate that day each year as a notable occasion.

---

## 6.5 The Lupercalia and the ritual race of the *luperci*

The Lupercalia, celebrated on February 15, was one of Rome's oldest festivals and entailed both purification and fertility rites. Goats, as well as a dog, were sacrificed to the god Pan or perhaps Inuus or Faunus, both of which are identified with Pan. This may have taken place at the Lupercal, the cave where Romans believed Romulus and Remus were found by the she-wolf. The cave's exact location is not known today, though it was between the Circus Maximus and the Temple of Magna Mater on the Palatine Hill. Ancient authorities (see, for example, Plutarch, *Life of Romulus* 21.3–8; Varro, *On the Latin Language* 6.34; Augustine, *City of God* 18.12) differ regarding aspects of the Lupercalia festival and their significance, including the particular route taken by the *luperci*, a group of priests who ran a sacred circuit of the city. The *luperci* performed this ritual either naked or nearly so, and lashed anyone they encountered during the race with goatskin thongs, especially women of childbearing age. It seems Romans of all ranks and both sexes came out to watch and, in some cases, participate in the ceremonies. In his biography of Caesar, Plutarch reports on a particularly memorable celebration of the Lupercalia in 44 BCE when Mark Antony, one of the *luperci*, offered a diadem to Julius Caesar who refused it for its connotations of monarchy.

Further reading: Littlewood 1975; North 2000: 47–50; Wiseman 1995b.

---

Plutarch, *Life of Caesar* 61.2–4

Many well-born young men and civic magistrates run a race through the city naked, striking those they encounter with hairy goatskin thongs in playful fun and laughter.

Many leading women purposely put themselves in their path and submit their hands to the blows, just as in school, believing that for pregnant women it is good for easy childbirth and for women who are barren to become pregnant. Caesar was watching these rites, seated upon the Rostra on a golden throne and dressed in triumphal attire. Antony was one of the runners of the sacred race for he was also a consul. When he came into the Forum carrying a diadem entwined with a laurel wreath and the crowd parted for him, he offered it to Caesar. The applause was not distinct, but faint and contrived. When Caesar rejected it, the whole populace applauded in turn. Antony offered it again and a few people applauded, but when Caesar did not accept it once again, everyone applauded. With this experiment complete, Caesar stood up and ordered that the crown be taken away to the Capitol.

## 6.6 Ritual dancing in the streets

The *salii* were twenty-four priests of Mars whose ritual responsibilities included care for sacred figure-of-eight shields called *ancilia*, which were kept in a shrine to Mars inside the Regia. Some associated their name with the Latin verb *salire* meaning "to leap" or *salitare* meaning "to dance" because of the ritual dances they performed in honor of the gods of war. For several days in March and October, the months marking the start and end of the campaigning season respectively, they processed through the streets of Rome wearing archaic military armor and carrying weapons, stopping to perform ritual dances to flute music while singing a special hymn called the *Carmen Saliare*. In the evening following their ritual procession and dance, they feasted in the Temple of Mars in the Forum of Augustus (see **6.10** in this volume). Dionysius of Halicarnassus describes the colorful appearance and rites of the Salii in terms he hoped would make sense to his Greek audience who were not familiar with many Roman customs.

Further reading: Scullard 1981: 85–9, 195.

---

Dionysius of Halicarnassus, *Roman Antiquities* 2.70.2–3
These Salii are a kind of dancers and singers of hymns for the gods of war. Their festival is around the time of the Panathenaea in the month called March.[2] It is celebrated at public expense and for many days during which they perform dances through the city to the Forum and the Capitoline Hill and to many other places both private and public. They wear embroidered tunics girded with belts made of bronze; overtop they fasten with brooches robes bordered with purple and striped in crimson, which they call *trabeae* (this robe is distinctively Roman and a mark of great honor among them). On their heads they wear high caps called *apices* that are narrowed into the shape of a cone, which the Greeks call *kyrbasiai*. Each of them has a sword hanging from his belt,

and in his right hand holds a spear or a staff or some other such weapon, and in his left a Thracian shield.

## 6.7 Prayers and sacrifices at the grove of Robigo to protect the crops

On April 25, the Robigalia festival was celebrated to appease Robigo, the divine personification of mildew or blight that affected vines and cereal crops (the former were associated with Bacchus/Dionysus and the latter with Ceres/Demeter). The ritual consisted of prayers to the deity and sacrifices of dogs, as well as sheep, performed by the *flamen* or priest of Quirinus (a deity associated with Romulus). A note about the festival in an early imperial calendar indicates that games involving runners were also held on this occasion. Although these rites took place in a grove five Roman miles north of the city at the fifth milestone on the Via Claudia, they are included here to give a sense of the diversity of ritual practices and spaces associated with the ancient city of Rome. They also show how natural rather than purpose-built spaces were sometimes selected for sacred functions.

Further reading: Scullard 1981: 108–10.

Ovid, *Fasti* 4.905–22

When I was returning to Rome from Nomentum on this day, a crowd dressed in white stood in my way in the middle of the road. The *flamen* was going to the grove of ancient Robigo to offer the entrails of a dog and the entrails of a sheep to the flames. I immediately approached him so that I would not be ignorant of the rite. Your priest, Quirinus, pronounced these words: "Harsh Robigo, spare Ceres' plants, and let the slender shoot tremble on top of the ground. Permit the crops to grow, nourished by the stars of a favorable sky, until they are ready for the sickle. Your power is not slight: the crops, which you have marked, the disheartened farmer counts among his losses. Neither the winds nor the rains have harmed Ceres so much, nor does she grow pale in this way once burned by marble frost, as when Titan warms the wet stalks. That is the moment of your anger, fearsome goddess. Be sparing, I pray, and keep scabby hands far from the harvest. Do not harm the cultivated fields: the potential to harm is enough."

## 6.8 Festivities in the grove of the Arval Brothers

This extract comes from a longer inscription on a marble tablet that records ceremonies on 19 May 87 CE, which was the second day of the festival of Dea Dia, a goddess of cereal crops. Priests called *fratres Arvales* (Arval Brothers) worshipped Dea Dia in her grove—a woodland clearing located near the fifth milestone on the Via Campania, five miles south of Rome. As with the previous entry for the Robigalia, the ceremonies conducted by the Arval Brothers for Dea Dia offer further insight into the wide range of practices and places connected to religious life for the inhabitants of ancient Rome, some of which spilled over to sites on the outskirts of the city. The account includes many details such as the full names of the Arval Brothers present and their ranks within the priestly college, the different sacrifices offered to the goddess, and even the special attire worn on this occasion. The grove contained a temple of Dea Dia, as well as a shrine for the imperial cult. It also had additional structures for the social and religious rituals that took place during the May festival and other times, such as a bath complex, a dining room (mentioned in this inscription), and a circus building for races.

Further reading: Beard, North, and Price 1998: 194–6; Scullard 1981: 30.

---

*Select Latin Inscriptions* 5037.15–29
In the consulship of Gaius Bellicus Natalis Tebanianus and Gaius Ducenius Proculus, fourteen days before the Kalends of June, in the grove of Dea Dia, when Gaius Iulius Silanus was master, with Gaius Nonius Bassus Salvius Liberalis taking charge, the Arval Brothers offered sacrifice to Dea Dia. Gaius Salvius Liberalis, who was serving as master in place of Gaius Iulius Silanus, in front of the grove sacrificed onto the altar two pigs to atone for the grove, which had been polluted and for the work that had to be done there; then he sacrificed a cow in honor of Dea Dia. Gaius Salvius Liberalis Nonius Bassus, Lucius Maecius Postumus, Aulus Iulius Quadratus, Publius Sallustius Blaesus, Quintus Tillius Sassius sat down in the *tetrastylum*[3] and feasted off the sacrifices, and once they had put on their *togae praetextae*[4] and wreaths made of ears of corn with woolen bands, they climbed up the grove of Dea Dia to a spot lying out of the way, and through Salvius Liberalis Nonius Bassus, who was serving as master, and Quintus Tillius Sassius, who was serving in place of the *flamen*, they sacrificed to Dea Dia a choice lamb, and once the sacrifice was complete, they all made an offering of incense and wine.

---

# Tradition and innovation under Augustus

## 6.9 Ceremonies in the Campus Martius to celebrate a new age

The Romans celebrated a *saeculum*, a period of 100 or 110 years, which was held to be the longest span of human life, with Saecular Games (*Ludi Saeculares*).

These involved sacrifices and theatrical performances. They are known to have taken place in 249 and 146 BCE, then several times during the Empire when emperors determined the date for the next celebration either based on the foundation of Rome or in relation to the previous celebration. The most famous Saecular Games are those staged by Augustus in 17 BCE. A lengthy inscription (excerpted here) records the prayers and sacrifices offered for the welfare of the Roman state and the emperor and his household. This text was later set up at the site where many of the ceremonies took place, an altar called the Tarentum in the northwest Campus Martius near the Tiber. Among Augustus's innovations to the games were seven additional days of festivities beyond the traditional three, which featured daytime and nighttime activities (see **4.13** in this volume). These included circus games and choral performances by 110 matrons, as well as groups of twenty-seven boys and the same number of girls who sang a hymn before the Temple of Apollo on the Palatine that had been specially written for the occasion by the Augustan poet Horace called the *Carmen Saeculare* or Song for the Ages.

Further reading: Beard, North, and Price 1998: 201–6; Putnam 2001; Severy 2003: 57–9; Zanker 1988: 167–72.

---

*Corpus of Latin Inscriptions* 6.32323.139–40, 147–9
On June 3, on the Palatine, the emperor Caesar Augustus and Marcus Agrippa sacrificed to Apollo and Diana nine offering cakes [each of three types], and prayed thus … Once the sacrifice had been completed, twenty-seven boys and the same number of girls, whose parents were still living and to whom notice had been given, sang a hymn. [They did so] in the same manner on the Capitol. Quintus Horatius Flaccus composed the hymn.

---

Horace, *Carmen Saeculare* 1–12, 61–72
Phoebus and Diana, mistress of the forests, shining glory of the heavens, O you always worshipped and deserving to be worshipped, grant what we pray for on this holy occasion when the Sibylline verses have instructed that chosen girls and virtuous boys sing a hymn for the gods who find the seven hills pleasing. O nurturing Sun, who on your gleaming chariot bring forth the day and hide it away, and are reborn another and the same, may you be able to look upon nothing greater than the city of Rome! … Phoebus, prophet adorned with his shining bow and pleasing to the nine Muses, who eases the body's weary limbs with his healing art, if he looks upon the altars on the Palatine with favor, always prolongs Roman strength and prosperous Latium for another cycle and a better age. And Diana, who holds the Aventine and Mount Algidus, attends to the prayers of the Fifteen Men[5] and lends friendly ears to the children's pleas.

## 6.10 A visit to the Temple of Mars Ultor

In the entry in his poetic calendar for May 12, Ovid celebrates the anniversary of the dedication of the Temple of Mars Ultor (Mars the Avenger) located in the Forum of Augustus. The temple was vowed by the young Augustus (then called Octavian) in 42 BCE for avenging the murder of Julius Caesar, his adoptive father. Not begun until the 20s BCE, it took more than twenty years to complete the building, which was dedicated in 2 BCE. Ovid envisions Mars, god of war, coming himself to see the magnificent monument replete with the figures of Aeneas and Romulus (Mars's son by the Vestal Virgin Ilia/Rhea Silvia) as founders of Rome, flanked by statues of the Julio-Claudian family and great men of the Republic. Although the porticoes on either side of the temple that housed these statues no longer exist, remains of the temple are still visible, including its white Italian marble steps and three of the Corinthian columns on the right side. The reconstruction model in Fig. 6.1 shows what the temple and the Forum of Augustus once looked like.

Further reading: Beard, North, and Price 1998: 199–201; Claridge 2010: 177–80; Coarelli 2014: 111–12; Richardson 1992: 160–2; Zanker 1988: 110–15, 192–6.

---

Ovid, *Fasti* 5.549–68

Am I deceived or are weapons resounding? I'm not: weapons were resounding. Mars comes and has presented the signs of war. The Avenger himself comes down from the heavens to his honors and magnificent temple in Augustus's forum. Both the god and his work are huge: Mars was not destined to live in any city other than his son's. This temple is worthy of trophies from the Giants. From here Mars fittingly stirs up fierce wars, whether someone impious from the East had harmed us, or someone

**Figure 6.1** The Forum of Augustus and the Temple of Mars Ultor. Reconstruction model by I. Gismondi. Photo credit: Alinari/Art Resource, NY.

from the West needs to be subdued. Mars, mighty in arms, surveys the pediments at the top of his temple and approves that invincible goddesses hold the highest points. He examines the weapons of different shapes on the doors, and arms from lands conquered by his soldiers. On this side he sees Aeneas weighed down by his dear burden, and so many ancestors of Julian nobility. Next he sees Ilia's son carrying the weapons of a [defeated] general on his shoulders, and the famous deeds placed beneath [statues of] great men arranged in rows. He takes in the sight of the temple adorned with Augustus's name and the structure seems greater when Caesar's name is read.

## 6.11 Sacrifices at the Ara Pacis Augustae

To celebrate Augustus's return to Rome following a three-year absence in Spain and Gaul, the Senate decreed the Ara Pacis Augustae (Altar of Augustan Peace) on 4 July 13 BCE. The altar was originally situated on the Via Flaminia (today the Via del Corso), the road by which Augustus had re-entered the city, and it faced the Campus Martius. Today it is located next to the Mausoleum of Augustus (see **11.11** in this volume) in a dedicated museum, having been reassembled there from the numerous fragments discovered during excavations in 1937–8 (Fig. 6.2). The Ara Pacis was formally dedicated on 30

**Figure 6.2** The Ara Pacis Augustae, currently in the Museum of the Ara Pacis in Rome. Photo credit: Scala/Art Resource, NY.

January 9 BCE, a date that coincided with the birthday of Livia, Augustus's wife. The monument consists of an altar surrounded by a high enclosure, both made of white marble. The enclosure has elaborately carved panels on each side that depict sacrificial processions of the imperial family, senators, and ordinary citizens, and mythological scenes relating to Rome's foundation such as Romulus and Remus suckled by the she-wolf at the Lupercal (see **6.5** in this volume) and Aeneas sacrificing to the *penates*, his household gods brought from Troy. Among the images on the Ara Pacis meant to reflect the prosperity and tranquility of Augustus's principate is a female figure seated with two infants on her lap whom some scholars identify as the goddess *Pax* (Peace).

Further reading: Castriota 1995; Claridge 2010: 207–13; Coarelli 2014: 299–302; Richardson 1992: 287–9; Zanker 1988: 114–25, 172–83.

Augustus, *Achievements* 12.2
When I returned to Rome from Spain and Gaul once affairs in these provinces had been favorably settled, while Tiberius Nero and Publius Quintilius were consuls [13 BCE] the Senate decreed that an altar of Augustan Peace be consecrated at the Campus Martius on account of my return; the Senate ordered the magistrates and the priests and the Vestal Virgins to perform an annual sacrifice there.

Ovid, *Fasti* 1.709–22
The poem itself has led me down to the altar of Peace: this day will be second from month's end [January 30]. Goddess Peace, your styled hair wreathed with laurels from Actium, be present and remain gentle throughout the world. So long as enemies are lacking, so too is cause for a military triumph: you will be a greater glory to our leaders than war. Let the soldier bear arms only to restrain others' arms, and let the fierce trumpet be sounded only in a parade. Let both the nearest and farthest lands tremble before Aeneas's descendants, and if any nation used to fear Rome a little, let her love Rome. Add incense, priests, to Peace's flames, and let a white sacrificial victim fall once its brow has been anointed. So that the household, which guarantees peace, may endure peacefully for years, invite gods who are favorably inclined to pious prayers.

### 6.12 The *lares* and *genius Augusti*: honoring the emperor on every corner

In 7 BCE, Augustus restructured the city of Rome, dividing it into fourteen districts (*regiones*), each further divided into wards (*vici*) of which there were

265 in total. At each crossroads, Romans had traditionally offered sacrifices to the tutelary deities thought to preside there called *Lares Compitales* (Lares of the Crossroads). With his reorganization of the city, Augustus transformed these cults, turning them into cults of his own *lares* and *genius* (guiding or protective spirit). A shrine was built at each crossroads and officials (usually slaves and former slaves titled as *magistri* or *ministri*, "priests" or "attendants") were appointed to oversee these local cults and perform sacrifices there as the inscriptions below attest. By having a shrine to the emperor's guardian deities at each crossroads, he now had a place throughout the city, which reflects Ovid's remarks below. Worship at Rome's crossroads shrines remained active into the third century CE (see also **2.8** in this volume).

Further reading: Beard, North, and Price 1998: 184–6; Severy 2003: 124–8.

Suetonius, *Augustus* 31.4
Augustus established that the Lares of the Crossroads should be decorated twice a year with spring and summer flowers.

Ovid, *Fasti* 5.143–6
I was looking for the two statues of the twin gods made fallen by the strength of many years passing. The city has a thousand *lares* and the *genius* of the leader who handed them down, and neighborhoods worship three divinities each.

*Corpus of Latin Inscriptions* 6.446[6]
The attendants of the *Lares Augusti* who first began their service on the Kalends of August: Antigonus, the slave of Marcus Iunius Eros; Anteros, the slave of Decimus Poblicius Barnas; Eros, the slave of Aulus Poblicius Damas; Iucundus, the slave of Marcus Plotius Anteros.

*Corpus of Latin Inscriptions* 6.430[7]
To the *Lares Augusti* of the emperor Caesar Nerva Traianus Augustus Germanicus [i.e., Trajan], consul for the second time [98 or 99 CE], by permission of Tiberius Allienus Sicinus Quintinanus, a tribune of the plebs, he approved the same. The *magistri* of the year 101–5 restored at their own expense the shrine of the *vicus* of the Colline Gate in the sixth *regio* from the base upwards once it had collapsed from age: Tiberius Sicinius Receptus, the freedman of Tiberius; Aulus Varro Felix, the freedman of Aulus; Publius Vettius Posidonius, the freedman of Publius; Gaius Turranius Geni[alis], the freedman of Gaius.

# Imported cults

## 6.13 The temple and rites for Magna Mater

Magna Mater (literally Great Mother) was a goddess native to Phrygia in Asia Minor who was also known by the Greek name Cybele. She was brought to Rome in 204 BCE along with a distinctive and subsequently controversial aspect of her cult: eunuch priests called *galli* who allegedly castrated themselves and engaged in self-flagellation. Stories of Magna Mater's arrival in Rome feature matrons welcoming her, among which Claudia Quinta stood out because of her chastity (see Livy, *History of Rome* 29.10–14; Ovid, *Fasti* 4.247–348). In 191 BCE, a temple was dedicated on the Palatine Hill to Magna Mater and an annual festival (the Megalesia/Megalensia or *ludi Megalenses*) established in her honor, which was celebrated on April 4. It included a procession of her cult statue by her priests, theatrical performances staged before her temple and perhaps at other locations in Rome, and chariot races held in the Circus Maximus. Little remains of the original temple which suffered considerable damage from a fire in 111 BCE; some of the concrete podium of the rebuilt structure is visible at present.

Further reading: Beard 1994; Beard, North, and Price 1998: 96–8, 160–6; Gruen 1990: 5–33; Richardson 1992: 242–3.

---

Livy, *History of Rome* 36.36.3–4
At about the same time [191 BCE], the Temple of Magna Mater from Mount Ida was dedicated ... It had been contracted for thirteen years earlier. Marcus Junius Brutus dedicated it and on account of the dedication, games were instituted called Megalesia, which Valerius Antias reports were the first theatrical performances.

---

Valerius Maximus, *Memorable Deeds and Sayings* 1.8.11
A statue of Claudia Quinta stood in the courtyard of the Temple of Magna Mater. Though the temple was twice consumed by fire (first when Publius Nasica Scipio and Lucius Bestia were consuls [111 BCE], and again in the consulships of Marcus Servilius and Lucius Lamia [3 CE]), the statue on its base was untouched by the flames.

---

Dionysius of Halicarnassus, *Roman Antiquities* 2.19.3–4
Every year the praetors hold sacrifices and games for her [the Great Mother] according to Roman customs, but a Phrygian man and woman serve as her priests. They go around the city begging for alms in her name, as is their practice, wearing images upon their chests and banging on drums while the songs of the Mother's followers are played

on the flute. By Roman custom and senatorial decree, no native Roman begs for alms in the Mother's name or processes through the city in a colored robe playing the flute or worships the goddess with Phrygian ecstatic rites.

## 6.14 Isis's female devotees at the Tiber River

At Rome, worship of Isis, a goddess of Egyptian origin, can be traced to the beginning of the first century BCE. The Greeks, who had established her cult by the fourth century BCE, identified her with Demeter, a mother goddess. She had strong associations with fertility and marriage among the Romans, and male authors like Juvenal insist she was especially appealing to women who were willing to commit extreme acts to please the goddess. Yet Isis was actually popular with both sexes, and hymns of praise found in her sanctuaries across the empire enumerate her many perceived innovations and spheres of influence including agriculture and seafaring. Worshippers were initiated into Isis's cult once they had performed a series of tasks that included bathing and purifying themselves; afterwards the secrets of the cult and the goddess's holy books were explained to them and they established a close, personal relationship with the deity. Initiation could take place in a private home or public temple, such as Isis's main temple located in the Campus Martius, which Juvenal calls "the proud king's field," near the "sheep pens," a reference to the area for voting booths called the Saepta (see **7.3** in this volume).

Further reading: Beard, North, and Price 1998: 278–82; Kraemer 1992: 71–9; Richardson 1992: 211–12; Turcan 1996: 75–129.

Juvenal, *Satires* 6.522–30
She will step down into the wintry water, breaking the ice, immerse herself three times in the morning Tiber, and wash her fearful head in the very eddies. Then she will creep, naked and trembling, on bloodied knees across the whole field of the proud king. If shining Io orders her, she will go to the ends of Egypt and carry water fetched from fiery Meroe so that she can sprinkle it in the Temple of Isis that stands tall next to the ancient sheep pens. Indeed, she believes that she is instructed by the voice of Mistress Isis herself!

## 6.15 Mithras's male initiates

The cult of Mithras was widely known throughout the Roman world by the beginning of the second century CE although many uncertainties about its origins and how the cult spread remain. The god seems to have been derived from an Indo-Iranian divinity named Mithra. Roman Mithras was hailed as the unconquerable sun god Mithras (*Sol Invictus Mithras*) and was regarded as a sun god, bull-killer, and cattle-thief. In art, he is depicted wearing a Phrygian cap and Persian trousers, and in the act of slaying a bull. Mithraic sanctuaries (called *mithraea*), which were often located in secluded areas and not readily visible to casual observers, typically featured a scene of Mithras killing a bull, which some scholars believe may be associated with the idea of salvation. Unlike worship of the Olympian gods, Mithraism was a so-called mystery religion, which meant that members had to be initiated into the cult, though it was only open to men. There were seven grades of initiation, each of which had a corresponding tutelary deity: Raven (Mercury), Bridegroom (Venus), Soldier (Mars), Lion (Jupiter), Persian (Moon), Courier of the Sun (Sun), and Father (Saturn). This hierarchy is preserved in a mid-third-century CE mosaic floor from a *mithraeum* in Ostia, dedicated by a man named Felicissimus. Nearly forty *mithraea* are known from the city of Rome datable to the second and third centuries CE while much smaller Ostia nearby boasted at least twenty, the earliest of which dates to the reign of Antoninus Pius in the mid-second century CE. Mithraism was particularly popular with soldiers, but does not seem to have appealed to the upper classes. Father, the highest grade in the initiatory sequence, is very well represented in the surviving evidence as two of these inscriptions reflect.

Further reading: Beard, North, and Price 1998: 266–308; Turcan 1996: 195–247.

---

*Corpus of Latin Inscriptions* 6.725

Marcus Aurelius Euprepes, a freedman of the emperor, in accordance with a vision set up [this] altar to the Unconquerable Sun Mithras when Bictorinus the Father and Ianuarius were holding the chief priesthoods. It was dedicated four days before the Nones of June when Lucius Eggius Maryllus and Gnaeus Papirius Ailianus were consuls.[8]

---

*Corpus of Latin Inscriptions* 6.734

To the unconquerable god Mithras: Gaius Lucretius Mnester and Marcus Aemilius Philetus, *summagistri* of Marcus Aemilius Chrysantus's first year, gave [it] as a gift.

---

*Corpus of Latin Inscriptions* 6.2271

To the spirits of the departed. Lucius Septimius Archelaus, freedman of the Three Augusti [i.e., Septimius Severus, Caracalla, and Geta], Father and priest of the unconquerable Mithras of the *domus Augusta*, made this for himself and Cosia Primitiva, his well deserving wife, and for their freedmen and freedwomen and their descendants.

## 6.16 Jewish places of worship in Trastevere

Rome was an ethnically and religiously diverse city that had a large Jewish population estimated at between 20,000 and 60,000 in the early decades of the first century CE. The majority lived across the Tiber in the area known today as Trastevere. Philo, a Hellenistic Jewish philosopher, praises Augustus's attitude towards Jews who had settled in Rome. This stands in stark contrast to the hostility shown by Caligula (officially named Gaius), the emperor in Philo's own day, whom he later describes in his account of the embassy he served on in 39/40 CE to address the oppressive conditions fellow Jews faced in the Egyptian city of Alexandria. Although not all imperial governments in Rome were as tolerant as Philo suggests Augustus was, Jewish social and religious life flourished in Rome for several centuries. Eleven synagogues are known from inscriptions such as the epitaph below; most come from one of the seven Jewish catacombs located on the outskirts of the city where Jews buried their dead.

Further reading: Beard, North, and Price 1998: 266–72; Dyson 2010: 287–90; Feldman and Reinhold 1996: 64–7; Noy 2000: 255–67.

---

Philo, *Embassy to Gaius* 155–6

Augustus knew that a great section of Rome on the other side of the Tiber was occupied and settled by Jews. Most were Roman citizens who had been emancipated; for having been brought to Italy as war captives, they were freed by their owners and not forced to break any of their ancestral traditions. Thus, he knew that they had houses of prayer and assembled in them, especially on their holy Sabbaths when, as a collective, they were taught their ancestral philosophy.

---

*Corpus of Latin Inscriptions* 6.29756

Veturia Paulla, placed in her eternal home, who lived eighty-six years and six months, a proselyte [i.e., a convert to Judaism] for sixteen years under the name of Sara, mother of the synagogues of the Campus and of Volumnius. In peace her sleep.

---

## 6.17 Rome's earliest Christian communities

By the middle of the first century CE, Christian groups were living in Rome, such as those the apostle Paul addressed in his *Letter to the Romans* and the "brothers" referred to in the opening of the excerpt from the book of *Acts* below. This text provides a history of the early Christian church, focusing on the deeds of Jesus's disciples Peter, John, and Paul. This passage comes from the concluding section, which reports Paul's missionary activities in Rome where he was brought as a captive following his arrest in Jerusalem. Nearly contemporary with Paul's stay was the great fire of 64 CE, during the emperor Nero's reign, which led to the execution of many Christians in Rome. Tacitus offers a lengthy account of the devastating fire, which destroyed large parts of the city, and of Nero's use of the Christians as scapegoats (see **10.3** in this volume). Hostility towards Christians resulted in a considerable degree of invisibility within Rome for the religion's earliest adherents who met in spaces not obviously recognizable as places for worship, especially private houses. By the third century CE, however, though intolerance persisted and at times intensified, purposely built churches began to appear in the city.

Further reading: Beard, North, and Price 1998: 236–44, 266–72; Dyson 2010: 290–4, 335–62.

---

*Acts* 28.14–16, 23–4, 30–1

And so we came to Rome. And the brothers there, having heard of us, came as far as Forum Appii and Tres Tabernae to meet us, and when Paul saw them he was thankful to God and took courage. And when we entered Rome, Paul was allowed to stay on his own with a soldier guarding him ... They [the local leaders of the Jews] appointed a day for him and many came to him at his lodgings. He expounded his views from early morning until evening, testifying to the kingdom of God and trying to persuade them about Jesus both from the law of Moses and from the prophets. While some were convinced by what he said, others disbelieved ... There [at Rome] he stayed for two whole years in his own hired dwelling, and he welcomed all who visited him, preaching the kingdom of God and teaching about the lord Jesus Christ, unhindered and with complete openness.

---

Tacitus, *Annals* 15.44

In order to quash the rumor [that he had ordered the fire], Nero substituted as the guilty and treated to the most select punishments those hated for their vices who are popularly called Christians. The originator of their name, Christus, had been executed by the governor Pontius Pilate when Tiberius was emperor. This deadly superstition, though suppressed for a time, broke out anew not only in Judaea, the source of this evil, but in Rome, too, where all horrible and shameful things flow together from everywhere and become fashionable. Thus, first those who confessed were arrested, then on their evidence a huge crowd was convicted not so much for the crime of arson as for their hatred of humankind. Those dying were made a mockery of: covered with the skins of wild animals, they died after they were torn to pieces by dogs; or they were nailed to crosses or set on fire when daylight faded, burned in place of nighttime torches. Nero offered his gardens for the spectacle and put on a public performance in the Circus at which he either mingled with the people or stood in a racing chariot dressed as a charioteer. From this, pity rose up towards the guilty, for although they deserved extraordinary punishment, it was as if they were destroyed not for the benefit of the state, but the savageness of a single man.

# The Political City

From its very beginnings, Rome was a political city where individuals vied with one another for leadership roles and laws passed or failed often amid fierce debate that shaped the city and its inhabitants in the present and for the future. Politics and political life were essentially everywhere in the city, overlapping and intertwining with spheres of activity that today tend to be separate, such as religion. Nearly any building could have political implications or political uses, not only those obviously connected with the business of the government such as the Curia (Senate House) where the Senate was convened (**7.1, 7.5**) or basilicas where law courts were held (**7.7**), but also temples, tombs, public squares, and private homes. A clear example of this is evident in some meetings of the Senate taking place in spaces other than the Curia. Cicero's choice of the Temple of Jupiter Stator (The Stayer) for one gathering held during the so-called Catilinarian conspiracy was particularly charged (**7.4**), but this was not always the case. The political face of the city can certainly be seen in the surviving monuments as well as those that no longer exist beyond references in ancient texts, where the popular assemblies met to vote on candidates for public office and to pass laws (**7.1, 7.3**) and prospective magistrates campaigned to win support (**7.2**), though with the end of the Republic, the power of the people and of individual officers of state diminished considerably. The political dimension to the city is also highly visible in the many buildings and monuments that reflect the efforts of leaders to garner or consolidate public support, especially by using the wealth gained from foreign conquests to expand and enhance central spaces while simultaneously commemorating victory through lasting memorials, such as Caesar's Forum (**7.8**). Whether in the Republic or the Empire, many of the buildings are products of elite competition, of a strong desire to put one's stamp on the city, differentiate oneself from rivals, and leave one's mark for prosperity. Naturally some of these projects were grand, even grandiose schemes, huge in scope and lavish in decoration, sometimes mirroring their author's reputation, as Domitian's palace on the Palatine (**7.10**) exemplifies. New construction was definitely important but restoration and enhancement of existing structures were also key means for political figures to bolster their reputations. This is one aspect of Roman political life that continued practices from the Republic, as we see with Paullus's basilica (**7.6**). In the Empire, Hadrian's activities in general illustrate this well and the Pantheon in particular (**7.11, 7.12**), a monument that reflects the involvement of several leaders over a long period of time, from Agrippa early in Augustus's principate to Septimius Severus and Caracalla at the beginning of the third century CE.

# Housing traditional political institutions: the popular assemblies and the Senate

## 7.1 Three key Republican monuments: the Comitium, Curia Hostilia, and Rostra

Aulus Gellius preserves Republican author Laelius Felix's explanations for the three main assemblies as well as information concerning where the centuriate assembly met specifically. This assembly was based on wealth or property and its functions included enacting laws, electing senior magistrates, and declaring war and peace. In Republican Rome, the Comitium was the primary place for political assembly. It was broadly rectangular in shape and basically open though some ancient sources (Livy, *History of Rome* 27.36.8; Pliny the Elder, *Natural History* 19.6.23) report that awnings were sometimes used to shade those assembled there from the sun. Located at the base of the Capitoline Hill in an area north of the Roman Forum, it was oriented by the cardinal points of the compass with the Curia Hostilia (the original Senate House) to the north and the Rostra (speaker's platform) and Graecostasis (a waiting area for foreign ambassadors) to the south, as Varro's description reflects. A circular amphitheater of steps rising on all sides where citizens stood in their assemblies occupied the center of the Comitium in the middle Republic (at least by the beginning of the third century BCE), and various honorific statues were set up in the general area. Once the Saepta Iulia was complete (see **7.3** in this volume), the public assemblies largely moved there. None of the Comitium, Curia Hostilia, or Rostra remains today.

Further reading: Dyson 2010: 30–2; Patterson 2000a: 8–28; Richardson 1992: 97–8, 102–3, 334–5.

Aulus Gellius, *Attic Nights* 15.27.5

It is also written in this same book [by Laelius Felix]: "When voting of men takes place according to families, the assemblies are called 'curiate' (*curiata*); when it is according to census ranking (i.e., wealth-based) and age, 'centuriate' (*centuriata*); when it is according to regions and localities, 'tribal' (*tributa*). Moreover, it is not proper to hold the centuriate assemblies inside the *pomerium* because the army must be mobilized outside the city and it is not lawful for it to be mobilized within the city. Therefore, it was customary for the centuriate assemblies to be held in the Campus Martius and the army to be mobilized there for the purpose of defense because the people were engaged in casting their votes."

Varro, *On the Latin Language* 5.155

The Comitium [is so named] from the fact that the Romans used to assemble there in the centuriate assemblies (*comitia centuriata*) and for the sake of legal trials. There are two kinds of Curia (Senate House): where the priests attend to divine matters, such as the Curiae Veteres, and where the Senate sees to human affairs, such as the Curia Hostilia which the king [Tullus] Hostilius first built. Before this is the Rostra, which [takes] its name from the beaks (*rostra*) of captured enemy [ships] that have been attached there. To the right of the Rostra from the Comitium there is a place built below where the ambassadors of [foreign] nations who had been sent to the Senate would wait; this is called the Graecostasis from some [of the nations, i.e., the Greeks], as is many [times the case].

## 7.2 Campaigning for office

Running for political office in antiquity, just as today, was not an easy task. The following excerpt comes from a long letter seemingly addressed to Cicero by his brother Quintus in late 65 or early 64 BCE as he prepared to stand for the consulship of 63, in which he was successful. Even though the authorship of the letter has been the subject of debate, it contains much valuable advice that is still relevant today such as the need to cultivate different constituencies of voters and the importance of being visible and staying in the public eye. The former can be seen in the author's treatment of the different groups of men who wait on the candidate over the course of the day and accompany him on his business through the city, beginning with those who come to his home for the *salutatio* or morning greeting (see **4.3** in this volume). The second group consists of those who go with the candidate to the Forum—the center of Roman political, economic, social, and religious life—literally those who "lead [him] down" because the Roman Forum occupied an area of low ground between the

Palatine, Velia, Quirinal, and Capitoline Hills. Visibility was further enhanced by the fact that a man canvassing for office wore a specially whitened toga called the *toga candidata* (cf. the English term "candidate"). The topography of the city and its relationship to political institutions is also evident in the Latin reference to the election (*in campo*) since the Campus Martius was where the *comitia* or assemblies met.

Further reading: Patterson 2000a: 53–70.

Quintus Cicero, *Handbook on Electioneering* 34–7

Since mention has been made about [clients and others] attending you, you must take care that every day you enjoy the company of every class, order, and age. For from [each group's] very ranks a guess will be able to be made how much strength and power you are going to have in the election itself. There are, moreover, three groups in this regard: first, those who call on you at your house in the morning; second, those who escort you to the Forum; and third, those who accompany you [about the city]. Among morning callers, who are rather ordinary and, according to current custom, come in great numbers, you must see to it that this very small duty on its own seems most agreeable to you. Those who will come to your house: make it clear that you notice them; tell them often and tell their friends who will report it back to them. Often when there are many rival candidates and people see that there is a certain one who especially notes these acts of attention, they devote themselves to him and desert the others, and gradually they emerge as his own men from everybody's and as firm supporters from phonies ... Now, the service of those who escort you to the Forum is much greater than that of the morning callers: make this clear and show them that it is more pleasing to you and, as far as is possible, go down to the Forum at specific times. Going down to the Forum every day with a large escort makes a great impression and lends great distinction. The third group to consider is the army of constant attendees. In this group, you will have those who do so voluntarily: take care that they understand you are forever in their debt for their very great favor. However, those who are in your debt, simply demand this service from them, that those who by their age and business are able to attend you accompany you themselves regularly, and those who are unable to do so themselves appoint their relatives to this duty. I sincerely want you always to have a crowd around you and think you should aim to achieve this.

## 7.3 Voting on the Campus Martius

Among the many plans Julius Caesar was unable to accomplish in his lifetime was the construction of a permanent voting enclosure on the Campus Martius for the centuriate and tribal assemblies. The new building, called the Saepta (officially the Saepta Iulia), was completed and dedicated in 26 BCE by Marcus Agrippa, Augustus's right-hand man. It was a large rectangular building 310 m by 120 m and colonnaded on its long sides. The Saepta subsequently served a number of functions beyond its original purpose, as several emperors used it for staging gladiatorial contests and in the Flavian period it housed a market for luxury goods (see **3.19** in this volume). Hadrian restored it along with a number of other prominent buildings (see **7.11** in this volume).

Further reading: Claridge 2010: 202; Dyson 2010: 141–3; Richardson 1992: 340–1.

---

Dio, *Roman History* 53.23.1–2
After this, Augustus became consul for the eighth time together with Statilius Taurus, and Agrippa dedicated the so-called Saepta. He did not undertake to repair any road, but adorned with stone tablets and paintings this structure already built in the Campus Martius for the *comitia tributa*, which were surrounded with colonnades by Lepidus, and he named it the Saepta Iulia for Augustus.

---

## 7.4 Alternate locations for meetings of the Senate

The Senate always met in a *templum*, an area that had been marked off as a sacred precinct by an augur who was a priest who read and interpreted signs from the gods which is known as augury. A building dedicated to Roman gods was thus a *templum*, giving us our modern term "temple," but so were other structures, including those perhaps associated more with politics than religion, such as the Curia, which was the normal meeting place for the Senate in the Republic. However, the first meeting of each year, as well as meetings about warfare, took place in the Temple of Jupiter Optimus Maximus (Best and Greatest) on the Capitoline Hill, while other temples were sometimes chosen either for practical reasons or on account of the symbolic resonances of the particular edifice. This was certainly the case on 8 November 63 BCE when the Senate met in the Temple of Jupiter Stator (Stayer [of Flight]) at Cicero's behest. There he delivered his second speech against Catiline, denouncing him and his plans (see **4.10** in this volume). Other meetings of the Senate about Catiline's conspiracy, including one to determine the fate of his associates, took place in the Temple of Concord, another carefully chosen locale for symbolic reasons.

Further reading: Claridge 2010: 157; Patterson 2000a: 22–3.

---

Cicero, *Against Catiline* 2.12

Yesterday, citizens, when I had nearly been killed in my own home, I summoned the Senate to the Temple of Jupiter Stator and reported the entire matter to the conscript fathers. Once Catiline had arrived, what senator addressed him? Who greeted him? Finally, who looked on him as a ruined citizen and not a most savage enemy instead? And furthermore, even the leading men of this order abandoned that area of the benches he had approached, leaving it bare and empty.

---

## 7.5 A Senate House for a new era

In 29 BCE, Augustus completed the Curia Iulia, the Senate House begun in 44 BCE by Julius Caesar as part of his new Forum. Coins from 28 BCE appear to depict the completed structure with the Chalcidicum Augustus mentions, a porch with widely spaced Ionic columns raised on a high podium that was accessed either by stairs or ramps. The present building one sees is from the late third century CE and dates to Diocletian's restoration following a damaging fire in 283 CE. Scholars believe Diocletian's restoration largely resembles the Julian original and could accommodate about 300 senators seated. The pediment at the front of the Curia had a winged Victory on a globe while another statue and altar of Victory were inside near which the round golden shield given to Augustus was dedicated, as he recorded in his *Achievements*.

Further reading: Claridge 2010: 71–4; Coarelli 2014: 57–9; Richardson 1992: 103–4.

---

Augustus, *Achievements* 19, 34

I built the Curia and the Chalcidicum next to it … In my sixth and seventh consulships [i.e., 28–27 BCE], after I had extinguished the civil wars, with universal agreement I took control of everything and transferred the state from my power into the control of the Senate and the Roman people. For this service of mine, by a decree of the Senate, I was named Augustus; I wrapped the doorposts of my house with laurel garlands, publicly fastened the civic crown[1] above my door and placed the golden shield in the Curia Iulia, an inscription on which solemnly affirmed that the Senate and Roman people gave it to me on account of my excellence and clemency, justice and piety.

# The administration of justice

## 7.6 "Truly magnificent": the Basilica Aemilia

Basilicas occupied both long sides of the Roman Forum—the Basilica Aemilia on the north end and the Basilica Iulia on the south, though little remains of either. These large colonnaded structures consisted of a rectangular hall whose interior was divided by rows of columns. Some were certainly used for legal proceedings, such as the Basilica Iulia. Because of its location, the Basilica Aemilia (generally called the Basilica Paulli by ancient sources) seems a likely space for the courts as well, but no legal hearing can be definitively assigned to it. This excerpt from Cicero's letter of 54 BCE reports progress on the Basilica Aemilia. It was begun in 55 BCE by Lucius Aemilius Paullus to replace an earlier building, the Basilica Fulvia, which had been completed in 179 BCE; in 34 BCE, Paullus's son Lucius Aemilius Lepidus Paullus finished the work his father had started. Cicero remarks on how beautiful the basilica was and Pliny the Elder (*Natural History* 36.24.102) later counted it among Rome's marvels for its columns of Phrygian marble, probably among other features. Plutarch notes Caesar's financial contribution to the project. When the basilica burned down twenty years after its completion in a fire that spread to the nearby Temple of Vesta (see **6.3** in this volume and cf. **10.4**), Augustus and friends of Paullus paid to restore it (Dio, *Roman History* 54.24).

Further reading: Bablitz 2007: 47–8; Claridge 2010: 69–71; Richardson 1992: 54–6.

---

Cicero, *Letters to Atticus* 4.16.7–8

Paulus has now almost roofed his basilica in the middle of the Forum with the ancient columns themselves [of the original basilica which was erected in 179 BCE]. However, that other basilica, which he contracted for, he has made truly magnificent. How so, you ask? There is nothing more pleasing than that building, nothing more glorious. So "Caesar's friends" (I mean me and Oppius, though you may explode) have spent 60 million sesterces on that building you used to praise to the skies to widen the Forum and extend it as far as the Hall of Liberty; we couldn't come to an agreement with the private owners for a smaller amount. We shall accomplish a most glorious thing. Further, in the Campus Martius we're planning to build covered marble voting booths (*saepta*) for the tribal assemblies and we'll surround them with a high colonnade a mile long. At the same time, the Villa Publica will be attached to this building.

Plutarch, *Life of Julius Caesar* 29.2–3
Once Marcellus [finished his year as consul], Caesar now readily made available funds from his Gallic campaigns to all those involved in public affairs to draw upon … and he gave 1,500 talents to Paullus when he was consul with which Paullus adorned his basilica in the Forum named in honor [of his family] where the Basilica of Fulvius had previously been built.

## 7.7 Trials and tribulations in the grand Basilica Iulia

When Caesar began work on his new Forum, he also turned his attention to building a new basilica on the southwest side of the old Roman Forum between the Temples of Saturn and Castor. This large basilica (49 m by 101 m) was dedicated by Caesar in 46 BCE though not yet complete; Augustus finished the work, as he indicates in his account of his own achievements, including rebuilding after a fire in 12 CE when it was renamed in honor of Gaius and Lucius, his deceased heirs. In the first century CE, the Centumviral Court (or Court of One Hundred, though it actually numbered 180 judges) met in the Basilica Iulia, a special civil court that mainly heard cases concerning inheritance. The building was typically noisy, as the passage from Quintilian dating to about 80 CE confirms; this is not surprising since seats would be filled with onlookers and supporters, some spilling into the upper gallery. The silence described by Pliny the Younger in his letter of 105 CE was thus highly unusual. On the steps of the basilica today one can still see game boards carved into the surface where people amused themselves while awaiting the outcomes of trials (cf. **3.12** in this volume).

Further reading: Bablitz 2007: 61–70; Claridge 2010: 92–3; Richardson 1992: 52–3.

Augustus, *Achievements* 20
I completed the Forum Iulium [Forum of Julius Caesar] and the basilica, which was between the Temple of Castor and the Temple of Saturn, buildings begun and nearly finished by my father [i.e., Julius Caesar]. When the same basilica was consumed by fire, I started to rebuild it on an enlarged site in the names of my sons, and if I do not complete it while living, I have given orders that it be completed by my heirs.

Quintilian, *The Orator's Education* 12.5.5–6
Our own age has had more eloquent speakers, but when he was speaking, Trachalus seemed to stand out among his peers. Such was his lofty stature, the passion in his eyes, the dignity of his brow, the distinction of his gesture, and indeed a voice not almost of a tragedian, as Cicero desired, but in fact beyond all tragedians I have heard. In any event,

I remember that when he was speaking in the Basilica Iulia before the first tribunal, and moreover the four panels of judges [of the Centumviral Court] were assembled, as is usual, and everywhere was brimming with noise, Trachalus was both heard and understood and even applauded by the four tribunals, which was most irksome for the other pleaders.

---

Pliny the Younger, *Letters* 5.9.1–2

I had come down to the Basilica Iulia in order to listen to those speeches I needed to respond to after a two-day adjournment. The judges were seated, the decemvirs[2] had arrived, and the lawyers were pacing up and down. There was a long silence. Finally, a messenger came from the praetor. The centumvirs were dismissed and the day's business concluded with my full approval, as I am never so prepared that I am unhappy with a delay.

---

# Leaving one's mark on the city

## 7.8 Caesar's Forum and the Temple of Venus Genetrix (the ancestress)

Using the spoils amassed from his campaigns in Gaul (58–51 BCE), Caesar began building a new forum in 54 BCE that would bear his family name: the Forum Iulium (Julian Forum), which was also called the Forum Caesaris (Forum of Caesar). The site was costly, for Suetonius indicates that he paid over 100 million sesterces for the land, and Cicero's letter dated to the same year the project was undertaken (see **7.6** in this volume) records that Cicero and Gaius Oppius were willing to contribute 60 million sesterces, though it is not clear precisely which part of the project this concerned. Caesar's plan was to expand the Roman Forum as far as the Atrium Libertatis with an annex for transacting public business and especially affairs of the Senate. His new forum consisted of a colonnaded court approximately 115 m by 45 m with the Temple to Venus Genetrix standing at its far end on a very high podium. As Dio notes, the goddess was considered the founder of the Julian family. During the civil war against Pompey, Caesar had vowed a temple to Venus not in her guise as Genetrix but as Victrix (Bringer of Victory), but in the end he chose to celebrate his divine ancestry. In addition to the statues mentioned by Appian that adorned the new temple, Caesar dedicated many other works of art including paintings and engraved gemstones. Although the forum itself was not yet complete, Caesar dedicated it and the Temple of Venus Genetrix in late September of 46 BCE. That same year the *ludi* in honor of his daughter Julia, who died in 54 BCE, were staged in the Circus Maximus (see **5.2** in this volume).

Further reading: Claridge 2010: 162–9; Dyson 2010: 107–14; Richardson 1992: 165–7.

---

Suetonius, *Julius Caesar* 26.2–3

Once he obtained this [i.e., the right to stand for the consulship while absent from Rome], already contemplating loftier things and full of hope, he omitted no kind of expenditure or favor toward anyone publicly or privately. From his war booty, he began his forum, the land for which cost more than 100 million sesterces. He announced a gladiatorial show and public banquet in memory of his daughter, which no one had done before him. So that anticipation of these events would be as great as possible, he even had preparations for the banquet seen to by his household staff although some were contracted out to the markets.

---

Appian, *Civil Wars* 2.102

He built the Temple to Venus Genetrix, as he had vowed when planning to fight [Pompey] at Pharsalus, and set out an area around the temple which he intended to be a forum for the Romans not for the sale of goods, but for business and social transactions as a public square functions among the Persians [who] seek justice or learn the laws there. He placed a beautiful statue of Cleopatra there next to one of the goddess, which remains in that place even today [i.e., 202 CE].

---

Dio, *Roman History* 43.22.2

He built for himself a forum named after him, and while it is much more beautiful than the Roman Forum, it increased the reputation of the latter so that it was called the Great Forum. And so once he completed both this forum and the Temple of Venus [Genetrix] as the founder of his family, he then dedicated [them] straightaway.

---

## 7.9 Augustus's magnificent new Forum

In 2 BCE, Augustus dedicated his Forum and the Temple of Mars Ultor (Mars the Avenger), which he had vowed in 42 BCE to celebrate victory over Caesar's assassins (see **6.10** in this volume), though the temple was not entirely finished at the time of dedication. Augustus purchased the site with war booty (Augustus, *Achievements* 21) but apparently was unable to acquire as much land as desired, for Suetonius records in his biography of the *princeps* (*Augustus* 56) that the Forum ended up being narrower than planned because some owners would not sell their properties and Augustus was unwilling to expropriate them. Nevertheless, it is estimated that the courtyard, albeit shorter and wider than that of Caesar's Forum, probably equaled it in actual area (8,000 m$^2$). Deep porticoes ran down the long sides of the rectangular space which was dominated by the very large Temple of Mars Ultor, one and a half times the size of the Temple of Venus Genetrix in Caesar's Forum, in the far end. The porticoes, which each had an exedra,[3] were paved in colored marbles and had numerous niches built into their walls to hold statues of great Romans from the legendary and historical past including Aeneas, Romulus, and members of the Julio-Claudian family. These porticoes, which were each 15 m by 110 m, seem the likely locales for the administration of justice Suetonius reports was one of the main functions of Augustus's new Forum. Today a large portion of the Forum of Augustus is inaccessible as it lies beneath the Via Dei Fori Imperiali.

Further reading: Claridge 2010: 177–80; Coarelli 2014: 108–13; Richardson 1992: 160–2; Zanker 1988: 110–14, 209–15.

---

Suetonius, *Augustus* 29.1–2

He put up a great many public buildings, among which these were especially notable: his Forum along with the Temple of Mars Ultor; the Temple of Apollo on the Palatine; the Temple of Jupiter Tonans [Jupiter the Thunderer] on the Capitol. The reason for building his Forum was the large number of people and legal cases, which seemed to require even a third, as two were insufficient. So even though the Temple of Mars was not yet completed, his Forum was rather quickly opened to the public and provisions were made so that public trials could take place there separately, as well as the selection of jurors by lot. He had vowed the Temple of Mars when he undertook the war at Philippi to avenge his father [i.e., Julius Caesar]. Therefore, he decreed that the Senate should deliberate about wars and triumphs here, those about to depart for provinces with military command should set out from here, and those who had returned victorious [from war] should bring their triumphal insignia to this place.

---

## 7.10 Palace of Domitian (Domus Augustiana)

The achievements of the Flavians, Rome's second dynasty, are still apparent throughout the city in major monuments such as the Colosseum and Arch of Titus (see **5.17** and **9.12** in this volume), as well as in the remains of the Palace of Domitian, which dominate the Palatine Hill. The extensive ruins actually offer only a hint at Domitian's massive remodeling and expansion of the Palatine. The palace was built over an eleven-year period on the site where Nero had previously built a palace that may have been a rebuilding of the Augustan palace there. This has resulted in some confusion in modern terminology though the Romans referred to Domitian's new palace as the Domus August(i)ana. Built around two peristyle courtyards, the palace complex featured impressive rooms for conducting public business such as the two reception or council halls that flanked the huge central audience chamber known as the Aula Regia (38 m by 31 m). There was also a great banquet hall, which Statius describes in the second excerpt below as being lavishly decorated in marble and stone of nearly every color. The poet marvels at the hall's height, which perhaps matched its length (31.6 m), and made him feel as though he were dining with Jupiter rather than Domitian in such an "august" space. A passage from an earlier poem captures the grandeur and opulence of the palace overall, which was filled with colored marble and gold. The scale of the palace buildings, both their height and expanse, was evocative of the gods and is also thought to reflect Domitian's growing pretensions to divinity.

Further reading: Claridge 2010: 145–53; Jones 1992: 95–6.

---

Statius, *Silvae* 1.2.147–58

Here is Libyan stone and Phrygian, here hard Laconian rocks gleam green, here fluid onyx and the veins similar in color to the deep sea, and porphyry glitters which Oebalian purple and the stirrer of the Tyrian dye-pot often envy. Pediments rest on countless columns, beams shine linked with Dalmatian ore. A coolness coming from the ancient trees shuts out the sun's rays, and crystal-clear fountains live in marble. Nature does not preserve her order: here Sirius[4] is chilly, midwinter warm, and the house moderates the changing seasons to its liking.

---

Statius, *Silvae* 4.2.18–31

An august building, huge, extraordinary, and not with one hundred columns but as many as might be able to support heaven and the gods above if Atlas were to let go. The Thunderer's neighboring palace[5] is astounded by this [sight], the gods rejoice that you are settled in a residence equal to their own: do not hasten to ascend to the lofty sky. Such a vast space lies open, so great the sweep of its extensive hall—wider than a spreading plain, embracing much of heaven and only inferior to its lord. He fills the dwelling and weighs it down with his great genius. Here the mountains of Libya vie and contend with stone from Ilium, at the same time dark Syene and Chios and rocks rivaling the greenish-grey sea, and [plain white marble from] Luna substituted only to support the columns. The view extends far beyond: with wearied eyes you can scarcely spot the roof and might think it the gilded ceiling of heaven.

## 7.11 Hadrian's many building projects

Political leaders could visibly leave their mark on the city both by erecting new buildings and restoring existing ones as important ways of strengthening their reputation while ruling and beyond. The emperor Hadrian was actively involved in both new construction and restoration during his twenty-one year reign, as his biographer details below. It is curious, though, that the biographer seems more interested in the emperor's efforts to restore many structures built under Augustus and to relocate the Colossus of Nero than in discussing Hadrian's new building activities, for he barely mentions the Pantheon and omits the Temple of Venus and Roma, two masterpieces associated with Hadrian's reign. According to Dio (*Roman History* 69.4.1–5), Hadrian considered himself somewhat of an architect and insisted on preparing plans for the Temple of Venus and Roma; Apollodorus, the leading architect of the day who had designed Trajan's Forum, Odeum, and Stadium, criticized the designs and ending up losing his life as a result. The Temple of Venus and Roma sat on a small hill at the foot of the Palatine Hill between the Roman Forum and the Colosseum. The massive building, with its Corinthian columns rising sixty Roman feet in height and its podium equal in area to the entire Forum of Augustus, housed two temples set back-to-back within a single structure, one to Roma (the personification of Rome) and the other to Venus. Nearly three centuries after its dedication, the temple still stood tall as the Christian writer Prudentius attests in his critique of traditional Roman religion, arguing that the child steeped in pagan practices at home later encounters the public aspects of his religion once he has grown up.

Further reading: Claridge 2010: 19–20, 118–21; Ramage and Ramage 2009: 235–41.

---

SHA, *Life of Hadrian* 19.9–13

Although he had built countless buildings everywhere, he never inscribed his own name except on the temple of his father Trajan. At Rome, he restored the Pantheon, the Saepta, the Basilica of Neptune, very many temples, the Forum of Augustus, the Baths of Agrippa, and all of these he dedicated in the names of the previous builders. He also built a bridge in his own name, a tomb near the Tiber [i.e., the Mausoleum of Hadrian: see **11.13** in this volume], and the Temple of Bona Dea [on the Aventine Hill]. He transferred the Colossus [of Nero] from the site where the Temple of Rome is now, raising it and keeping it upright through the help of the architect Decrianus, its weight so immense that he even brought out twenty-four elephants for the task. When the face of Nero had been removed to whom it had previously been dedicated, he consecrated this statue to the Sun, and he also planned to make another such statue to the Moon with the architect Apollodorus as its designer.

---

Prudentius, *Against Symmachus* 1.215–22

Now leaving home, he was amazed at the public festivals, the holidays and games (*ludi*). He saw the lofty Capitol and the priests crowned with laurels standing by the temples of their gods, the Sacra Via resounding with the lowing of cattle before the shrine to Roma (for she herself is worshipped with blood in the manner of a goddess—the name of the place is regarded as a divinity—and the Temples of Venus and Roma raise themselves to equal height and incense is burned to a pair of goddesses at the same time).

## 7.12 The work of many hands: the Pantheon

Along with the Colosseum (see **5.17** in this volume), the Pantheon is one of the most recognizable monuments in Rome, though its function remains unclear. It is a unique and distinctive structure comprising two rather different elements: a classical porch that is rectangular in plan, supported by sixteen huge Corinthian columns with shafts of Egyptian granite; and a circular drum—a round interior covered with a dome whose interior diameter measures 44.4 m, which is the same as the height from the floor to the circular *oculus* in the roof. The *oculus*, which is 8.3 m across, was the building's only source of natural light and probably also admitted rain and birds. Looking up at it gave one a sense of awe, as Dio suggests. The grandeur of the interior is still evident today (see Fig. 7.1). The Pantheon's long history illustrates how a single building could be associated with multiple successive political leaders, yet each in a different way. The first building on the site was constructed by Marcus Agrippa from 27 to 25 BCE, as the initial inscription below attests. Pliny the Elder praises various features he would have seen firsthand in this original building before it was destroyed by fire in 80 CE only to be rebuilt by Domitian then burned again in 110 CE from a lightning strike. Though Hadrian's biographer pays it little attention, as noted above, the Pantheon, which he rebuilt around 125 CE, was one of Hadrian's great achievements. As was his custom, he retained the original dedicant instead of dedicating the building in his own name, which is why Agrippa's simple but bold testament to his work in rather large, visible lettering sits over the porch. Another inscription in much smaller lettering lies beneath it and this documents restoration of the building by the emperors Septimius Severus and Caracalla in 202 CE.

Further reading: Claridge 2010: 226–32; Coarelli 2014: 286–9; Ramage and Ramage 2009: 235–8; Richardson 1992: 283–6.

*Corpus of Latin Inscriptions* 6.896.1
Marcus Agrippa, son of Lucius, consul for the third time, made [this].

**Figure 7.1** Interior of the Pantheon with partial view of the dome. Photo credit: Scala/Art Resource, NY.

Pliny the Elder, *Natural History* 36.4.38

Diogenes of Athens adorned the Pantheon of Agrippa, and his Caryatids [which form] the columns of the temple, are commended for their uniqueness, just as the statues placed on the pediment, but on account of the height of the structure, these are less celebrated.

Dio, *Roman History* 53.27.2–3

Agrippa completed the so-called Pantheon. It was perhaps named thus because it had statues of many gods among its sculptures, including one of Mars and one of Venus, but I think it is because the dome resembles the heavens. Agrippa resolved to set up a statue of Augustus there and to name the building after him, but when he did not accept either [honor], Agrippa placed a statue of Julius Caesar there and statues of both Augustus and himself in the *pronaos*.

*Corpus of Latin Inscriptions* 6.896.2–3

The emperor Caesar Lucius Septimius Severus Pius Pertinax Augustus Arabicus Adiabenicus Parthicus, *pontifex maximus*, with tribunician power for the tenth time, *imperator* for the eleventh time, consul for the third time, Father of the Country, and proconsul; and the emperor Caesar Marcus Aurelius Antoninus Pius Felix Augustus, with tribunician power for the fifth time, consul, and proconsul restored the Pantheon and all its ornaments after it had been damaged from old age.

# Urban Infrastructure

Ancient writers often mentioned the greatness and importance of Rome's urban infrastructure, and it was this infrastructure that significantly impacted the daily lives of the urban population. These were not sites for occasional use. In the introduction, we noted that Rome is a living organism that changes over time. If we continue with this metaphor, we could consider the infrastructure of the city to be like the skeleton of this organism. It is the framework of the city that made much of urban life possible. Aqueducts (**8.1–8**) brought in a large volume of fresh water to the city, while sewers (**8.9–12**) and latrines (**8.13**) tried to deal with the city's overflow and waste. Street and road development (**8.14–19**) allowed easier transport of people, goods, and animals, both inside and outside the city. Bridges (**8.20–2**) provided access across the Tiber and to the city, and walls (**8.23–4**) encircled the city. Ancient writers, such as Vitruvius and Frontinus, have provided us with significant evidence of ancient Roman engineering in action. Urban infrastructure progressed in varying degrees from its early years to the reigns of numerous emperors interested not only in changing the lives of Rome's people, but also in leaving their own marks on the city. Since the city was built and rebuilt over many years whether because of strategic changes made to the city or the need to rebuild after a fire, the construction industry was crucial to a changing cityscape. There were skilled artisans of all sorts, from architects to workers in wood, to producers of brick stamps to makers of pipes.

Further reading: Aldrete 2009: 25–42; DeLaine 2000; Grewe 2016.

## Rome's aqueducts

### 8.1 The aqueducts: an introduction

A number of ancient writers mention the greatness of the Roman aqueducts and they do so rightly. The aqueducts were responsible for bringing a supply of clean, fresh water to the city. Yet as Harry Evans reminds us (1997: 2), the Romans were not the first to carry water over long distances. Of course, this does not diminish the significance of the Roman aqueducts, eleven in total through the third century CE. The first aqueduct in Rome was built in 312 BCE by Appius Claudius Caecus, a censor. In 537 CE, the city of Rome was invaded and the Goths cut the lines of the aqueducts. The aqueducts were later restored and some were used for centuries. From the 1930s through the 1970s, two new lines were constructed: the Acqua Vergine Nuova followed by the Acqua Peschiera-Capore (see Aicher 1995: 169–70). While the romantic images of Rome often showcase the aboveground aqueducts, many of them were underground. The remains of aqueducts outside the city are grander (for instance, the Parco degli Acquedotti), and there are still a few spots inside the city where you can trace the ancient aqueducts. Peter Aicher's volume (1995) on the aqueducts well describes the ruins that remain at Rome today (in particular the "field guide" in part 3 of the book). The major ancient work on the aqueducts is Frontinus's *On the Aqueducts of Rome* (for more on this work, see **8.2**).

In the pages that follow you will find passages on a selection of individual aqueducts. You will read about the building and upkeep of the aqueducts, the problems associated with them, and the significance of the system. Dodge (2000: 171) provides an excellent chart on the eleven ancient aqueducts, which includes their sources and technical details (such as length, slope, and distribution in the city). For a discussion of the technical aspects of aqueducts, read Trevor Hodge's *Roman Aqueducts and Water Supply* (2002), though his work is not limited to the aqueducts of the city of Rome.

Further reading: Aicher 1995; Bruun 1991; Bruun 2013; Dodge 2000; Evans 1997; Hodge 2002; Stambaugh 1988: 129–30; Taylor 2001.

---

Strabo, *Geography* 5.3.8

These people [the Romans] thought ahead, especially about things that those people [the Greeks] thought little about: the paving of roads, aqueducts, and sewers that were able to wash out the dirt of the city into the Tiber … The sewers, vaulted with cut stone, left some roads [big enough to be] passable for wagons of hay. So much is the water brought in by the aqueducts that rivers flow through the city and the sewers and nearly every house has a cistern and pipes and plentiful watercourses. Marcus Agrippa paid the most attention to these things.

---

Frontinus, *On the Aqueducts of Rome* 4
From the foundation of the city, for 441 years, the Romans have been content with the use of the waters, which they drew either from the Tiber or wells or springs. The memory of the springs still exists and is cultivated with honor. They are believed to bring health to sick bodies, just as the springs of the Camenae and Apollo and Juturna. Now, moreover, the following flow into the city: the Aqua Appia, Anio Vetus [Old Anio], Marcia, Tepula, Julia, Virgo, Alsietina which is called also the Augusta, Claudia, and Anio Novus [New Anio].

Frontinus, *On the Aqueducts of Rome* 16
With so many necessary structures for transporting so many waters, clearly you should compare the useless pyramids or the other idle, but celebrated, works of the Greeks.

Frontinus, *On the Aqueducts of Rome* 124
I believe that it will be doubtful to no one that the closest aqueducts [to the city], that is, the ones that stand from the seventh milestone in squared stone, must be protected the most since they are of the greatest necessity and each one supports very many waters. If it is necessary to interrupt these, they will deprive the greater part of the city of its waters.

## 8.2 *Curator aquarum* (commissioner of the waters)

Anyone who wants to know more about Roman water systems should begin with a reading of Sextus Julius Frontinus's *On the Aqueducts of Rome*. This work is a detailed description (or as Frontinus himself described it, a commentary) of the aqueduct system in the city of Rome. Frontinus was appointed commissioner of the waters, *curator aquarum*, by the emperor Nerva in 97 CE, and his work is therefore an excellent source on this topic. His work provides wide-ranging information, from descriptions of individual aqueducts to issues of distribution and use of water to legal questions; he even reflects on his own role as the water commissioner. Long before Frontinus became an official state water commissioner, Marcus Agrippa, close general and eventual son-in-law of the emperor Augustus, was in charge of the waters, using his own crew of slaves to care for them. Frontinus (*On the Aqueducts of Rome* 98) tells us that upon Agrippa's death, he gave this crew of slaves to Augustus as part of his inheritance and when Augustus died, he in turn gave them to the state.

Further reading: Evans 1982; Peachin 2004; Rodgers 2009.

Suetonius, *Augustus* 37

So that more men might take part in the managing of the state, Augustus devised new offices: the care of public works, of the roads, of the waters, of the channel of the Tiber, of distributing grain to the people, a prefect of the city, a group of three men for choosing senators, and another for reviewing the bands of knights, whenever needed.

Suetonius, *Augustus* 42.1

But so that you might know that he was an emperor promoting health rather than one courting favor, he corrected with a very stern voice the people who were complaining about the scarcity and high price of wine, [saying] that enough was provided by his son-in-law Agrippa, who made many aqueducts so that men would not be thirsty.

Frontinus, *On The Aqueducts of Rome* 98

Marcus Agrippa, after his aedileship, which he performed after his consulship, was the first permanent commissioner [*curator*] of his own works and structures. Since the supply allowed it, he apportioned how much water would be given for public works, for the basins, and for private uses. He held his own crew of slaves[1] for the caretaking of the waters who would maintain the channels, the water tanks, and the basins.

Frontinus, *On The Aqueducts of Rome* 103

Now I will list[2] to what the water commissioner should pay attention—to both the law and the decrees of the Senate applicable to informing his work. The following things must be noted about the right to draw water by private people: no one without written permission from Caesar, that is, no one may draw public water not granted, and no one may draw more water than granted … In both, moreover, great attention to many kinds of fraud must be set in place … so that the water may flow day and night without interruption.

## 8.3 Overall care and maintenance of the aqueducts

As we can tell from Frontinus's writings, as well as those of Pliny the Elder, the aqueducts required a great deal of care and upkeep. The water commissioner was responsible for deciding what needed to be taken care of and to whom the work should be assigned. He oversaw many attendants and contractors of this water system. There were attendants for taking care of the pipes, others to guard the aqueducts, and people to manage them both inside and outside the city.

Further reading: Peachin 2004: 15–18; Rodgers 2009: 264–5.

Pliny the Elder, *Natural History* 36.24.121–3
Quintus Marcius Rex, ordered by the Senate to repair the channels of the Aqua Appia,
the Aqua Anio, and the Aqua Tepula, brought forth, during the time of his praetorship,
a new aqueduct named after him,[3] with water tunnels led through the mountains.
Agrippa in his aedileship added the Aqua Virgo and with the rest of the waters brought
together and improved, he made 700 basins, in addition to 500 fountains, 130 water
tanks, many of them splendid in appearance. On these works, he placed 300 bronze
or marble figures and 400 marble columns, and all these things he did in the space
of a year. He himself adds, in the commemoration of his aedileship, that there were
games for fifty-nine days and 170 baths were made free, a number now at Rome they
have increased to infinity ... If anyone measured diligently the abundance of waters
in public places, in the baths, in pools, in conduits, in homes, in gardens, in suburban
villas, he will acknowledge that nothing more amazing has been made in the whole
world, given the distance traveled by the water, the arches constructed, the mountains
dug through, and the valleys made level.

Frontinus, *On the Aqueducts of Rome* 96
I find that the guardianship of individual aqueducts was usually hired out to contractors
and that the necessity was placed on them of having a certain number of slave workers
for the aqueducts outside the city and a certain number in the city.

Frontinus, *On the Aqueducts of Rome* 117
Moreover both crews are split into several sorts of attendants: overseers, superintendents
of water tanks, inspectors, pavers, plasterers, and other workers. From these, it is
necessary that some are outside the city to care for those things that are not of great
labor[4] but demand timely support. The men in the city around the stations of water tanks
and structures will direct the tasks[5] especially for sudden emergencies so that extra water
may be able to be turned from several regions to one where necessity has fallen.

Frontinus, *On the Aqueducts of Rome* 119–20
Since we explained what things seemed to pertain to the crew, we will turn, as I had
promised, to the care of the channels, a matter worthy of more zealous concern, since it is
excellent proof of the greatness of the Roman empire. Many and large works are frequently
in decay, which should be attended to before they begin to need great help. Nevertheless
very often the works must be controlled with a sensible moderation, since we should not
always trust the ones seeking to build the structure or to enlarge it. For that reason, the
commissioner should be provided with information not only from skilled men, but also
from his own experience. He should not only use architects from his own office, but he
should call upon the reliability no less than the expertise of very many people,[6] so that he
may determine what must be done immediately, what may be put off and, again, what

ought to be done by contractors or by domestic workers. Works [the need for repairs] come from these reasons: either by the violence of owners[7] or by old age or by the force of storms or the fault of badly done work, which happens more often in recent works.

## 8.4 Stealing water from the aqueducts and damaging them

According to Frontinus, there were issues with the theft of water, as well as people who damaged the various parts of the aqueducts. Even those involved in the care of the aqueducts, the *aquarii* or water men, were said to be involved in committing fraud. The *lex Quinctia* of 9 BCE, quoted by Frontinus (*On the Aqueducts of Rome* 129), deals with damage to the aqueducts and the penalties associated with causing such damage.

Frontinus, *On the Aqueducts of Rome* 114
There is, further, the intolerable fraud of the water men [*aquarii*]. When water has been transferred to a new owner, they place a new opening on the water tank and they leave the old one from which they extract water to be sold. I believe, therefore, that this especially must be corrected by the commissioner, indeed not only for the care of the waters themselves but also as it pertains to the care of the water tank, which when pierced repeatedly and without reason, is made faulty.

Frontinus, *On the Aqueducts of Rome* 75.3
But very many of the owners, from whose fields the water is led around, pierce the channels of the water course whence it happens that the public aqueducts are suspended for private men or for the use of their gardens.

Frontinus, *On the Aqueducts of Rome* 129.4
After this law has been passed, whoever knowingly with bad intent will have pierced, ruptured, or caused to be pierced or ruptured, or will have done worse to the channels, drains, arches, pipes, tubes, water tanks, and basins of public waters, which are led to the city … that person will have to pay a fine of 100,000 sesterces to the Roman people.

## 8.5 Water for certain uses

Frontinus describes how certain waters could be delivered to specific places in the city for particular uses. He further alerts us to multiple aqueducts serving one area of the city at the same time. He also notes that the health of the city rises along with the care of the aqueducts.

Frontinus, *On the Aqueducts of Rome* 87–8

[Prior to these sections, Frontinus devotes multiple chapters to how much water is delivered to certain places for particular uses inside and outside the city] This supply of the waters, computed all the way to the time of the emperor Nerva, was being distributed in this way. Now by the foresight of the most diligent prince, whatever was being intercepted by the cheating of the water men or corrupted by idleness, has been added as if by a new discovery of springs. And the abundance of water has been nearly doubled, and the portions have been distributed with so much care that those regions that single aqueducts were serving, now are being given several. Just as with the Caelian and the Aventine Hills to which the Claudia alone was being led on the Neronian arches, whenever some repair interrupted [the water], the most populous hills were thirsty. Now several waters and especially the Marcia, restored on a great structure, are led all the way from the Spes Vetus to the Aventine … The queen and mistress of the world [Rome] feels every day the care of her most pious prince Nerva and the health of this same city will feel it more with the increase in the number of water tanks, works, structures, and basins … Not even the waste waters are useless. There is a different appearance of cleanliness, the air is purer. The causes of the unhealthy climate, on account of which city air was notorious among the ancients, have been removed.[8]

Frontinus, *On the Aqueducts of Rome* 91.5–92

We have observed the Aqua Marcia itself, most pleasing in its splendor and cold, serving the baths and fullers, and even functions too vile to repeat. Therefore, it was decided that the waters all be separated and then for them to be regulated individually so that the Marcia especially might be devoted entirely to drinking and then the rest of the waters would be assigned to suitable uses according to their own quality. So it is with the Anio Vetus [Old Anio], for several reasons (since the further downstream[9] it is received, the less healthy it is), that it would go to the watering of gardens and for the dirtier things of the city itself.

## 8.6 The Aqua Marcia and its waters

The Aqua Marcia was built in 144–140 BCE by the praetor Quintus Marcius Rex. According to Pliny the Elder and Frontinus, it was known for having the coldest and healthiest water. It ran aboveground for part of its path and carried water to the Capitoline. The inscriptions indicate the repairing of the aqueduct by the emperors Augustus, Titus, and Marcus Aurelius.

Further reading: Aicher 1995: 36–7; Richardson 1992: 17–18.

*Corpus of Latin Inscriptions* 6.1244

*Imperator* Caesar Augustus, son of the deified Julius, *pontifex maximus* [chief priest], consul twelve times, with tribunician power nineteen times, *imperator* fourteen times, repaired the channels of all the waters.

*Corpus of Latin Inscriptions* 6.1245

*Imperator* Caesar Marcus Aurelius Antoninus Pius Felix Augustus, Parthicus Maximus, Britannicus Maximus, *pontifex maximus*, took care to lead the Aqua Marcia, that was hindered by various events, to his sacred city [Rome], once the spring was cleaned, the mounts cut out and dug through, and the aqueduct restored, and a new spring was acquired, the Fons Antoninianus.

*Corpus of Latin Inscriptions* 6.1246

*Imperator* Titus Caesar Vespasian Augustus, son of the deified Vespasian, *pontifex maximus*, with tribunician power nine times, *imperator* fifteen times, censor, consul seven times, consul designate eight times, father of the country, repaired the channel of the Aqua Marcia that was destroyed by old age and he led back the water that had ceased to be in use.

Pliny the Elder, *Natural History* 31.24.41–25.42

The Aqua Marcia (among the gifts of the gods to the city) has been honored with the highest prize by the public crier of the city for the coldest and healthiest of all waters in the whole world. This aqueduct was once called the Aqua Aufeia, and the source itself was the Pitonia. It rises in the furthest mountains of the Paelignii and crosses the Marsi and the Fucine lakes, traveling to Rome with certainty. Then plunged into the cave near Tibur, it appears, traveling for nine miles on the arches of the aqueduct. One of the kings, Ancus Marcius, first began to lead it into the city, afterwards Quintus Marcius Rex, when he was praetor, repaired it and again Marcus Agrippa. The same Agrippa also led in the Aqua Virgo ... Just as the Aqua Virgo is distinguished to touch,[10] so the Aqua Marcia is distinguished to drink.

## 8.7 Agrippa constructs the Aqua Virgo

The Aqua Virgo was built by Agrippa in 19 BCE. Today, visitors to Rome who are unaware may see the story of the aqueduct without realizing it. Facing the Trevi fountain, on the viewer's upper-right side is a relief of the maiden, the *virgo*, showing the source of the aqueduct, the Aqua Virgo, that brings water to the fountain. On the upper-left side, there is a relief of Agrippa planning construction of the aqueduct. The nearby Città dell'Acqua archaeological site, underground at Vicolo del Puttarello, 25, shows a piece of a water tank, as well as the remains of an ancient apartment building. There is also an arch on the Via del Nazareno.

Further reading: Aicher 1995: 39–41, 68–74; Claridge 2010: 221–3; Richardson 1992: 19; Shipley 1933.

---

Dio, *Roman History* 54.11.7
Agrippa led in the water called the Virgo [the maiden], at his expense.

---

Frontinus, *On the Aqueducts of Rome* 10.3
It was called Virgo, because to the soldiers seeking water a young girl showed them certain courses of water, which once they followed and had dug, they discovered a huge amount of water.

---

*Corpus of Latin Inscriptions* 6.1252
Tiberius Claudius Caesar Augustus Germanicus, son of Drusus, *pontifex maximus*, with tribunician power five times, *imperator* eleven times, father of the country, consul designate four times, rebuilt from the foundations the arches of the Aqua Virgo that were destroyed by Gaius Caesar [Caligula] and restored them.

## 8.8 Aqueduct inscriptions at Porta Maggiore

At what is called today the Porta Maggiore (see Fig. 8.1) are the double gates of the Porta Praenestina and the Porta Labicana. The gates were two arches of the Aqua Claudia and the Anio Novus and they crossed the roads Via Labicana and Via Praenestina. The construction of both aqueducts began during the rule of the emperor Caligula and was completed under the emperor Claudius.

Further reading: Aicher 1995: 42–4; Richardson 1992: 11; 16–17.

---

*Corpus of Latin Inscriptions* 6.1256
Tiberius Claudius Caesar Augustus Germanicus, the son of Drusus, *pontifex maximus*, with tribunician power for the twelfth time, consul for the fifth time, *imperator* for the twenty-seventh time, father of the country, took care, at his own expense, to lead into the city the Aqua Claudia from the springs which are called the Caerulean and the Curtian from the forty-fifth milestone, likewise the Anio Novus from the sixty-second milestone.

**Figure 8.1**  Porta Maggiore. Photo credit: Scala/Art Resource, NY.

*Corpus of Latin Inscriptions* 6.1257
*Imperator* Caesar Vespasian Augustus, *pontifex maximus*, with tribunician power for the second time, *imperator* for the sixth time, consul for the third time, consul designate for the fourth time, father of the country, restored for the city, at his own expense, the Curtian and Caerulean waters that had been led by the deified Claudius and afterwards had been interrupted and falling apart for nine years.

*Corpus of Latin Inscriptions* 6.1258
*Imperator* Titus Caesar Vespasian Augustus, *pontifex maximus*, son of the deified Vespasian, with tribunician power for the tenth time, *imperator* for the seventeenth time, father of the country, censor, consul for the eighth time, took care that the Curtian and Caerulean waters led by the deified Claudius and afterwards restored for the city by his father the deified Vespasian, be led back in a new form from the source of the waters at his own expense when they had fallen apart from the foundation because of age.

# Sewers

## 8.9 Early sewer

The Cloaca Maxima, the Greatest Sewer, is said to have been constructed by one of the early kings of Rome, Tarquinius Priscus. The building of the sewer made possible the drainage of the Forum and surrounding areas.

Further reading: Bradley 2012; Gowers 1995; Reimers 1989; Richardson 1992: 91–2; Robinson 1992: 101–3.

---

Dionysius of Halicarnassus, *Roman Antiquities* 3.67.5
Tarquinius began to dig the sewers by which all the collected water from the narrow streets is conducted into the Tiber, a marvelous work beyond description. In the three most magnificent structures of Rome, from which the greatness of her rule is displayed, I place the aqueducts and the paving of the roads, and the sewers. Not only do I bring up this thought for the usefulness of the constructions, on which I will speak at a suitable time, but for the great expense of them, which is judged from one example if someone takes Gaius Acilius as the authority who says that at some time when the sewers were neglected and no longer flowing, the censors paid 1,000 talents for their cleaning and repair.

---

Livy, *History of Rome* 1.38.6
And Tarquinius Priscus drained the lowest spaces of the city around the Forum and other valleys between the hills (since they were not easily carrying away the waters from the flat places) with sewers that led into the Tiber from the summit.

---

Livy, *History of Rome* 1.56.2
[In the time of Tarquinius Superbus] the plebs were less annoyed that they were building the temples of the gods with their own hands than when they were transferred to other tasks that were lesser in appearance, but of much greater work: the making of rows of seats in the Circus and the making of the Cloaca Maxima underground, the receptacle of all the filth of the city. Scarcely can this new magnificence[11] make anything equal to these two works.

---

## 8.10 On the size and enduring nature of the Roman sewer system

During the time of the emperor Augustus, Agrippa was responsible for repairs to the sewers and, according to Pliny the Elder, he examined the sewers himself by sailing along them underground. This is a marker of their size.

Pliny the Elder, *Natural History* 36.24.104–6
But at that time old men were amazed at the enormous space of the ramparts, the substructures of the Capitol, and moreover the sewers, the greatest work of all to mention, since hills were dug up and as we said a bit earlier, the city was a hanging city and was sailed underneath in the aedileship of Marcus Agrippa after his consulship. Seven streams flowing into one channel cross [the city]. With a downhill rush of torrents they are compelled to snatch and take away all things from their path. On top of that, when they are stirred up by a lot of rain, they touch the bottom and sides [of the sewer]. Sometimes the overflowing Tiber flows back and the different streams of waters fight within and still, the steadfast strength withstands it. Above [the sewers], huge structures are dragged, but the excavated tunnels do not give in. Buildings falling headlong on their own or struck by fires agitate them. The ground is shaken by earthquakes; however, they have lasted nearly impregnable 700 years from the reign of Tarquinius Priscus.

Dio, *Roman History* 49.43.1–2
In the next year, Agrippa willingly became aedile and he repaired all the public buildings and all the roads, taking nothing from the treasury, and he cleared out the sewers and sailed underground into the Tiber.

## 8.11 Care of the sewers and damage to the sewers

Several ancient writers give a sense of who was responsible for taking care of the sewers, including the cleaning of them.

Further reading: Koloski-Ostrow 2015b: 70–4.

Pliny the Elder, *Natural History* 36.2.6
A sewer contractor compelled Scaurus to pay security for anticipated damage, when those [columns for his house] were being dragged to the Palatine.

Frontinus, *On the Aqueducts of Rome* 111
I wish that no one draws fallen water,[12] except those who do it with my support or that of earlier rulers. For it is necessary that some part of the water flows out of the water tanks, since this pertains not only to the healthfulness of our city, but also to the use of cleaning the sewers.

Ulpian, *Digest* 43.23.1.2
The praetor, through these interdicts, will take care that the sewers are both cleaned and repaired, both of which pertain to the healthfulness and protection of cities, for the filth

of the sewers, if they are not repaired, threatens to make the sky unhealthy and to make buildings collapse.

## 8.12 Sewer anecdotes

While not everyday occurrences, the anecdotes below show events involving the sewers.[13]

---

Suetonius, *On Grammarians* 2
Crates of Mallos, a contemporary of Aristarchus, so far as I think, first brought the study of grammar into the city of Rome. He was sent to the Senate by King Attalus between the second and third Punic Wars at the time of the death of Ennius, when, in the area of the Palatine, having fallen into the opening of a sewer, he broke his leg.

---

SHA, *Life of Elagabalus* 17.1–2
Then an attack was made on Elagabalus and he was killed in a latrine to which he had fled. Then he was dragged through the public spaces. Injury was added to his cadaver when soldiers threw it into the sewer. But when by chance the sewer did not accept it, a weight was added so that it would not float and it was thrown from the Pons [Bridge] Aemilius into the Tiber, so it would never be able to be buried. The body was also dragged through the spaces of the Circus before it was thrown into the Tiber.

---

# Finding the facilities: latrines

## 8.13 Making and using the latrine

The archaeological remains of public latrines in the city of Rome are limited, but there are records of 144 in the Regionary Catalogues from the fourth century CE. The literary sources on the subject are also limited. As many scholars have noted, 144 public latrines would have not been many for a city of approximately one million inhabitants. Dio, in the passage below, seems to be discussing the latrine at Largo Argentina, near the Theater of Pompey. Another example of a latrine is on Via Garibaldi in Trastevere that was discovered in 1963. Koloski-Ostrow (2015b: 13–17) provides a full listing of all the latrine remains in the city. The passages of Seneca and Martial below are part of the limited literary evidence on the specifics of ancient latrines. It is believed that the sponges were part of the ritual for the self-cleaning of the body after using the latrine.

Further reading: Dodge 2000: 191; Dyson 2010: 232; Hobson 2009; Jansen, Koloski-Ostrow, and Moorman 2011; Koloski-Ostrow 2015b.

---

Dio, *Roman History* 47.19

The room in which Caesar was slaughtered, straightaway they closed it and later transformed it into a latrine.

---

Seneca, *Letters* 70.19–20

Men of the basest sort, with a great impetus, have escaped into safety and when it was not permitted to die at one's leisure nor to choose the instrument of their death at their own judgment, they have seized those things at hand, and what things were not harmful by nature, they made them their own weapons by force. Recently in a school for gladiators who fight wild beasts, one of the Germans, when he was being prepared for the morning spectacles, went away to relieve his body; nothing else was granted to him to do in solitude without a guard. There he stuffed into his throat that piece of wood with a sponge attached, which was placed for cleaning one's private parts, and with his throat blocked, he crushed his breath. This was to make an insult to death.

---

Martial, *Epigrams* 12.48.7

The unhappy sponge on the doomed rod.

# Roads and streets

## 8.14 The types of streets in a city

In looking at a map of the ancient city, one will see various words to refer to the kinds of streets and areas of the city, from particular streets to cul-de-sacs to slopes. In the passage below, Varro attempts to explain the etymology of the names for a few of these paths.

---

Varro, *On the Latin Language* 5.145

In a town there are *vici* [quarters] from the word *via* [street], because there are buildings on either side of the street [*via*]. Streets without outlets [*fundulae*] are from the word *fundus*, "bottom" because they do not have an exit and there is no passage through. An alley [*angiportum*] is either because it is narrow [from the word *angustus*] or from leading [from the word *agere*] and entrance [from the word *portus*].

---

## 8.15 On paved roads and milestones

According to the historian Livy, contractors were hired to pave the roads. Just as there were people to care for the aqueducts and the sewers, there were superintendents to care for the roads.

Further reading: Keppie 1991: 60–9; Laurence 1999; Laurence 2013; Quilici 2008; Tilburg 2012.

---

Livy, *History of Rome* 41.27.5–6
First of all, the censors contracted people for paving the roads in the city with flint,[14] and for paving roads with gravel outside the city, and for making bridges in many places … and they took care of paving the Clivus Capitolinus[15] with flint.

---

*Corpus of Latin Inscriptions* 6.1598[16]
Superintendent for the pavements.

---

Plutarch, *Life of Gaius Gracchus* 7.1–2
He was especially eager concerning road-making and he paid attention at the same time to necessity, grace, and beauty. For the roads led straight through the country with stability. They were paved with shaved stone and were compressed with mounds of solid sand … Besides these things, he measured out all the roads by miles (the mile falls a little short of eight stades)[17] and he set down stone pillars as marks of the measurement. He arranged other stones at less distance from each other on each side of the road, so that people would be able easily to mount their horses from them, not needing someone to help them.

## 8.16 The Via Appia

As Livy tells us, the censor Appius Claudius was responsible for the building of the Via Appia in 312 BCE and the road was named after him. The road originally extended from Rome south to Capua and was eventually extended to Brundisium.[18] This road was the first of a series of major roads through Italy, marked with milestones noting the distance from Rome. Along the stretch of the road right outside of the city, there were villas and funeral monuments, of which there are physical remains, including inscriptions.

Further reading: Coarelli 2014: 365–400; Kaster 2012; Richardson 1992: 414.

---

Livy, *History of Rome* 9.29.6–7

In that year was the celebrated censorship of Appius Claudius and Gaius Plautius. However, the name of Appius is of happier memory to coming generations because he made a road and he led water into the city and he accomplished these things by himself.

---

Statius, *Silvae* 2.2.12

Now [I am] longing to turn my steps where the Appia, the queen of long roads, is well traveled on its known passage.

---

*Corpus of Latin Inscriptions* 6.8466

To the spirits of the dead of Marcus Ulpius Eutychus, freedman of Augustus, keeper of archives of the Via Appia. He lived scarcely forty years. Flavia Daphne made this [tombstone] for her well-deserving husband.

---

*Corpus of Latin Inscriptions* 6.8468

To the spirits of the dead of Gnaeus Cornelius Musaeus, son of Gnaeus, contractor of the Via Appia, Herennia Priscilla made this [tombstone] for her well-deserving husband.

---

## 8.17 The Sacra Via and its life

The Sacra Via, the Sacred Way, was a route from the Palatine to the Roman Forum and was the "oldest axial road of the Forum" (Coarelli 2014: 81). It was known for being a residential area with luxury shops. Numerous epitaphs mention the artisans who sold their goods there, including workers in gold (see **3.1** in this volume for more examples). On the Sacra Via and its connection to the triumphal procession, see **9.7** in this volume.

Further reading: Coarelli 2014: 81–2; Holleran 2012: 55–6; Popkin 2016: 30; Richardson 1992: 338–40.

---

Varro, *On the Latin Language* 5.47

Caeriolensis has been named from the joining of the Carinae. The word Carinae is possibly from "ceremony" [*caerimonia*], because from this place arises the top [*caput*] of the Sacra Via, which stretches from the chapel of Strenia to the citadel, by which the sacred items in all months are carried to the citadel and through which the augurs, having set out from the citadel, are accustomed to take the omens. Of this Sacra Via, this part alone is known commonly, which is at the first ascending road to someone going from the Forum.

*Corpus of Latin Inscriptions* 6.9207
Marcus Caedicius Iucundus, goldsmith from the Sacra Via lived scarcely thirty years.

*Corpus of Latin Inscriptions* 6.9545
Stranger, stop and look at this heap of earth to the left, where are contained the bones of a good man, compassionate, loving, of small means. I ask you, traveler, that you do nothing bad to this monument. Gaius Ateilius Euhodus, freedman of Serranus, dealer in pearls from the Sacra Via, has been placed in this monument. Traveler, farewell. From his will it is permitted that no one be buried nor placed here except those freedmen to whom I gave and allotted in this will.

Ovid, *The Loves* 1.8.99–100
Let him see especially the gifts, which another man has sent. If no one has given any, you must ask for some from the Sacra Via.

Propertius, *Elegies* 2.24.13–14
Sometimes she desires to beg me for ivory dice and some common shiny gifts from the Sacra Via.

## 8.18 Via Lata/Via Flaminia

The Via Flaminia stretches north from Rome, extending from the Piazza del Popolo. Inside the Aurelian Wall, it was called the Via Lata (which is the modern Via del Corso).

Further reading: Coarelli 2014: 19; Richardson 1992: 415–16.

*Corpus of Latin Inscriptions* 6.1333
Lucius Aemilius, son of Lucius … commissioner of the Via Flaminia.

Cicero, *Letters to Atticus* 1.1.2
Thermus … commissioner of the Via Flaminia.

Augustus, *Achievements* 20
In my seventh consulship, I built the Via Flaminia from the city [of Rome] to Arminium and all the bridges except the Mulvian and Minucian.

Livy, *Summaries* 20
Gaius Flaminius, censor, built the Via Flaminia and the Flaminian Circus.

Dio, *Roman History* 53.22.1–2
In the year already mentioned, seeing that the roads outside the walls were hard to pass because of neglect, Augustus ordered some of the senators to repair some of them through their own financial means. He took care of the Via Flaminia, since he was going to march out through it. This happened straightaway at that time and on account of this, likenesses of him were made for the arches on the bridge over the Tiber and in Arminium. But the other roads were repaired later, either by the public, since none of the senators spent their money with pleasure, or by Augustus, some want to say.

## 8.19 Via Labicana

Ancient writers sometimes provide details as to the location of a road. The ancient Via Labicana was located at the present Porta Maggiore where one can find the tomb of Eurysaces the Baker (see **11.10** in this volume). The modern Via Labicana goes from the Colosseum and crosses with Via Merulana.

Further reading: Coarelli 2014: 21; Richardson 1992: 416.

Strabo, *Geography* 5.3.9
Then the Via Labicana meets with the Via Latina starting from the Esquiline Gate. From this point, there is also the Via Praenestina. On the left, the Via Labicana leaves this road and the Esquiline Plain and goes forward 120 stades more.

Frontinus, *On the Aqueducts of Rome* 1.21
The Anio Vetus, on this side of the fourth milestone, is below the Anio Novus, which from the Via Latina to the Via Labicana crosses over between the arches and has its own cistern.

# Bridges

## 8.20 The first bridge over the Tiber River, the Pons Sublicius

The Pons Sublicius was the oldest bridge that crossed the Tiber. The location of the bridge is uncertain and it is thought that it was made of wood. It was originally built by Ancus Marcius, one of Rome's early kings, and the name seems to come from the word *sublica*, a pile or long pole. As told by Livy below, the Pons Sublicius had a key role in the legend of Horatius Cocles, who defended Rome there from the attacking Etruscans. The bridge is also said to have featured in certain religious rituals, as told by Dionysius of Halicarnassus.

Further reading: Griffith 2009; Hallett 1970; Laurence 2013: 249; Richardson 1992: 299; Robinson 1992: 71–2; Roller 2004; Tucci 2011.

---

Varro, *On the Latin Language* 5.83

The *sacerdotes* [priests] as a whole were named from "sacred rituals" [*sacra*]. The *pontifices* [high priests], as Quintus Scaevola the *pontifex maximus* said, were from the word "to be able" [*posse*] and the word "to do" [*facere*] as if the word were *potentifices*. I think the word is from "bridge" [*ponte*]. For by them the bridge of piles [Pons Sublicius] was first made, as it was often repaired by them.

---

Livy, *History of Rome* 1.33.5–6

At last, Ancus, having made an effort with all his troops, conquered first in battle and from there returned to Rome, powerful with enormous plunder. Then many thousands of Latins were received into the state, to whom were given dwellings near the altar of Murcia, so that the Aventine might be joined to the Palatine. The Janiculum[19] was also added not because of the want of space, but so that this citadel might not ever belong to the enemy. It was determined that it be joined to the city not only with a wall, but also, on account of the convenience of the passage, with the bridge resting on piles [Pons Sublicius], at that time the first bridge made over the Tiber.

---

Plutarch, *Life of Numa* 9.2–4

[Concerning the origin of the title *pontifices* (priests)] Most people choose a laughable reason for the names that is nothing other than the men who build bridges, called from the sacrifices made at the bridge, sacrifices that are the holiest and oldest. For the Latins call a bridge a *pons*. They say, to be sure, that the safekeeping and repair of the bridge, just as anything else of the inviolate and ancestral sacred rites, belong to the priests. The Romans believed that the destruction of the wooden bridge was not right, but even accursed. It is said that the whole thing was fastened together with nails through wooden beams, without iron, according to some oracle. The stone bridge was completed much later by Aemilius the quaestor. They say also that the wooden bridge was not from the time of Numa, but was completed by [Ancus] Marcius, grandson of Numa, when he was king.

---

Livy, *History of Rome* 2.10.1–5; 9–10

When the enemy [the Etruscans] were at hand, everyone, on their own, moved from the fields into the city. They surrounded the city itself with guards. Some places seemed safe because of the walls, others because of the Tiber in the way. The Bridge of Piles [Pons Sublicius] almost gave a path to the enemy, if it had not been for one man, Horatius Cocles. On that day, by the fortune of the city of Rome, he held that defense. He was placed, by chance, on post at the bridge when he saw that the Janiculum was captured by a sudden attack and that the swift enemy were running down from there and that the crowd of his own people were abandoning their weapons and their ranks. He detained them one at a time, stood in their way, implored them and called on the faith of gods and men, [saying] that with their defense deserted they were fleeing in vain. If they were to leave the bridge behind them, there would soon be more of the enemy on the Palatine and Capitoline than on the Janiculum. And so he advised them and ordered them to break apart the bridge by sword, by fire, by whatever means they were able. He said that he would receive the attack of the enemy as much as could be resisted by one body. Then he rushed to the entrance of the bridge, and prominent among the visible backs of those withdrawing from the fight, he engaged his arms to enter the battle in hand-to-hand combat. He amazed the enemy with the marvel of his boldness ... Then shame set the battle line in motion and with a raised shout from all sides, the Etruscans threw all their weapons against one enemy [Cocles], all of which had clung onto the one shield that was thrown in the way. He, no less determined, occupied the bridge with an enormous step. Now they were attempting to push off the man with an attack when at the same time the crashing noise of the broken bridge and also the shout of the Romans raised up by the joy of their completed work held back the attack with sudden dread. Then Cocles said, "O Father Tiberinus,[20] I pray solemnly that you accept these weapons and this soldier in your gracious river." Thus armed in this way, he jumped into the Tiber and with many weapons falling on him from above, he swam across safely to his own men, having dared something that would have more fame than belief to coming generations.

---

Dionysius of Halicarnassus, *Roman Antiquities* 1.38.3

Then even until my time, still the Romans continue doing this, namely making offerings a little later than the spring equinox in the month of May on what is called the Ides. On this day, after having sacrificed according to the law, the ones called *pontifices*, the most distinct of priests, and with them the maidens who guard the undying fire,[21] the praetors, and the other citizens for whom it is right to be present at the sacrifices throw from the sacred bridge [Pons Sublicius] into the current of the Tiber images fashioned in the shape of men, thirty in number, called the *Argei*.

---

Pliny the Elder, *Natural History* 36.23.100

Likewise in Rome on the Pons Sublicius, it is a strict rule [that no nails are used], after it was torn away with difficulty when Horatius Cocles was defending it.

## 8.21 The first stone bridge in Rome, the Pons Aemilius

The Pons Aemilius, identified as the Ponte Rotto, was the first stone bridge in Rome and part of it still stands today. According to Livy, its construction was started by Marcus Fulvius Nobilior in 179 BCE.

Further reading: Claridge 2010: 257–8; Erasmo 2015: 83; Richardson 1992: 296–7.

---

*Corpus of Latin Inscriptions* 6.878
*Imperator* Caesar Augustus, son of the deified Caesar, *pontifex maximus*, by decree of the Senate, repaired this bridge.

---

Livy, *History of Rome* 40.51.4
Marcus Fulvius arranged more works and of greater use: a harbor and piles for a bridge over the Tiber, on which after a number of years, Publius Scipio Africanus and Lucius Mummius as censors, arranged for the placing of arches.

---

## 8.22 Pons Fabricius

The bridge is still preserved in Rome and is the oldest surviving bridge. It is now called the Ponte dei Quattro Capi. The builder of the bridge was also the commissioner of roads (*curator viarum*) and the bridge was constructed in 62 BCE. The inscription below appears over the arches on each side.

Further reading: Erasmo 2015: 87–8; Tuck 2013: 230.

---

*Corpus of Latin Inscriptions* 6.1305
Lucius Fabricius, son of Gaius, commissioner of roads, took care to make the bridge.

---

Dio, *Roman History* 37.45.3
At the time these things happened [Julius Caesar divorced his wife], a stone bridge, the one going to the small island on the Tiber, was constructed and called the Fabrician.

# City walls

## 8.23 Servian Wall

The Servian Wall is, in the legendary history of the city, attributed to the sixth king of Rome, Servius Tullius (sixth century BCE), but archaeological evidence points to a dating of the fourth century BCE. Halfway between the gates of the Porta Collina (Colline Gate) and Porta Esquilina (Esquiline Gate) was the Porta Viminalis, which is at the center of the modern Piazza dei Cinquecento, where the remains of the wall can be seen today (Coarelli 2014: 15). Here, outside the main train station, Termini, there is a large piece of the wall to the left of the station. Additional remains are located in the basement level of Termini Station. Coarelli (2014: 13–18) takes the reader on a detailed itinerary around the remains of the wall.

Further reading: Coarelli 2014: 13–18; Dyson 2010: 298–9; Richardson 1992: 262–3.

---

Livy, *History of Rome* 1.44.3–4
It seemed that the city had to be extended for this great number of people. Servius added two hills, the Quirinal and the Viminal. Later, he enlarged the Esquiline, and he himself lived there so that the place would have more worth. He surrounded the city with a rampart, trenches, and a wall and thus he extended the boundary of the city [*pomerium*].

---

Vergil, *Aeneid* 1.7
The walls of lofty Rome.

---

Vergil, *Georgics* 2.534–5
Rome has become the most beautiful of all things and with one wall surrounded the seven hills.

---

Dionysius of Halicarnassus, *Roman Antiquities* 4.14.1
Tullius, when he surrounded the seven hills with one wall.

---

Strabo, *Geography* 5.3.7
The first people walled the Capitol, the Palatine, and the Quirinal Hill, which was so easy to ascend that Titus Tatius, when he came to avenge the violence of the seizure of the maidens, took it at first assault. Ancus Marcius added the Caelian Hill and the Aventine Hill, and the plain between them, separated both from one another and from what was walled before. But he added them out of necessity, for it was not a good idea to leave hills so fortified by nature outside the walls for someone wanting to make them strongholds. Nor was he able to fill up the whole circle as far as the Quirinal. Servius exposed the defect and he filled the void by adding the Esquiline Hill and the Viminal Hill. These places were easy to attack for those outside of them. On this account they dug a deep trench and they took in land on the inside of it, and they extended the

mound of earth for six stades on top of the inside of the trench. They added a wall and towers from the Colline gate to the Esquiline. In the middle of the trench, there is a third gate, named for the Viminal Hill.

## 8.24 Aurelian Wall

Construction on the Aurelian Wall was started in 271–2 CE, during the reign of the emperor Aurelian. There were structures already established in the path of the wall at the time of its construction and these structures were woven into the wall itself. According to Richardson (1992: 261), one sixth of the circuit of the wall consists of earlier structures, such as houses, the walls of the Praetorian Camp, the Castrense Amphitheater, and the Pyramid of Cestius. Construction on the wall began as Aurelian prepared for war with Queen Zenobia of Palmyra.[22] Since the wall was repaired many times during its later history, the ancient path remains preserved. Coarelli (2014: 18–27) takes the reader on a detailed itinerary around the remains of the wall. The wall is used today as a point of demarcation. If you are traveling from the main airport, Fiumicino, you can take a taxi for a flat rate, but only to places within the Aurelian Wall. Any place outside the wall will be at a different rate.

Further reading: Coarelli 2014: 18–27; Dey 2011; Richardson 1992: 260–2; Richmond 1930; Todd 1978.

SHA, *Life of Aurelian* 21.9
With the advice of the Senate received, Aurelian extended the walls of the city.

SHA, *Life of Aurelian* 39.2
Aurelian extended the walls of the city so much that they have a circuit of almost fifty miles of walls.

## 8.25 Customs boundaries

There are inscriptions on boundary stones known as *cippi* from the time of Marcus Aurelius and Commodus that point to evidence of customs taxes on products (see also **6.1** in this volume on the boundary of the *pomerium*).[23] The *cippi* from this spot match the line of the wall (Dey 2011: 82). The gates of the city may have served the role of tax collecting, but did not seem to serve the purpose of regulating people's comings and goings (Moatti 2013: 78).

Further reading: Holleran 2012: 88–92; Richardson 1992: 261.

*Corpus of Latin Inscriptions* 6.1016a–c

*Imperator* Caesar Marcus Aurelius Antoninus Augustus Germanicus Sarmaticus and *Imperator* Caesar Lucius Aurelius Commodus Augustus Germanicus Sarmaticus have ordered these stones to be established on account of the disputes between traders and purchasers that had arisen in order to mark a boundary with a customs tax.[24]

# Victory and the City

The victories of Rome's generals and emperors have left a distinct stamp on the physical space of the city. As one walks through the city, it is difficult to miss the arches (**9.11–14**) and columns (**9.15–16**) that dot the landscape, or the numerous obelisks (**9.17**) that remain. On these monuments one can often see clear representations, whether in images or inscriptions, of conquered peoples. Moreover, the literary evidence for the triumphal procession is significant. The triumphal procession (**9.1–10**) was a grand parade held in the streets of Rome by a victorious general or emperor. It was a religious ritual, but also an opportunity for a conquering general returning from campaign to display to the gathered masses the achievements of Rome's battles abroad. As both captives and the spoils of war were carried in the streets, the large crowds of spectators of all ages and social classes would have been a spectacle unto themselves. The spaces of the city also played a significant role in the procession.

## The Roman triumph

### 9.1 The spectacle of the triumph

The triumphal procession was a very visual event and had the possibility to solidify the Roman identity of the spectators lining the streets. Appian recounts the triumph of Scipio Africanus over Carthage in 202 BCE, and describes the procession as an opportunity for the general to show the spoils of war to the people of Rome. In addition to the mention of gold, silver, animals, and other material items, images were carried in the parade to bring to life the deeds of war for the Roman people who had not participated in it. Pliny the Elder describes the spectacular triumph of Pompey over Pontus in 61 BCE. Likewise, Polybius depicts the triumph as a means to bring the vividness of the deeds before the eyes of the people.

Further reading: Beard 2007; Brilliant 1999; Östenberg 2009; Pittenger 2009; Popkin 2016; Versnel 1970.

Livy, *History of Rome* 30.15.12

There was nothing more magnificent among the Romans than a triumph.

Appian, *Punic Wars* 9.66

The manner of the triumph, which the Romans still continue using [in the second century CE], is as follows. All the people were crowned, trumpeters and wagons of spoils led the way, towers were carried as representations of the captured cities, as well as pictures of the things that took place. Then came gold and silver, coined and uncoined, and, if it existed, something else of that kind. Then came crowns given to the general by the cities or the allies or the army itself on account of his excellence. Then came the white oxen, and also the elephants, as well as many of the Carthaginian and Numidian leaders who were captured. Lictors[1] clothed in purple tunics went before the general and a chorus of cithara players and pipers, as a copy of an Etruscan parade. They were girded and wearing golden crowns and they walked in formation equally with song and dance. They call themselves Lydian, I think, because the Etruscans were colonists of the Lydians. Of them, someone in the middle, wearing a purple robe and armlets and twisted necklaces made of gold, gesticulated artfully to laughter as if triumphing over the enemy. After him came a large number of censers for incense and the general in his intricately engraved chariot. He was crowned in gold and costly stones and dressed according to the ways of the country in purple, woven with golden stars. He carried a scepter made of ivory and laurel, which the Romans always use as a sign of victory. Boys and girls rode in the chariot with him and on horses on either side were young unmarried kinsmen. Then they accompanied him, however many were with him in the war—secretaries, and officers, and shield-bearers. After them the army came in troops and companies, all crowned and carrying laurel; the best men received prizes. They praised some of their commanders, they mocked others, and they censured some. For the triumph is simple; it is permitted for people to say what they want. When Scipio arrived at the Capitoline, he put an end to the procession and he entertained his friends, as is custom, in the temple.

Pliny the Elder, *Natural History* 37.6.12–14

Nevertheless that victory of Pompey first turned the fashion to pearls and gems, just as that of Lucius Scipio and Gnaeus Manlius did for engraved silver and Attalic clothes [woven with gold], and bronze couches, and just as that of Lucius Mummius did for Corinthian goods and paintings. In order for this to be known more clearly, I will put forward words from the public records of the triumphs of Pompey. Accordingly, in the third triumph (over the pirates, Asia, Pontus, and the peoples and kings noted in the seventh volume of this work), which he held on his birthday on the day before the Kalends of October, in the consulship of Marcus Piso and Marcus Messala, he displayed a three-foot wide and four-foot long game board, with the gaming pieces made of two gems. And lest anyone doubt that these materials are exhausted, since today there is no gem nearly approaching to this size, on this gaming board there was a golden moon of thirty pounds. He displayed three golden couches, vessels of gold, and nine display tables of gems, three golden statues of Minerva, Mars, and Apollo, thirty-three crowns of pearls, a square golden mountain with deer, lions, and fruits of every sort, with a golden vine surrounding it, a grotto of pearls, on whose peak was a sundial. And there was an image of Pompey in pearls.

---

Polybius, *Histories* 6.15.8
What are called triumphs, through which the generals bring the vividness of their successful deeds before the eyes of the citizens, they [the generals] are not able to administer them, as is clear, nor even to hold them at all, if the Senate does not agree to them and does not give money for them.

---

## 9.2 Hostages led in the triumphal procession

Some of the people led in the procession would have been prisoners of war, but others would have been hostages, given to the conquering Romans as part of a treaty to end the war. Whereas regular prisoners could be executed at the end of the procession, hostages, at least those given in certain types of treaties, were protected. They were typically people important to the defeated ruler. Plutarch describes the triumph of Aemilius Paullus over King Perseus in 167 BCE, while Appian recounts the triumph of Pompey in 61 BCE after the Third Mithridatic War.

Further reading: Beard 2007: 7–40, 108–42; Östenberg 2009: 163–7.

---

Plutarch, *Life of Aemilius Paullus* 33.3
The chariot of Perseus followed them [gold and gems] and his armor and his diadem laid upon the armor. Next after a small pause were led the children of the king as slaves and with them a crowd of weeping attendants, teachers, and tutors, stretching out their hands to the spectators and teaching the children to beg and entreat.

---

Appian, *Mithridatic Wars* 17.117
Led forward before Pompey himself were the commanders, the children, and the generals of the kings who had done battle, about 324 of them. Some were captives, but others were given as hostages. There was Tigranes, the son of Tigranes, and five sons of Mithridates (Artaphernes, Cyrus, Oxathres, Darius, Xerxes) and his daughters (Orsabaris and Eupatra).

---

## 9.3 Women led in the triumphal procession

In **9.2**, we see family members led as hostages, but more significant are the occasions when a woman was the opponent being conquered rather than merely a member of a larger retinue of hostages. Dio describes how Arsinoe, the sister of Cleopatra, was led in the triumph of Julius Caesar over Egypt in 46 BCE, arousing the pity of the spectators. She was later released. Years later in 30 BCE, Caesar's heir, Octavian, led not Cleopatra, then Queen of Egypt, but an image of her, since Cleopatra had already taken her own life. Her children with the Roman general and Octavian's rival Marc Antony were also part of the procession, but they were alive and were later raised at Rome.

Further reading: Östenberg 2009: 141–4.

---

Dio, *Roman History* 43.19–20.1

And Julius Caesar celebrated triumphs over the Gauls, Egypt, Pharnaces, and Juba in four parts separately in four days. The rest [of the spectacle] gladdened the ones watching to some degree, but Arsinoe, the Egyptian led among the prisoners, the number of lictors, and the procession of belongings of the citizens killed in Africa, troubled them terribly. The number of lictors provided the most offensive crowd to them, seeing that not yet before had they seen so many at the same time. And Arsinoe, being a woman and considered a queen, in chains, was something that had not yet been seen in Rome and brought great pity, and with this as a motive, they lamented their own experiences. She was let go on account of her brothers, but the others and Vercingetorix were put to death. Therefore on account of the things I have mentioned, the crowd was ill disposed but considered them as very small in comparison with the number of captives and the magnitude of his achievements.

---

Plutarch, *Life of Antony* 86.3

For in Augustus's triumph, an image of Cleopatra herself was carried and of the asp clinging to her.

---

Dio, *Roman History* 51.21.7–9

On the second day [of Augustus's triple triumph, he celebrated] the naval victory of Actium and on the third day the subjugation of Egypt. All the triumphal processions were remarkable on account of the spoils from Egypt, so many gathered that it was enough for all of the processions, but the most expensive and the most becoming was the one of Egypt. As for the rest: Cleopatra on a couch in a representation of death was carried so that in some way she, along with the other prisoners and with her children Alexander Helios and Cleopatra Selene, could be seen as part of the procession.

---

## 9.4 I came, I saw, I conquered (*veni, vidi, vici*)

This famous phrase, often quoted by students of Latin learning the perfect tense of verbs, can be found in the writings of the biographer Suetonius. In his work on the life of Julius Caesar, he describes the triumphal processions of Caesar who celebrated a quadruple triumph in 46 BCE, with victories over Gaul, Egypt, Pontus, and Numidia.

---

Suetonius, *Julius Caesar* 37.2

On the day of his Gallic triumph, as he was riding past the Velabrum, Caesar was almost cast out of his chariot because of a broken wheel and he ascended the Capitol by torchlight, with forty elephants on his right and left carrying candlesticks. In his Pontic triumph, among the litters of the procession, he displayed a placard with three words: "I came, I saw, I conquered," signifying not the deeds of the war, as with the rest, but a mark of how quickly it was accomplished.

---

## 9.5 Examples of triumphal processions

Provided below are three examples of triumphal processions. The first triumphs, described by the historian Velleius Paterculus, are those of Julius Caesar. In the second passage, the Jewish historian Josephus writes about the triumph in 71 CE of the emperor Vespasian and his son, the future emperor Titus, over the Jews in the Roman province of Judaea. A connection can be made between the ritual items led in this procession, such as the menorah, and those that are depicted on the Arch of Titus (on this arch, see **9.12** in this volume. See also **3.21** on the housing of items from the Jewish Temple in the Temple of Peace). The third triumph is not a real one, but rather one imagined by Pliny the Younger as part of his praise of the emperor Trajan.

Further reading: Lovatt 2016: 368–70; Östenberg 2009: 29–30.

---

Velleius Paterculus, *Roman History* 2.56.1–2

Caesar, conqueror of all, having returned to the city of Rome, pardoned all who had taken arms against him, a thing which goes beyond human belief. He filled the city with the most splendid spectacles of a gladiatorial display, of a *naumachia* [mock naval battle], of cavalry and infantry, and of a contest of elephants and feasts given for many days in celebration. He led five triumphs: he displayed the ornaments of the Gallic triumph from wood, the Pontic one from acanthus, the Alexandrian one from tortoise shell, the African one from ivory, and the Spanish one from smoothed silver.

---

Josephus, *The Jewish War* 7.129–34; 146–55

After the prayers, Vespasian, having spoken for a short time with everyone in public, released the soldiers to the customary meal prepared for them by the rulers, and went to the gate from which, on account of the triumph always being conducted through it, it took its name [Porta Triumphalis]. There the rulers tasted food and they put on their triumphal clothing and they sacrificed to the gods set up beside the gate. They sent forth the procession, driving through the theaters so that the view would be easier for the masses. It is impossible to describe well the multitude of those sights and the magnificence in all of them … One could see a mass of gold, silver, and ivory, prepared in all sorts of forms, not as if carried in a procession, but as one might say, as a flowing river. And the robes carried were woven from very rare purple cloth, others embroidered into precise paintings with Babylonian skill … The skill and the magnificence of the structures showed to the people what happened in the war, as if they had been present. On each of the stages, the general of a conquered city was positioned in the way he was captured. Many ships followed. The rest of the spoils were carried in floods, but all the ones captured in the temple of Jerusalem were conspicuous: a golden table with a weight worth many talents,[2] a lampstand likewise made of gold, but the work was changed from the customs of everyday use. There was a middle pillar fixed on a pedestal, the thin branches of the candlesticks had been lengthened in the form of a trident, each of them forged with a lamp at the tip. There were seven of them, showing the Jews' esteem for the number seven. In addition to these things, the law of the Jews was carried as the last of the spoils. Besides these, many men passed by carrying images of victory; the construction of all of them was from ivory and gold. Thereafter, Vespasian rode in on a chariot first and Titus followed and Domitian rode alongside. He himself was adorned magnificently, having also a horse worthy to see. The end of the procession was at the Temple of Capitoline Jupiter, at which when they arrived, they came to a stop. For it was an old custom to wait until someone reported the death of the general of the enemies. This was Simon, the son of Gioras who, after having taken part in the procession among the prisoners, had a noose put on him and was dragged to the place near the Forum and tortured by the ones leading him. It is Roman law to kill there the ones sentenced to death for wrongdoing. After his death was reported and everyone shouted in triumph, they began the sacrifices, and after having obtained good omens and with the customary prayers, they went to the palace.

Pliny the Younger, *Panegyric* 17

Now I seem to see a triumph laden not with the spoils of provinces and the gold extorted from allies, but with enemy arms and the chains of captured kings. I seem to recognize the remarkable names of leaders and their bodies not unbecoming of the names. I seem to watch the litters of spoils loaded with the enormous undertakings of the barbarous peoples and each man following his own deeds with his hands bound. Soon I see you elevated and standing on your chariot behind the broken peoples. Before the chariot, moreover, are the shields you yourself pierced. Nor would the spoils[3] be lacking if any of the kings dared to come to fight you. Not only would he shudder at your weapons, even with the whole field and the whole army before you, but also because of your threatening eyes.

## 9.6 The result of triumphal money on the Roman economy

The abundance of money to which Suetonius refers is the result of the conquering of Egypt and part of Octavian's triple triumph of 29 BCE.

Suetonius, *Augustus* 41.1

Augustus frequently showed generosity to all ranks at favorable opportunities. For in the Alexandrian triumph, since the royal treasury was carried in the Alexandrian triumph, he obtained such an abundance of money that the interest rate was diminished, and most property increased in price.

# Locating the triumphal procession

## 9.7 Watching the triumph on the Sacra Via

The city itself played an important role in the event. While the precise route remains debated in scholarly literature,[4] the procession was likely to have made certain known stops: the Triumphal Gate (the Porta Triumphalis), the Circus Flaminius, the Circus Maximus, the Sacra Via, and culminating on the Capitol.

Further reading: Beard 2007: 92–106; Favro 1994; Östenberg 2009: 13–14; Popkin 2016: 24–45.

Propertius, *Elegies* 3.4.11–13; 21–2

Father Mars, and the fated lights of sacred Vesta, I pray, let that day come before my end, on which I see the wheels of Caesar weighted with spoils ... Let this booty belong to those whose labors earned it: it will be enough that I am able to applaud on the Sacra Via.

Horace, *Epodes* 7.7–8

Or so that the untouched Briton might go down the Sacra Via in chains?

## 9.8 The Circus Flaminius and the triumph

The Circus Flaminius is sometimes mentioned as a staging area for the procession, but there is no clarity on this issue (Popkin 2016: 40). Literary sources do mention the area in connection with the triumph, whatever its purpose.

---

Livy, *History of Rome* 39.5.17
On that day, before he was brought into the city, Marcus Fulvius bestowed military gifts upon many tribunes, prefects, cavalry, centurions, Romans, and allies in the Circus Flaminius.

---

Livy, *History of Rome* 45.39.14
Will the king of the Macedonians, Perseus, with his children and the other crowd of prisoners and the spoils of the Macedonians, be left in the Circus Flaminius?

## 9.9 Passing through the Porta Triumphalis

There continues to be debate among scholars about the location of the Triumphal Gate (the Porta Triumphalis). Can we identify one fixed position, or was it simply the name given to any gate through which the triumphing general passed?

Further reading: Östenberg 2009: 12–13; Sobocinski 2009.

---

Pliny the Elder, *Natural History* 8.2.4
Procilius denies that in the triumph of Pompey the joined elephants were able to go out from the gate.

---

Plutarch, *Life of Pompey* 14.4–5
When many people were displeased and feeling irritated, as they say, Pompey, wishing even more to distress them, attempted to enter in triumph mounted upon a chariot of four elephants that he led from Africa, as great captives of the kings. But the gate was rather narrow and he gave up on this idea and came on his horses.

---

Martial, *Epigrams* 8.65
Here where the gleaming Temple of Fortuna Redux [Fortune the Bringer Back] shines widely, it was recently a happy space. Here stood Caesar, handsome with the dust of the northern war, pouring beautiful splendor from his mouth. Here Rome, her hair wreathed in laurel and shining with elegance, greeted the leader with her voice and hand. Other gifts bear witness to the great merit of the place: a sacred arch

stands and triumphs over the conquered peoples. Here twin chariots have a crowd of elephants and he himself, golden, suffices for the enormous yoked teams. This gate, Germanicus,[5] is worthy of your triumphs. It is fitting that the city of Mars has these entrances.

## 9.10 Executed foreign leaders and the Carcer (the prison)

The Carcer was the prison at the base of the Capitoline Hill used for temporary holding before a prisoner was executed (see also **11.17** in this volume). The underground part was called the Tullianum and was the place of execution. Triumphal processions made a stop at the Carcer to unload prisoners to be executed. Cicero describes this stop in his speech against the former governor of Sicily, Verres. Plutarch writes about the death of Jugurtha, king of Numidia, as part of the victory of Marius, while Dio mentions the death of Vercingetorix, a Gallic chief, as part of the triumph of Julius Caesar.

Further reading: Cadoux 2008; Claridge 2010: 163; Richardson 1992: 71.

Cicero, *Against Verres* 2.5.77
But even those men who triumph and keep the leaders of enemies alive longer, so that by leading them through the triumph the Roman people are able to see the most beautiful spectacle and success of victory, still when they begin to turn their chariots from the Forum to the Capitol, they order that those prisoners be led to the prison [*carcer*]. The same day brings an end of the right of command for the victors, and brings an end to life for the conquered.

Plutarch, *Life of Marius* 12.2–4
Marius crossed over from Africa with his army on the Kalends of January, which the Romans observe as the beginning of the year. He took up the office of consul and he entered in triumphal procession. He exhibited a spectacle beyond belief to the Romans: Jugurtha as a prisoner. While he was alive, no one had hoped to conquer the enemy, so wily was the man at being in good fortune and he had passion mixed with much trickery. But, as they say, once he was led in triumph, at that time he lost his senses. And after the triumph, thrown into prison, some tore off his clothes by force, others, hastening to take his golden earring by force, tore off his earlobe together with it. Once he was pushed into the pit, naked, full of confusion and grinning, he said, "Hercules, how cold is your bath." He struggled with hunger for six days and until the final second clinging to the desire to live, he had a punishment worthy of his impious acts.

---

Dio, *Roman History* 40.41.3

Caesar did not pity him [Vercingetorix] at this moment, but directly bound him in chains and after this, having sent him to the triumph, killed him.

---

# Arches

## 9.11 Arch of Claudius

This arch was dedicated to the emperor Claudius in 51/52 CE to mark the conquest of Britain and was located on the Via Lata. A large fragment of the inscription below is located at the Palazzo dei Conservatori in the Capitoline Museums in Rome.

Further reading: Coarelli 2014: 255; Keppie 1991: 46–7; Richardson 1992: 24.

---

Dio, *Roman History* 60.22.1

The Senate, having learned of Claudius' achievements, called him Britannicus and gave him a triumphal procession. They voted for an annual festival to take place and for there to be triumphal arches, one in the city, the other in Gaul, from where, having set sail, he crossed over to Britain.

---

*Corpus of Latin Inscriptions* 6.920

The Senate and the Roman people [gave this arch] to Tiberius Claudius Caesar Augustus Germanicus, son of Drusus, *pontifex maximus* [chief priest], with tribunician power eleven times, consul five times, *imperator* twenty-two times, father of the country, because he received the submission of eleven conquered kings of Britain without any loss and first led back into the power of the Roman people the barbarous peoples across the ocean.

---

*Corpus of Latin Inscriptions* 6.922

To Claudius Caesar Britannicus.

---

## 9.12 Arch of Titus

This arch was dedicated to the emperor Titus for his victory over Jerusalem and stands on the Sacra Via. Reliefs on the arch depict the items taken from the temple of Jerusalem, including the menorah. There is also a representation of Titus himself in the triumph he held with his father Vespasian. You can still see the arch and its reliefs today in the Roman Forum area.

Further reading: Claridge 2010: 121–3; Coarelli 2014: 97–8; Richardson 1992: 30; Tuck 2016: 113–15.

---

*Corpus of Latin Inscriptions* 6.945

The Senate and the Roman people [gave this arch] to the deified Titus Vespasian Augustus, son of the deified Vespasian.

---

*Corpus of Latin Inscriptions* 6.944

[On another arch to Titus that was near the Circus Maximus, but is no longer standing] The Senate and the Roman people [gave this arch] to *Imperator* Titus Caesar Vespasian Augustus, *pontifex maximus*, son of the deified Vespasian, with tribunician power ten times, *imperator* seventeen times, consul eight times, father of the country, because with the paternal precepts, and advice, and auspices, he conquered the nation of the Jews and destroyed the city of Jerusalem, either attempted in vain or untried altogether by all the leaders, kings, people before him.

## 9.13 Arch of Septimius Severus

This arch stands in the Roman Forum and its remains are significant. It was established in 203 CE for the emperor Septimius Severus and his sons Caracalla and Geta. The arch is a distinctive triple arch with a dedicatory inscription at the top of it. The inscription is worthy of extra notice since its original words were edited and the traces of the changes remain visible. After one son, Caracalla, murdered his brother Geta, traces of Geta's name were removed as an attempt to permanently erase his memory, a practice called *damnatio memoriae*. Other titles for Septimius Severus and Caracalla were added.

Further reading: Claridge 2010: 78–9; Coarelli 2014: 60–3; Favro 2011; Richardson 1992: 28.

---

*Corpus of Latin Inscriptions* 6.1033

The Senate and the Roman people [gave this arch] to *Imperator* Caesar Lucius Septimius Severus Pius Pertinax Augustus, son of Marcus, father of the country, Parthicus Arabicus, and Parthicus Adiabenicus, *pontifex maximus*, with tribunician power eleven times, *imperator* eleven times, consul three times, proconsul and to *Imperator* Caesar Marcus Aurelius Antoninus Augustus Pius Felix, son of Lucius, with tribunician power six times, consul, proconsul, father of the country. To the best and strongest princes, on account of the state renewed and the empire of the Roman people extended by their remarkable capacities at home and abroad.

## 9.14 Arch of Constantine

This arch was erected in 315/316 CE for Constantine's conquering of Maxentius, who ruled Rome before him. Like the Arch of Septimius Severus, it is a triple arch. The arch is located near the Sacra Via and still stands today. Reliefs on the arch show battles, soldiers, and captives. The structure is made from reused pieces of earlier monuments. Even the sculptures are from multiple periods of Rome's history (possibly from the times of Trajan, Hadrian, and Marcus Aurelius), taken from other monuments and adapted for new purpose.

Further reading: Claridge 2010: 308–12; Holloway 2008; Richardson 1992: 24–5.

*Corpus of Latin Inscriptions* 6.1139
[On the front of the arch]
The Senate and the Roman People dedicated this arch distinguished by triumphs, to the *Imperator* Caesar Flavius Constantine the great, Pius Felix Augustus, because by the instinct of divinity[6] and a greatness of mind, with his own army, he avenged the state with just arms on the tyrant [Maxentius] and his whole faction at one time.
[On one side]
To the liberator of the city.
[On another side]
To the founder of peace.

# Columns

## 9.15 Trajan's Column

Trajan's Column dates to 113 CE and serves as a marker of Trajan's battles in Dacia (modern Romania) (see Fig. 9.1). A visitor to Rome can still see it intact at the Forum of Trajan off the Via dei Fori Imperiali. The reliefs in a helical frieze on the column show events from Trajan's campaigns in a continuous sequence of 155 scenes. The column provides a significant visual marker of the life and equipment of the Roman army. There is a spiral stairway within the column by means of which one can reach the top. There are small windows along the shaft of the column allowing light into the staircase. It is said that in antiquity, there was a statue of Trajan himself at the top, but nothing remains of this statue. In 1588, a statue of St. Peter was placed at the top and still remains there today. According to ancient sources, the ashes of Trajan were buried at the base.

**Figure 9.1** Column of Trajan. Photo credit: Scala/Art Resource, NY.

Further reading: Claridge 2010: 186–90; Coarelli 2014: 118–20; Ramage and Ramage 2009: 209–20; Richardson 1992: 176–7.

*Corpus of Latin Inscriptions* 6.960

The Senate and the Roman people [gave this column] to *Imperator* Caesar Nerva Trajan Augustus Germanicus Dacicus, *pontifex maximus*, son of the deified Nerva, with tribunician power seventeen times, *imperator* six times, consul six times, father of the country, to proclaim that a hill of such great height and location was removed for such great structures.

Dio, *Roman History* 68.16

Trajan also built libraries and set up in the Forum a huge column both as a tomb for himself and a memorial for his work in the Forum. For since the entire area there was hilly, he had dug down such a distance as the column's height and created a level site for his Forum.

## 9.16 Column of Marcus Aurelius

This column is located in Piazza Colonna. Today there is a statue of St. Paul at the top where once there may have been a statue of Marcus Aurelius. The column marks two campaigns of Marcus Aurelius north of the Danube River, one against the Marcomanni and another against the Sarmatians. Like the column of Trajan, it has an internal staircase leading to a viewpoint.

Further reading: Claridge 2010: 219–21; Richardson 1992: 95–6.

*Corpus of Latin Inscriptions* 6.1585a.5–6

The one-hundred foot column of the deified Marcus and Faustina.

*Corpus of Latin Inscriptions* 6.1585b.18–19

For Adrastus, procurator of the column of the deified Marcus.

# Obelisks

## 9.17 The obelisks of Augustus

There are a number of Egyptian obelisks still in the city of Rome. Although the obelisks have been moved from their original places in later periods, they are reminders of the agendas of Rome's leaders at various points in the city's history.

For example, the obelisk that was placed in the Circus Maximus by Augustus stands today in the Piazza del Popolo. Following in the footsteps of ancient Rome, Benito Mussolini had one taken from Axum in Ethiopia during World War II and placed in the Piazza di Porta Capena near the Circus Maximus. It was returned to its home in 2005. Under Mussolini, a modern obelisk was also erected with the words "Mussolini Dux" (Mussolini the Leader) inscribed on it. It remains outside the Foro Italico.

Further reading: Richardson 1992: 272–6.

---

Pliny the Elder, *Natural History* 36.14.70–4
Above all things, there came the difficulty of carrying away the obelisks by sea to Rome ... Moreover, the obelisk that the deified Augustus placed in the Circus Maximus was cut by king Psemetnepserphreus, who ruled when Pythagoras was in Egypt. It is eighty-five feet and nine inches minus the base of the same stone. The obelisk that is in the Campus Martius is lesser by nine feet and was cut by Sesothis. Both inscribed obelisks contain an explanation of natural matters by the philosophy of the Egyptians. To the obelisk that is in the Campus, the deified Augustus added an extraordinary method for understanding the shadows of the sun and in this way the size of the days and nights. Stone was paved to the length of the obelisk, so that at the sixth hour on the shortest day, the shade might be equal to it ... The third obelisk in Rome is in the Vatican circus of the emperors Gaius [Caligula] and Nero and it is the one out of all of them that was broken in moving it.

---

*Corpus of Latin Inscriptions* 6.701 and 6.702 (one side facing south and one north)
*Imperator* Caesar Augustus, son of the divine Caesar, *pontifex maximus*, *imperator* twelve times, consul eleven times, with tribunician power fourteen times, gave [this obelisk] as a gift to the sun once Egypt was brought into the power of the Roman people.

---

Ammianus Marcellinus, *Roman History* 17.4.12; 16
When Octavian Augustus brought two obelisks from the city of Heliopolis in Egypt, one of them was placed in the Circus Maximus, the other in the Campus Martius ... Following generations brought others, of which one was erected in the Vatican, another in the gardens of Sallust, and two at the Mausoleum of Augustus.

# The City Under Siege: Natural and Man-made Disasters

The eruption of Mount Vesuvius in 79 CE, which devastated the Campanian cities of Pompeii and Herculaneum, has forever linked antiquity with "disaster" in both history and popular imagination. Yet the city of Rome should perhaps be more readily associated with catastrophic events, some of which claimed a far greater number of lives. Indeed, Rome was often under siege—not in the military sense, but because of a range of natural and man-made threats that seem to have struck with surprising regularity including fires, floods, and plagues. The scope of the destruction and extent of loss, both human and material, varied considerably as is well illustrated in the case of fires which ancient sources mention as routine dangers for urban dwellers (**10.8, 10.9**). Some seem to have been relatively contained while others destroyed huge areas, radically altering the cityscape (**10.3–5**). Official responses were likewise diverse with some emperors directly involving themselves and their relatives in cleanup and recovery efforts, and others offering financial aid but not getting their hands dirty (**10.10, 10.11**). There were attempts to prevent certain disasters from reoccurring (**10.1, 10.12**), though seemingly with little success as floods, fires, and food shortages continued to beset leaders throughout Rome's history. Disasters were often interconnected and one calamity might soon bring about another. The flooding of the Tiber, for instance, weakened the foundations of buildings leading to collapses (**10.6**), and outbreaks of disease followed on floods and fires (**10.7**). Several disasters in succession might be lamented but simply deemed very unfortunate if they happened under the leadership of a popular or "good" emperor such as Titus (**10.10**), but similar circumstances while a "bad" emperor was in power, such as Nero or Domitian, reflected his innately bad character and could presage his demise (**10.2, 10.7**).

# Calamities and catastrophes

## 10.1 Problems with the grain supply

Food shortages were regular features of ancient Mediterranean society and occurred because of a sharp decrease in available food rather than a decrease in the amount of food produced. Although famines were rare, food shortages were common: between 123 and 50 BCE, for instance, the Romans suffered a food crisis approximately one year in five. Food shortages had both natural causes, such as climate and the physical environment which could contribute to harvest failures, and human causes including the level of agricultural technology, transport and trade, disruption of the normal movement of essential food items because of war and piracy, maladministration, and profiteering. Maintaining year-round grain supplies for the city of Rome, which had an estimated population of one million people, was a significant task, as is clear from the excerpt from Suetonius's biography of the emperor Claudius. Wheat was a staple of the Roman diet and a large number of citizens depended upon state-sponsored handouts to survive. Under Augustus, for example, the number of eligible citizens registered for the grain dole was 200,000 (see also **2.22** in this volume).

Further reading: Garnsey 1988; Toner 2013: 48–57.

---

Suetonius, *Claudius* 18–19

He always paid most careful attention to the city and its grain supply. When the Aemilian area[1] stubbornly kept burning, he remained for two nights in the Diribitorium,[2] and when the assistance from a body of soldiers and his own slaves was not sufficient, he summoned the plebs from all the districts through the magistrates and, having set bags of money before them, he urged them to give aid, paying each one a suitable fee for his services. When the grain supply was rather meager because of persistent bad harvests, he was once detained in the middle of the Forum by a mob, which so attacked him with insults and at the same time with crusts of bread that he was scarcely able to escape into the Palace except by a backdoor. He thought up every possible means of bringing in grain, even in the winter season. For he promised merchants secure profits by undertaking the loss himself if any should occur for them due to storms, and for those building merchant ships he also offered large incentives in accordance with each person's status: to a citizen, exemption from the *lex Papia Poppaea* [the Papian and Poppaean Law]; to a Latin, the rights of Roman citizenship; to women, the privileges afforded to those with four children—and these terms are still observed today.

## 10.2 Wild and destructive weather foretells misfortune

When disasters occur today, most people attribute them either to nature in the case of hurricanes, tornados, and earthquakes, or to humans in the case of massive oil spills or nuclear power plant accidents. While people might turn to religion to help cope in the aftermath of a disaster, generally they do not look to religion for an explanation or signs that they should have foreseen the event and acted either to prevent or avoid it. In the Roman world, however, the gods and phenomena associated with them were thought to play roles both in causing some disasters and especially in predicting them. Romans believed the gods communicated their will to humans by sending messages ("signs") that ritual specialists interpreted. An unusual or unnatural occurrence could be a sign that the gods were angry with humankind and signal a dire future event. In a lengthy chapter of his biography of Domitian, Suetonius enumerates the many odd incidents that foretold the emperor's assassination, including a period of destructive weather detailed below. In addition to documenting what happened, Suetonius, and likewise Tacitus, also used disasters as an index of an emperor's character: for a stereotypically "bad" emperor such as Domitian or Nero, calamities either precipitate the leader's demise or reveal his selfish or destructive nature (cf. **10.3** in this volume); in contrast, for a "good" emperor such as Domitian's brother Titus, disasters present opportunities to show appropriate concern and take action for those suffering (see **10.10** in this volume).

Further reading: Beard, North, and Price 1998: 37–8; Toner 2013: 108–23.

---

Suetonius, *Domitian* 15.2

Over eight successive months, so many lightning strikes occurred and were reported that Domitian cried out, "Let him now strike whom he wishes." The Capitoline was struck and the temple of the Flavian line, likewise his residence on the Palatine—even his own bedroom, and the inscription was also torn off the base of his triumphal statue from the force of a storm and fell down onto a nearby monument. A tree, which had toppled over when Vespasian was still a private citizen and sprung up anew, then suddenly fell to the ground once again. Fortuna of Praeneste, accustomed throughout the span of his reign to grant him a propitious omen and always the same one when he entrusted the new year to her protection, now on the last occasion returned a most dire one and not without mention of bloodshed.

## 10.3 Two destructive fires, two different responses

Fire was a constant threat in Rome for many reasons including overcrowding, limited enforcement of building regulations regarding the height and spacing of structures (among other serious issues), and construction materials such as wood, brick, and stone, which all posed risks. In particular, the upper floors of apartment buildings (called *insulae*) were regularly constructed with wooden frames, which would burn quickly and easily once a fire began (see **2.9–13** in this volume, especially **2.10**). Ancient sources routinely mention fires at Rome, and although the city had an organized fire brigade (see **2.18–20** in this volume), numerous large-scale blazes are known, some of which devastated significant parts of the city. The historian Tacitus reports on major fires under two Julio-Claudian emperors and their responses to these calamities: Tiberius in 37 CE and Nero in 64 CE (cf. **10.10** in this volume). The fire under Nero is often referred to by modern scholars as the Great Fire. From Tacitus's long and detailed narrative, which is excerpted here, it certainly appears to have been spectacular. In addition to capturing the scope of damage and destruction to properties and infrastructure, and how this changed the appearance of the urban landscape permanently, Tacitus also notes the emperor's efforts to address the needs of those affected by the conflagration by erecting temporary shelters and bringing in supplies, and his attempts to prevent similar disasters from occurring in the future by various reforms. Yet despite his measures, major fires continued to be problems in Rome with further significant blazes reported in 69 and 80 CE.

Further reading: Canter 1932; Newbold 1974; Oleson 2011.

---

Tacitus, *Annals* 6.45

The same year the city was struck by a serious fire. The part of the Circus that borders on the Aventine burned down as well as the Aventine itself, a catastrophe Caesar [Tiberius] turned to his own glory by paying out the values of the houses and apartment buildings. One hundred million sesterces were spent on that generosity which was that much more agreeable to the masses because he was modest in expenditures on buildings of his own and did not even build at public expense with the exception of two works: the Temple of Augustus and the stage of Pompey's theater—and because of either his disdain for popularity or his old age, he did not dedicate them once completed. The four husbands of Caesar's granddaughters were chosen to estimate individual losses: Gnaeus Domitius, Cassius Longinus, Marcus Vicinius, and Rubellius Blandus; by nomination of the consuls, Publius Petronius was added.

Tacitus, *Annals* 15.38–9, 40–1

Disaster followed. Whether due to chance or because of some criminal act by the emperor [Nero] is not certain (for both versions have supporters), but it was more grievous and terrible than all the calamities that have befallen this city through the destructive force of the fire. It sprung up first in that part of the Circus that touches the Palatine and Caelian Hills where the flames were fed through shops filled with goods. There the fire began at once and, strengthened immediately by the winds, it quickly destroyed the length of the Circus. For there were neither mansions fenced by protective enclosures nor temples surrounded by walls or any other means to slow its progress. First the fire swept through the level parts of the city in its attack; then, rising up into the hills, it once again ravaged the lower parts. It kept ahead of all remedies because of the catastrophe's speed and because the city was vulnerable from its narrow streets winding this way and that and irregular blocks which were typical of old Rome … Nero was staying in Antium at the time and did not return to the capital until the fire was approaching the mansion by which he had connected the Palatine and the Gardens of Maecenas.[3] Nevertheless, it could not be stopped even from swallowing up both the Palatine and the house and everything surrounding them. But as relief to the people who had been driven out of their homes and were fleeing the fire, he opened up the Campus Martius and the buildings of Agrippa,[4] even his own gardens, and he constructed emergency shelters, which received the helpless masses. Necessities were brought up from Ostia and neighboring municipalities, and the price of grain was lowered to three sesterces. But these measures, although popular, failed in their aim because a rumor had spread that at the very moment when Rome was aflame, Nero had entered upon his private stage and, comparing present misfortunes to ancient calamities, had sung of the destruction of Troy … Rome, in fact, is divided into fourteen regions of which four remained intact, three were razed to the ground, and in the other seven the few traces of dwellings that survived were mangled and half-burned. It would be difficult to calculate the number of homes and apartment buildings and temples lost. But the fire consumed sites sacred in their extreme antiquity: the temple Servius Tullius had dedicated to Luna (on the Aventine); both the Great Altar and shrine Arcadian Evander had consecrated to the present Hercules (in the Forum Boarium); the Temple of Jupiter Stator vowed by Romulus, the Palace of Numa, and the shrine of Vesta with the Penates of the Roman people (on the northern side of the Palatine).

## 10.4 The loss of cultural heritage

Fires resulted in numerous losses, among which was a vast amount of cultural heritage in the form of works of art and literature and precious artifacts crafted from silver and gold that were housed in temples, libraries, and storerooms in the city (see **3.14–17** in this volume). Although some of these could be replaced with considerable effort, as the excerpt concerning damage to Rome's libraries under Domitian shows, many treasures consumed in fires and other disasters were lost forever. The passages from Herodian and Galen regarding a massive fire in 192 CE under the emperor Commodus reveal some of the ways such a disaster could affect individuals differently with respect to cultural heritage. Herodian notes the economic impact such a fire could have as people lost wealth in the form of objects they had dedicated, and he repeatedly states that Rome's "most beautiful" buildings were destroyed—beautiful architecturally, but presumably also because of their fine interiors adorned with paintings and valuable artifacts. Galen instead concentrates on the fire's impact on knowledge and culture when he records the loss of many of his books, medical instruments, and remedies kept in a storeroom near the Sacra Via, as well as books destroyed in libraries on the Palatine. The losses from his storeroom were so significant for him that he not only catalogued them in his treatise *On the Avoidance of Grief,* parts of which are included here, but also mentioned particular lost items in several other treatises. Herodian's narrative of the fire situates it within a discussion of the portents that signaled how dire Commodus's rule was, a theme evident in disaster narratives for other unpopular emperors (cf. **10.3** in this volume).

Further reading: Tucci 2008.

Suetonius, *Domitian* 20
At the beginning of his rule, he neglected liberal studies, although he saw to it that the libraries, which had been destroyed by fire, were restored at tremendous expense. Copies [of lost works] were sought from everywhere and scribes were sent to Alexandria to transcribe and correct them.

Herodian, *Histories* 1.14.2–5
Without a rainstorm happening beforehand or clouds gathering together, a small earthquake first occurred, then either a thunderbolt struck at night or a fire from the earthquake broke out somewhere. The entire Temple of Peace was burned down, the largest and most beautiful of the buildings in the city. It was also the richest of the temples, having been adorned with votive offerings of both gold and silver [placed] there for safekeeping, as each person stored there what he had. But on that night, the fire made many poor men from wealthy ones. While all lamented [lost] public property together, each person [kept thinking] about his own private losses. Once the fire burned down the temple and all its precincts, it spread to a major part of the city and the most beautiful buildings. When the Temple of Vesta was also consumed by fire, the statue of Pallas, said to have been brought from Troy, was exposed to view, which the Romans both revere and keep hidden. People in our age laid eyes upon it

first after it came to Italy from Troy, for the Vestal Virgins snatched up the statue and carried it along the Sacra Via to the emperor's palace. Very many other most beautiful parts of the city also burned down as the fire fed on everything for a considerable number of days and did not stop its fury until the rains came down.

---

Galen, *On the Avoidance of Grief* 10, 18
When I was leaving for Campania, I deposited in the storeroom everything I had at home—instruments and remedies and books and not a small number of silver objects—so that they would be safely guarded while I was away. Accordingly, it happened that all those things piled up there together with valuables previously stored there were destroyed ... The books on the Palatine were destroyed on the same day as mine, for the fire not only ruined the storerooms along the Sacra Via but also, before them, those near the Temple of Peace, and after them, those around the Palatine and the *domus* called Tiberiana in which there was a library filled with many other books.

---

## 10.5 Civil unrest leads to a massive fire

One of the features of disasters in Rome that recurs in ancient narratives is the way one could easily produce another such as when a fire destroyed grain supplies thus prompting a food shortage. Sometimes both the initial disaster and the resultant one were the work of human hands as Herodian indicates in his account of a huge fire in 238 CE, which began in the midst of civil unrest. The fire claimed many lives and destroyed numerous buildings including the Temple of Peace, which Septimius Severus had restored after the fire of 192 CE.

Further reading: Toner 2013: 40.

---

Herodian, *Histories* 7.6–7
If there were any wooden balconies (and there were many in the city), [the soldiers] set fire to them. Because the buildings were close together and a great many made of wood in rows, the fire very easily burned down most of the city. So many who had been rich were made poor after losing their wonderful and abundant properties, some valuable in the rents they brought in and others in the extravagance of their workmanship. A great many people burned alive together since they were unable to flee because the escape routes were already overwhelmed by flames. All the wealth of some rich men was plundered by criminals and poor citizens who mixed in with the soldiers to make off with their property. The part of the city the fire destroyed was greater than the size of any of the largest cities as a whole.

---

## 10.6 The flooding of the Tiber

Between the age of Julius Caesar and the reign of Constantine, ancient authors record twenty separate times when the Tiber flooded. It is likely, though, that there were additional floods not reported by sources. According to one expert (Aldrete 2007: 14), "the basic scientific facts of the geology, hydrology, and topography of Rome as well as more contemporary records of Tiber flooding and rainfall patterns suggest that floods might have been quite common in ancient Rome, with major incidents occurring every few years." Significant flooding was disruptive and destructive causing property damage, homelessness, deaths from drowning and disease once flood waters retreated, health hazards from contaminated water sources, and compromised food supply due to the damage and spoilage of grain that could lead to shortages and even famine. The excerpts below touch upon many of these consequences of serious flooding. The first pair of sources, Cicero and Dio, offers rather differ perspectives on a flood in 54 BCE. Cicero's letter to his brother Quintus is concerned with documenting the extent of the flooding which was considerable for the public fishpond he mentions was a little over a half a mile inland from the Tiber while the Temple of Mars lay beyond the walls of the city along the Via Appia more than a mile and a half from the bank of the river. Dio's account instead concentrates on the human impact of the inundation in terms of lost lives and damaged property. This is similarly the case for Tacitus and Plutarch's reports of the flood of 69 CE, which emphasize how one disaster could lead to another as flooding brought upon scarcity and starvation.

Further reading: Aldrete 2007.

Cicero, *Letters To His Brother Quintus* 3.7.1
At Rome, and especially along the Appian Way up to the Temple of Mars, there has been extraordinary flooding. The promenade of Crassipes was swept away, also gardens and numerous shops. There is a huge amount of water all the way up to the public fishpond.

Dio, *Roman History* 39.61.1–2
In the meantime, either because extraordinarily heavy rains had occurred somewhere upstream above the city, or because a violent wind from the sea had driven back the effluence, or more probably, as was generally supposed, because of the power of some divinity, the Tiber suddenly rose to such an extent that all the lower parts in the city were flooded and even many higher areas were inundated. And so the houses, because they were built from brick, became very wet and collapsed, and all the draft animals were submerged and drowned. Of the people, so many who did not flee to higher

ground perished: some were caught in their homes, others on the roads and lost their lives. As the dire situation lasted for many days, the remaining houses also became unstable and caused ruin for many people either immediately or afterwards.

---

Tacitus, *Histories* 1.86

But there was especial fear both because of the present destruction and also future due to the sudden flooding of the Tiber which, swollen to immense size, once the wooden bridge[5] had been destroyed, was pushed back by the debris that blocked the river like a dam. It filled not only the low-lying parts of the city, but also areas normally safe from calamities of this kind. Many people were carried away from out in the open, more were trapped in shops and in their beds. Among the common people there was starvation from the lack of employment and scarcity of foodstuffs. The foundations of apartment buildings were weakened by the stagnant waters then collapsed when the river receded.

---

Plutarch, *Life of Otho* 4.5

Most people considered the misfortune regarding the Tiber as a dreadful sign. For it was a time when the rivers are especially full, but it had not previously risen so high nor ruined and destroyed so much. It overflowed its banks and flooded a great part of the city and particularly the area where grain is sold to the public such that a terrible shortage endured for many days.

---

## 10.7 Epidemics

The density of population in the ancient city of Rome, overcrowding, and poor sanitation combined to have a very negative impact on the quality and duration of life, which was drastically lower than it is today. Though Rome's buildings were beautiful, its streets appear to have been dirty and disease-ridden, strewn with animal and human feces and rotting animal carcasses (see also **2.1** in this volume). These, as well as other factors, contributed to compromised water supply and food contamination resulting in gastrointestinal diseases, which were rampant and the main cause of death among infants and young children. In addition to these common yet serious health problems, epidemics were regular occurrences throughout the Republic and Empire, and with devastating effects. Tacitus describes a major outbreak in 65 CE, the year after the deadly fire under Nero, which the biographer Suetonius (*Nero* 39.1) reports claimed some 30,000 lives. Yet the casualties were relatively modest in comparison with those estimated for the Antonine plague a century later (perhaps an epidemic of smallpox) which may have killed as many as 300,000 or several thousand people per day by the time it ended.

Further reading: Duncan-Jones 1996; Scheidel 2003; Scobie 1986.

---

Tacitus, *Annals* 16.13

The gods distinguished this year fouled by so many horrible deeds even with storms and disease. Campania was devastated by a whirlwind which tossed farmhouses, fruit trees, and crops all about and ruined them, and brought its fury to the vicinity of Rome. There all classes of people were ravaged by the virulence of a plague though no contagion could be discerned in the air. But houses kept filling with lifeless bodies and roads with funerals. Neither sex nor age freed one from danger. Slaves and likewise the freeborn masses quickly had their lives snuffed out amid the wailing of wives and children who were often cremated on the same funeral pyre after they had sat by their side to comfort them and wept.

---

## 10.8 Worrying about the roof over your head

Building collapses seem to have been common occurrences in ancient Rome. Floods and fires left buildings weakened (see **10.6** in this volume), and the excessive number of upper stories and poorly chosen construction materials made them structurally unsound. Wealthy Romans generally did not live in apartment buildings called *insulae*, which Umbricius, the narrator of Juvenal's satire, suggests were often ready to collapse (see **2.9–13** in this volume on *insulae* and **2.14** and **2.15** on elite housing). Some landlords of such properties must have been indifferent to the poor condition of their buildings and the serious risks they posed to their tenants. Cicero, for example, jokes in a letter to his friend Atticus (*Letters to Atticus* 14.9) that even the mice have moved out after two of his properties collapsed; others showed cracks, presumably in the walls or foundations, but Cicero claimed he was not concerned. Those with means were not entirely immune from the misfortunes of collapses and fires (see **10.3** and **10.4** in this volume), yet when these did occur, they often had the advantage of access to resources and a support network of affluent friends, which enabled them to recover more easily. In contrast, average Romans could literally lose everything in one of these routine calamities, as Juvenal bemoans.

Further reading: Oleson 2011; Toner 2013: 87–97.

---

Juvenal, *Satires* 3.190–225

Who now fears or ever feared a building collapse at cool Praeneste or Volsinii among wooded mountain heights, or at unpretentious Gabii or the hilltop of steep Tibur? We inhabit a Rome for the most part supported by slender props, for so the building manager prevents buildings from falling down. And once he has covered over a yawning ancient crack, he bids us to sleep unconcerned in a structure on the verge of collapse. One ought to live where there are no fires, no nighttime fears. Already Ucalegon is calling for water and carrying out his rickety furniture, and already your third floor is smoking. But you're completely unaware: for if the alarm is sounded at the bottom of the stairs, the place which is protected from the rain by a single roof-tile, where gentle doves lay their eggs, this will be the last to burn. Cordus had a bed (too small for Procula), six small earthenware jugs as decoration for his sideboard and, underneath, a little reclining Centaur, Chiron, made from the same "marble," and a box, now old, keeping his little Greek books safe though the boorish mice were nibbling away at the immortal poems! Cordus had nothing: who would disagree? And yet that unfortunate man lost the entirety of his "nothing." However, truly the height of his misery is that no one will help him with food, no one with hospitality or shelter when he's naked and begging for scraps. If Assaracus's grand mansion has perished, his mother appears disheveled in mourning, the nobles are in black, and the praetor adjourns his hearings. Then we lament Rome's mishaps and loathe its fires. While the flames are still burning, someone runs up and gives a gift of marble and collects donations: this one offers nude, gleaming statues, another some distinguished work by Euphranor or bronzes by Polyclitus, antique ornaments of Asian gods; another man will give him books and bookcases and a Minerva to set in their midst, another a pile of silver. Persicus, the richest man in the world, replaces lost items with more and better things, and now not without reason, he's suspected of setting fire himself to his very own house! If you can tear yourself away from the games in the Circus, a fabulous house at Sora or Fabrateria or Frusino[6] can be had for as much as you now pay in rent for a single year for your shady little plot.

## 10.9 Profiting from loss

Disasters such as fires and floods offered opportunities for small-scale exploitation of others' misfortune by looting and theft of property that was portable. Plutarch, however, reports on a much more concerted effort to capitalize on people's losses and profit tremendously from them. In the first half of the last century BCE, Marcus Licinius Crassus was considered the wealthiest man in Rome. Much of his wealth came from buying the property of those proscribed under the dictator Sulla in the 80s BCE, but Crassus was also very shrewd. He realized the demand for high-quality housing in Rome by the wealthy so was ready during fires with a permanent team of purchasers and rebuilders who were prepared to assist in buying up and redeveloping properties he would then sell at high profit.

Further reading: Frier 1980: 21–34; Oleson 2011; Toner 2013: 41–2.

Plutarch, *Life of Crassus* 2.4
Seeing that conflagrations and collapses were natural and familiar calamities at Rome because of the size and number of buildings, he purchased slave architects and builders. Then, when he had over five hundred of these, he bought up houses that were on fire and the ones bordering those on fire, which, because of fear and uncertainty, their owners let go for a small sum. As a result, a very large part of Rome came into his possession.

# Dealing with disasters: administration and prevention

## 10.10 Imperial responses

In the wake of disasters, the government was expected to respond quickly and ideally with generosity to assist survivors and help return an area to its former glory. Economic aid was one welcome means, as illustrated in Dio's brief notice concerning a major fire in Rome during Tiberius's reign. Yet a leader's attitude in the midst of a crisis and its aftermath in particular seems to have mattered considerably as well, especially if he showed compassion for those affected, as Suetonius maintains Titus amply did when Rome was struck by fire and plague. He is praised for his deft handling of so many serious calamities during his short reign, for in addition to those that befell the capital, the region of Campania was reeling from the eruption of Mount Vesuvius in 79 CE.

Further reading: Mitchell 1987; Toner 2013: 45–66.

Dio, *Roman History* 58.26.5
In the consulship of Sextus Papinius and Quintus Plautius [37 CE], the Tiber swamped many parts of the city such that people went about in boats, and a much larger area around the Circus and on the Aventine was destroyed by fire such that Tiberius gave 100 million sesterces to those who suffered as a result of it.

Suetonius, *Titus* 8.3–4
During his reign, certain misfortunes occurred and dreadful ones at that, such as the eruption of Mount Vesuvius in Campania and a fire in Rome that lasted three days and as many nights and, moreover, a plague of a size hardly occurring at any other time. Amid so many and great difficulties, he displayed not only the deep concern of a *princeps*, but also the singular feeling of a parent, now comforting through his edicts, now offering aid as far as his ability allowed. From men of consular rank, he appointed by lot superintendents for the restoration of Campania. The properties of those overcome by Vesuvius, who did not have surviving heirs, he directed to

the reconstruction of communities affected by the eruption. In the course of the fire at Rome, the only statement he made publicly was that he was ruined. All of the decorations from his imperial properties he assigned to temples and public buildings, and he put several men from the equestrian order in charge so that things would be completed sooner. He employed any divine or human resource for curing ill health and alleviating afflictions, and every kind of sacrifice and remedy was sought out.

## 10.11 Efforts at urban renewal

Not only was much of Rome's rich cultural heritage threatened when common disasters such as fires and floods struck (see **10.4** in this volume), but potentially much of its recorded history as well. Although some losses were irreplaceable, with significant effort certain items could be restored as Suetonius reports of the emperor Vespasian's initiative regarding government documents. This excerpt also offers a different perspective on imperial responses to disaster, for it is not so much by opening the state's coffers but rather by getting his hands dirty—literally—that Vespasian helped to bring about some urban renewal. Vespasian's son Domitian also took steps to rebuild and restore buildings damaged prior to or during his principate, including the Capitol damaged by fire in 80 CE, according to the imperial biographer.

Further reading: Toner 2013: 45–66.

Suetonius, *Vespasian* 8.5
As the city was ugly due to earlier fires and building collapses, he allowed anyone to take possession of vacant lots and to build on them if the owners had failed to do so. He himself undertook restoration of the Capitol: he was the first to lend a hand in clearing away the rubble and even carried off some of it on his own head. He oversaw the replacement of 3,000 bronze tablets which had gone up in flames [in the temple fire] and had copies sought out from all over: these were very fine and very old public records of the empire which contained decrees of the Senate and ordinances of the people, from almost the foundation of the city, concerning alliances, treaties, and special privileges granted to individuals.

Suetonius, *Domitian* 5
He restored numerous impressive buildings, which had been destroyed by fire among which was the Capitol which had burned again; but all of these he restored with an inscription in his own name only and without any record of the original builder. Moreover, he erected a new temple on the Capitoline Hill to Jupiter Custos [Jupiter the Guardian] and a forum which is now called the Forum of Nerva,[7] likewise a temple

to the Flavian family, a stadium, a music hall, and a pool for staging sea battles. Later, from the stone used in this last structure, the Circus Maximus was built up after both sides were destroyed by fire.

## 10.12 Disaster prevention

Despite the location of the Republican Temple of Vulcan outside Rome's city walls in the hopes of keeping buildings safe, as Vitruvius reports, fires in the city were commonplace as we have seen. At all points of time, leaders had to contend with fires as regular threats to the city in addition to the Tiber flooding, as well as occasional catastrophic events such as earthquakes. Though these excerpts suggest that successive imperial governments took an active interest in preventing disasters from recurring, overall there seems to have been a lack of administration and foresight (in contrast, note the official attention to maintenance of the city's aqueducts: see in particular **8.2**, **8.3**, and **8.8** in this volume). Many crises were dealt with on an *ad hoc* basis and the measures necessary to truly prevent the recurrence of avoidable disasters, such as massive fires or Tiber flooding, were not given the serious attention they needed and so lapsed after a set of measures was put in place.

Further reading: Aldrete 2007; Toner 2013: 52–3.

Vitruvius, *On Architecture* 1.7.1
For the Etruscan *haruspices*,[8] in the writings of their disciplines, it was thus specified that the temples of Venus, Vulcan, and Mars be located outside the wall so that young men and mothers of families may not become accustomed to sexual pleasure in the city, and by calling forth the power of Vulcan outside the ramparts by means of religious rites and sacrifices, that the buildings may seem to be freed from fear of fires. But since the divinity of Mars has been dedicated outside the ramparts, there will not be armed quarrels among the citizens, but he will keep the ramparts defended from the enemy and from the danger of war.

Suetonius, *Augustus* 30.1–2
He divided the area of the city into regions and wards; the former were looked after by magistrates selected each year by lot while he appointed "masters" for the latter chosen from the plebs in each neighborhood. To deal with fires, he came up with a system of night watchmen and guards; to control flooding, he widened the channel of the Tiber River and cleaned it out once it had filled up with debris and become narrow from buildings jutting forth. Moreover, so that it would be easier to approach the city from

any direction, he undertook repairing the Flaminian Way as far as Ariminum, and divided the remainder among those men who had received triumphs to see to paving them using their share of war booty. He restored sacred buildings that had fallen to ruin over a long period of time or been destroyed by fire, and adorned both these and others with the most sumptuous gifts, placing as a single offering in the shrine of the Temple of Capitoline Jupiter 16,000 pounds of gold, as well as gemstones and pearls worth 50 million sesterces.

Suetonius, *Nero* 16.1

He devised a new appearance for the buildings of the city so that in front of apartments and houses there were also porticoes from the flat roofs of which fires could be kept from approaching; and these he built at his own expense. He also had resolved to extend the city walls as far as Ostia and to bring sea water from there into the old city through a channel.

# Death and the City

The most obvious marks of death in the city of Rome are the monuments created to remember the city's elites, especially the emperors. Strolling through Rome, you can still admire the burial places of the emperors and the more affluent dwellers, such as the Mausoleum of Augustus (**11.11–12**), the Mausoleum of Hadrian (**11.13**), the Pyramid of Cestius (**11.9**), and the Tomb of Eurysaces (**11.10**), to name a few examples. Not as convenient to visit for the casual visitor to the city are the tombs of the non-elite such as the multi-chamber *columbaria* (**11.7**). For an experiential approach to Rome's "funerary cityscape," read the work of Christopher Johanson (2011), who takes the reader on two imagined walks through the city. On these walks, one encounters not only the monuments associated with death, but also the rituals involved (**11.1–5**). Monuments and rituals of death in Rome were concerned with the deceased and their eternal memory, and also with how that lasting image affected the living descendants. As you will see below, there were traditional spaces in the city for these rituals. In this chapter, you will also find sites that are part of the city's spaces dealing with capital punishment (**11.14–17**), such as the Tarpeian Cliff (**11.14**), the Colline Gate (**11.16**), the Gemonian Stairs (**11.15**), and the Carcer (**11.17**).

Further reading: Edwards 2007; Erasmo 2008; Erasmo 2012; Hope 2007; Johanson 2011; Keppie 1991: 98–109; Patterson 2000b.

## Funeral rituals

### 11.1 Eulogies at the Rostra and the funeral procession

A public funeral for a Roman aristocrat included a procession of the deceased to the Forum where a eulogy was delivered from the Rostra by a close male relative. As Seneca describes in the first passage below, the funeral procession was similar in some ways to a triumphal procession. This was an opportunity to celebrate the deceased's accomplishments and service to the state, but also to celebrate his lineage by commemorating noble ancestors and their deeds. The procession, which wended its way through the city *en route* to the Forum, was a dramatic and highly visible event that featured actors who impersonated the ancestors of the deceased by wearing masks that resembled them, and by dressing in togas appropriate to the political or military offices the ancestors had held. Although public funerals were primarily staged for male aristocrats, noble women could also receive such honors, as was the case for Julia, grandmother of Augustus, eulogized by him as a young man; for Octavia, sister of Augustus, whose eulogy was delivered by Drusus; and for the empress Livia, who was eulogized by her great-grandson Caligula.

Further reading: Bodel 1999; Erasmo 2012: 1–29; Favro and Johanson 2010; Lindsay 2000; Sumi 2002; Toynbee 1996.

Polybius, *Histories* 6.53.1–3
Whenever someone among them of distinguished rank dies, in the course of his funeral he is carried into the Forum to the so-called Rostra with every kind of honor, sometimes in a visibly upright position, rarely in a reclined position. With all the people standing around, a grown-up son, if the deceased has left one and he happens to be present, or if not then one of his relatives who is there, goes up onto the Rostra and speaks about the virtues of the dead man and his achievements during his lifetime. As a result of this, many people, not only those who shared in the deceased's accomplishments but also those who did not, are so moved to sympathy when the facts are recalled and brought before their eyes that the loss seems not to be a private matter for the mourners, but a common loss for the people.

Propertius, *Elegies* 2.13b.17–24
Therefore, whenever death will close my eyes, learn what rites you should keep for my funeral. At that time, do not let a long procession walk with my ancestor portrait, nor let the trumpet be an empty complaint of my death; then do not let a bier with an ivy headrest be spread out for me, nor let my dead body rest on an ornamented bed. Let the series of pleasant smelling dishes be lacking, let the small rites of a common funeral be present.

Pliny the Elder, *Natural History* 10.60.122
[A talking raven, which used to fly to the Rostra in the Forum and greet by name the emperor Tiberius, Germanicus, and Drusus, was killed by a nearby shop owner.] The funeral of the bird was celebrated by countless people in a funeral procession, the covered bier on the shoulders of two Ethiopians with a flute player ahead of them and

with wreaths of all sorts all the way up to the pyre, which had been built on the right side of the Via Appia at the second milestone in the field called Rediculus.

Suetonius, *Augustus* 8.1
When he was four years old, he lost his father. When he was twelve years old, in front of the assembly, he praised his grandmother Julia, who had died.[1]

Dio, *Roman History* 54.35.4–5
In that year, Augustus gave Julia in marriage to Tiberius and he placed his sister Octavia, when she died, in the shrine of Julius, with a curtain on the corpse. And he himself gave the funeral oration in that place and Drusus gave one from the Rostra. The public mourning brought about the change of the senators' clothing. Her sons-in-law carried out her body, but Augustus did not accept all the things voted for her.

Suetonius, *Caligula* 10.1
Caligula accompanied his father also on the Syrian expedition. When he returned from it, he first remained at the dwelling of his mother and then, after she was banished, at the dwelling of his great-grandmother Livia Augusta, whom he praised from the Rostra when she died, though he was still a young man at the time.

## 11.2 Famous funerals in the city

The passages below depict elaborate funerals. Suetonius describes that of Julius Caesar after his assassination in 44 BCE (on this murder, see **5.14** in this volume) and Dio recounts the funeral of the emperor Pertinax, who died in 193 CE. Pertinax served as emperor for three months in that same year.

Suetonius, *Julius Caesar* 84.1; 84.3–5
Once the funeral was declared publicly, a funeral pyre was erected in the Campus Martius near the tomb of Julia, and on the Rostra a golden structure was set up, in the likeness of the Temple of Venus Genetrix. Within it was an ivory bed covered with gold and purple and at the head a trophy along with the garment in which Caesar had been killed … The magistrates and those who performed public offices carried the bier into the Forum. Some resolved to burn the bier in the chapel of the Temple of Capitoline Jupiter, some in the Curia of Pompey. Suddenly two men girded with swords and carrying two javelins set a fire below it with burning tapers, and immediately the crowd of those standing around threw together dry twigs and the tribunals along with the benches and whatever else there was available. Then the flute players and the stage artists removed the clothing that they had taken from the supplies of the triumphs and worn for the present use. They tore them, and threw

them into the flames. The legionary veterans did the same with their armor with which they were adorned to celebrate the funeral. Most of the women followed suit with their jewels, which they were wearing, and with the amulets and outer garments of their children. In the highest public mourning, a multitude of foreign peoples, in groups, lamented in their own custom, and especially the Jews, who visited the funeral pyre for continuous nights.

Dio, *Roman History* 75.4–5

Having settled himself, Septimius Severus built for Pertinax a hero shrine. He commanded that the latter's name be said in connection with all prayers and all oaths and that a golden image of him be led into the Circus on a chariot of elephants and that three gilded thrones be carried into the rest of the theaters for him. And further, even though he died earlier, it was done as follows: in the Roman Forum a wooden pedestal was constructed close to the one made of stone and on it a shrine was placed, unwalled, surrounded with colonnades, and made from ivory and gold. On it a similar bier and all around it were the heads of wild beasts from land and sea. It was carried out adorned with purple and golden coverings. And on it was a wax likeness of Pertinax in triumphal attire. An attractive boy was keeping away the flies from it with the feathers of a peacock, as if Pertinax were really sleeping. While he was laid out, Severus and we senators and our wives went forward dressed for mourning. The women sat in the roofed colonnades and we sat in the open air. After this, first were statues of all notable ancient Romans, then a chorus of children and men passed by singing a hymn-like dirge for Pertinax. After this were the subject peoples in twenty bronze likenesses, dressed in the fashion of their countries. And the classes in the city itself followed: that of the lictors, of the secretaries, and of the heralds and many others of such sort. Then the likenesses of other men came, for whom some deed or invention or habit had made them well known. And after this there were the cavalry and the armed infantry, and the racehorses, and the offerings to the dead, which the emperor and we and our wives and the cavalry held in high regard and the districts and the guilds in the city sent. A raised platform followed them, set in gold and furnished with ivory and stones from India. When these things passed by, Severus mounted the Rostra and read a eulogy of Pertinax. We cried out many things in the middle of his words, some commending then wailing for Pertinax, most of all when he finished speaking. At the end, when the bier was about to be moved, the chief priests and the magistrates, the ones in place and the ones appointed for next year, brought down the bier from the platform and gave it to some cavalry to carry. The rest of us went before the bier, some beating their breasts and others playing the flute in mourning. The emperor followed after everyone and in this way we reached the Campus Martius. A funeral pyre had been made ready, three-tiered like a tower adorned with ivory and gold with some statues and on its highest point a gold-plaited chariot, the very one which Pertinax drove. Then into this the funeral gifts were thrown and the bier was placed and after this

Severus and the relatives of Pertinax kissed the statue and Severus mounted the platform. We the Senate, except the magistrates, were on benches so that we could see what was happening safely at the same time as carefully. The magistrates and the knights were arranged suitably by order, and the cavalry and infantry passed around the pyre, unfolding in pathways, civil and warlike. Then the consuls set fire to it and when this was done, an eagle flew from it. Pertinax was thus made immortal.

## 11.3 *Imagines*: ancestral images

*Imagines* were wax masks of a family's ancestors. These masks, normally kept at home in the *atrium* (reception room), were brought out for the funeral procession of a deceased family member. Actors wore the masks and walked as part of the procession. The *imagines* provided a visual connection between the newly deceased, the family's ancestors, and the family still alive and present at the procession.

Further reading: Flower 1996; Kaplow 2008.

Pliny the Elder, *Natural History* 35.2.6
These things were otherwise in the atria of our ancestors. *Imagines* were for looking at, not the statues of foreign artists, nor bronze or marble statues. The likenesses formed in wax were arranged in individual closets, so that the *imagines* would be the ones in attendance at the funeral of a family. And always, when someone died, every person in the family who had ever existed was present.

## 11.4 Disposing of the dead at Rome

Both cremation and burial were practiced in ancient Rome. Numerous passages by ancient writers discuss the funeral pyre burning the body of the deceased. Cicero tries to explain the reason for not burying or burning the dead within the city. Exceptions to keeping the dead inside the city could be made for emperors or important people. The inscription in this section is from a boundary stone found on the Esquiline Hill warning people not to dump bodies (or trash) inside the city (Salomies 2014: 161–2). Pliny the Elder links the establishment of the practice of cremation to the fear of having one's body dug up after burial. Martial describes the wretched way the bodies of the poor were carried out of the city. Valerie Hope (2007) provides an excellent step-by-step look at death, from dying to the funeral to the afterlife.

Further reading: Aldrete 2009: 83–92; Bodel 2011; Erasmo 2012: 30–60; Hope 2007.

---

Cicero, *On the Laws* 2.58

Marcus: The law in the Twelve Tables says that a dead man is not to be buried nor burned in the city.[2] I believe it is because of the danger of fire. However, the fact that it adds "nor burned" points out that the one who is cremated, is not buried, but covered with earth.

Atticus: What about those famous men who were buried in the city after the Twelve Tables?

Marcus: I believe, Titus, that there had been those to whom, before there was this law, it [the right to be buried in the city] had been given on account of excellence, such as Poplicola and Tubertus, and their descendants kept the right by law, or there were those who came after, like Gaius Fabricius, who were exempted from the laws on account of excellence. But as the law forbids being buried in the city, so it has been decreed by the college of priests that it is not right for a burial place to be made in a public place. You know that beyond the Colline Gate, there is the Temple of Honor. It has been recorded that there had been an altar in this place. When a thin piece of metal was found near it and on the metal was written "Of honor," this was the reason why this temple was dedicated. But since there had been many graves in this place, they were dug up. The college of priests determined that a public place could not be bound by private religion.

---

*Corpus of Latin Inscriptions* 1² 839

[Found on the Esquiline Hill]

By the determination of the Senate, Lucius Sentius, son of Gaius, presided over the marking off of the boundaries of this place. A good deed. Let no one intend to make a place for burning bodies or intend to throw excrement or a corpse within the boundaries closer to the city.

---

Pliny the Elder, *Natural History* 7.54.187

Cremation itself was not an old practice among the Romans. People were buried under the earth. But after they learned that those buried in faraway wars were dug up, then cremation was instituted. And many families kept the old rituals, in the Cornelii family, no one before the dictator Sulla is said to have been cremated. It is also said that Sulla had wished cremation because he was afraid of retaliation for having dug up the dead body of Gaius Marius.

---

Martial, *Epigrams* 8.75.9–10

Four branded men were carrying the corpse of a poor person, just like the thousand bodies the miserable funeral pyre receives.

---

Dio, *Roman History* 48.43.3
It was forbidden for a senator to fight as a gladiator and for a slave to carry the rods of a lictor, and the burning of dead bodies within fifteen stades of the city.

Ulpian, *Digest* 47.12.3.5
The deified Hadrian determined a penalty of forty gold pieces on those who bury in a city, which he ordered to be paid to the public treasury.

SHA, *Life of Antoninus Pius* 12.3
He forbade the dead from being buried within cities.

## 11.5 Questioning a person's immortal fame in tombs

A tomb is often read as a marker of the everlasting fame of the deceased. Some ancient writers, such as Juvenal and Seneca, question the ability of stone to preserve a person's memory.

Further reading: Hope 2007: 71–84.

Juvenal, *Satires* 10.140–6
So much greater is the thirst for fame than for courage. Who indeed embraces courage itself if you remove the rewards? However, in the past, the thirst for glory of a few men has overwhelmed the country, and likewise has the desire for praise and for an inscription that will cling to the stone guardians of their ashes, which the evil strength of the barren fig tree has the power to break into pieces since deaths have been given also to the tombs themselves.

Seneca, *Consolation to Polybius* 18.1–2
Now then, immerse yourself more deeply in your studies, surround yourself with them as if they were fortifications of your mind, so that pain may not find an entrance from any part of you. Also bring forth the memory of your brother with some monument of your writings. This is the only work in human affairs that no storm may harm, that no old age may consume. The rest, which stands through the construction of stones and marble masses, or mounds of earth built up to a great height, they do not endure a long day. Of course they themselves perish. The memory of genius is immortal.

# Death in Rome's landscape

## 11.6 Esquiline burial spot

A number of sources mention a burial spot on the Esquiline Hill. According to Varro, there were pits in this region (*puticuli*), in which the remains of the poorer members of Rome's society would have been placed. Archaeologist Rodolfo Lanciani in the late 1800s uncovered in this region pits with remains of people and animals (Bodel 2011: 131–3; Hope 2007: 132).

Further reading: Aldrete 2009: 83; Bodel 2011: 131–4; Hope 2007: 132–3; Hope 2011.

---

Varro, *On the Latin Language* 5.25

Outside the towns are little pits [*puticuli*], from the word *puteis* [pits], because men were buried there in pits, unless as Aelius writes, the little pits were called thus because the dead bodies thrown out were rotting [*putrescebant*] there. This public place is beyond the Esquiline.

---

## 11.7 *Columbarium* of Pomponius Hylas

A *columbarium* is a tomb with numerous niches to hold the urns of the deceased. The deceased in these types of tombs were slaves or freedmen usually from large, affluent households including the imperial household. There are remains of well-preserved *columbaria* within the walls of Rome. One such *columbarium* is that of Pomponius Hylas, located on the Via Latina. The name derives from an inscription within the tomb, but the other inscriptions contained within the *columbarium* are not related. Inscriptions numbered 6.5539–57 from the *Corpus of Latin Inscriptions* are from this *columbarium* and range from the period of the emperor Tiberius to that of the emperor Antoninus Pius. Not far from this *columbarium* are located the three *columbaria* at Vigna Codini (the former Codini vineyard).

Further reading: Borbonus 2014; Joshel and Petersen 2014; Newton and Ashby 1910; Penner 2012; Toynbee 1996: 113–18.

---

*Corpus of Latin Inscriptions* 6.5552

[The tomb of] Gnaeus Pomponius Hylas and Pomponia Vitalinis, freedwoman of Gnaeus.[3]

---

---

*Corpus of Latin Inscriptions* 6.5546
Quintus Granius Nestor made this [tomb] for himself and his well-deserving wife Vinileia Hedone.

---

*Corpus of Latin Inscriptions* 6.5539
For Paezusa, hairdresser of Octavia, daughter of Caesar Augustus, she lived for eighteen years.

---

## 11.8 Tomb of the Scipios

One can see tombs of Rome's elite families on the Via Appia. An example of such a tomb is the Tomb of the Scipios, that of the family the Cornelii Scipiones. As Cicero notes, it is outside of the Porta Capena. It is located inside the later-constructed Aurelian Wall. The tomb contained multiple generations of the family, including the consul Lucius Cornelius Scipio Barbatus.

Further reading: Claridge 2010: 365–8; Coarelli 2014: 367–73; Patterson 2000b; Richardson 1992: 359–60.

---

Cicero, *Tusculan Disputations* 1.13
Having come out of the Porta Capena, when you see the tombs of Calatinus, the Scipios, the Servilii, the Metelli, do you think that they are wretched?

---

*Corpus of Latin Inscriptions* 6.1284
Lucius Cornelius, son of Gnaeus.

---

*Corpus of Latin Inscriptions* 6.1285
Lucius Cornelius Scipio Barbatus, born from his father Gnaeus, a brave and wise man, whose appearance was equal to his excellence, consul, censor, aedile among you, who captured Taurasia and Cisauna in Samnium. He subjugated all of Lucania and led away hostages.

---

Livy, *History of Rome* 38.56.4
At Rome, outside the Porta Capena there are three statues on the memorial of the Scipios, of which two are said to be Publius and Lucius Scipio, the third the poet Quintus Ennius.

---

## 11.9 A tomb with an Egyptian design: The Pyramid of Cestius

The tomb of Cestius is a large marker in the landscape of Rome (see Fig. 11.1). It stands out from the space around it thanks to its distinctive shape: a pyramid.

A number of scholars have posited that the shape is a reflection of a passion for things in an Egyptian style. As the inscription below notes, it was the tomb of Gaius Cestius, a praetor in the time of Augustus. The monumental remains of this pyramid continue to stand today very near to the Metro station Piramide, to which it lends its name, and the Via Ostiense. In ancient Rome it would not have been the lone pyramid in the city. Another one, called the Meta Romuli, located between the Vatican and the Mausoleum of Hadrian, was supposedly larger than the Pyramid of Cestius.

Further reading: Claridge 2010: 397–401; Coarelli 2014: 346–7; Dyson 2010: 140; Richardson 1992: 252–3; Ridley 1992.

**Figure 11.1** Pyramid of Cestius. Photo credit: Alinari/Art Resource, NY.

*Corpus of Latin Inscriptions* 6.1374a
[The inscription below can be found on two sides of the monument]
Gaius Cestius Epulo, son of Lucius, from the Poblilia tribe, praetor, tribune of the people, *septemvir*[4] of the sacred banquets.

*Corpus of Latin Inscriptions* 6.1374b
In accordance with his will, the work was completed in 330 days at the direction of his heirs: Lucius Pontus Mela, son of Publius in the Claudian tribe and the freedman Pothus.

## 11.10 Tomb of the Baker, Eurysaces

The tomb of a freedman, Marcus Vergilius Eurysaces, and his wife Atistia, stands near the Porta Maggiore, at the intersection of the Via Praenestina and Via Labicana. The tomb includes scenes of his work as a commercial baker, pictured in stages, including the kneading of dough and the baking of bread. There is also a portrait of a man and a woman associated with the tomb thought to be Eurysaces and his wife. The remains are easily visible from the road.

Further reading: Coarelli 2014: 204–5; Patterson 2000b: 268; Petersen 2003; Petersen 2006: 84–122; Richardson 1992: 355.

*Corpus of Latin Inscriptions* 6.1958
[On the two sides]
This is the monument of Marcus Vergilius Eurysaces, baker, contractor.[5]

*Corpus of Latin Inscriptions* 1.1206
Atistia was my wife. She lived as a wonderful woman, the remains of whose body which still exist are in this breadbasket.

# Death and the Emperors

## 11.11 Mausoleum of Augustus

The Mausoleum of Augustus was created many years before Augustus died in 14 CE, with construction started (28 BCE) after his victory at Actium against Marc Antony and Cleopatra (31 BCE). A number of members of his family were buried there before and after him, including his nephew Marcellus, his sister Octavia, his son-in-law Agrippa, and his wife Livia. On the outside of the Mausoleum were two bronze tablets inscribed with his *Res Gestae*, meaning the things he achieved. Today the words of the *Res Gestae* in Latin can be seen inscribed on the outside of the Ara Pacis Museum in Rome. The original Mausoleum had a large bronze statue of Augustus on top. Restoration of the Mausoleum, closed to the public for many years, has been announced. The area around the Mausoleum, the Piazza Augusto Imperatore, was constructed during the rule of Benito Mussolini.

Further reading: Coarelli 2014: 302–4; Cooley 2009; Davies 2004: 13–19; Painter 2005; Richardson 1992: 247–9; Zanker 1988: 72–7.

Strabo, *Geography* 5.3.8
The most worthy of mention is called the Mausoleum, a large mound on a high foundation of white marble near the river, thickly covered to the top with evergreen trees. On the top there is a bronze statue of Caesar Augustus and under the mound are the urns of him, his family, and those close to him. Behind, a large grove has wonderful places for walking. In the middle of the plain is an enclosure of white stone around his pyre. It is surrounded in a circle by a fence made of iron and within it is full of black poplar trees.

Suetonius, *Augustus* 100.4
The chief men of the equestrian order, with loosened tunics and bare feet, gathered his remains and placed them in the Mausoleum. He had it constructed in his sixth consulship between the Via Flaminia and the bank of the Tiber and at that time he had the surrounding woods and walks made open for public use.

Suetonius, *Augustus* 101.1; 101.3–4
In the consulship of Lucius Plancus and Gaius Silius, on the third day before the Nones of April, one year and four months before he died, a will was made by him [Augustus]. It was written partly by his own hand and partly by that of his freedmen Polybius and Hilarion in two ledgers and deposited with the Vestal Virgins. They produced them with three rolls sealed in like manner, which were all opened and read in the Senate ... He forbade his daughter Julia and his granddaughter Julia to be placed in his Mausoleum, if anything should happen to them. As for the three rolls, in one he included orders for his funeral, in another a list of his achievements, which he wished to be inscribed on bronze tablets which would be placed in front of the Mausoleum, in the third, a summary of the whole empire.

Augustus, *Achievements* 1
Below is a copy of the achievements of the deified Augustus, by which he placed the world under the rule of the Roman people, and of the expenses he incurred for the Roman people and state, as inscribed on two bronze pillars, which have been placed at Rome.

## 11.12 *Ustrinum* (crematorium) of the house of Augustus

Strabo (*Geography* 5.3.8, see above **11.11**) describes the location of the crematorium of the emperor Augustus. Excavations from 1777 yielded stones with the inscriptions below, but the precise location of the *ustrinum* remains uncertain.

Further reading: Noreña 2013; Rehak 2006: 33–4; Richardson 1992: 404.

---

*Corpus of Latin Inscriptions* 6.888
Tiberius Caesar, son of Germanicus Caesar, was cremated here.

---

*Corpus of Latin Inscriptions* 6.889
Gaius Caesar, son of Germanicus Caesar, was cremated here.

---

*Corpus of Latin Inscriptions* 6.891
Livilla, daughter of Germanicus Caesar, was cremated here.

---

## 11.13 Mausoleum of Hadrian

The Mausoleum of the emperor Hadrian, now the Castel Sant'Angelo, sits on the right bank of the Tiber, connected to the Campus Martius by the Pons (bridge) Aelius. Among the surviving inscriptions are those of a number of people buried in this place. The mausoleum was not completed during the life of Hadrian, but was finished at the order of his successor Antoninus Pius, who had Hadrian's body moved there. In addition to Hadrian and his wife Sabina, the bodies of a number of later emperors were placed there. The site of the mausoleum served varied purposes in later years, including that of a fortress and a papal castle.

Further reading: Boatwright 1989: 161–81; Claridge 2010: 410–15; Coarelli 2014: 360–2; Davies 2004: 34–40; Erasmo 2015: 53–6; Richardson 1992: 249–51.

---

Dio, *Roman History*, 69.23.1
Hadrian lived for sixty-two years, five months, and nineteen days, and he ruled for twenty years and eleven months. He was buried near the river itself, near the Aelian Bridge. There he built his tomb, since the one of Augustus was full and no longer was anyone placed in it.

---

*Corpus of Latin Inscriptions* 6.984
*Imperator* Caesar Titus Aelius Hadrianus Antoninus Augustus Pius, *pontifex maximus* [chief priest], with tribunician power twice, consul three times, consul designate three

times, father of the country, [made this] for his parents, the *imperator* Caesar Trajan Hadrian Augustus, son of the deified Trajan Parthicus, grandson of the deified Nerva, and for the deified Sabina.

---

*Corpus of Latin Inscriptions* 6.973
[Inscription from the Pons Aelius]
*Imperator* Caesar Trajan Hadrian Augustus, son of Trajan Parthicus, grandson of the divine Nerva, *pontifex maximus*, with tribunician power for the eighteenth time, in his third consulship, father of the country, made this.

---

# Capital punishment

## 11.14 The Tarpeian Cliff

The Tarpeian Cliff was a spot on the Capitoline Hill from which criminals were thrown as punishment for their crimes.

Further reading: Richardson 1992: 377–8.

---

Livy, *History of Rome* 6.20.12
The tribunes threw Manlius from the Tarpeian Rock and the same place was in one man a memorial of exceptional glory and an extreme punishment.

---

Dionysius of Halicarnassus, *Roman Antiquities* 7.35.4
And having said these things, Sicinius ordered that Marcius be led to the crest of the hill above the Forum. The spot is an extraordinary overhanging cliff from where it was custom to throw those condemned to death.

---

Tacitus, *Annals* 6.19
Sextus Marius, the richest man in Spain, was indicted for incest with his daughter and thrown from the Tarpeian Rock.

---

## 11.15 Gemonian Steps

The Gemonian Steps were a flight of steps up to the Capitoline Hill where bodies of executed criminals were left. Valerius Maximus and Dio provide information about their location.

Further reading: Richardson 1992: 345.

---

Valerius Maximus, *Memorable Deeds and Sayings* 6.9.13

Quintus Caepio surpassed Crassus in the harshness of his death. By the magnificence of his praetorship, the brilliance of his triumph, the splendor of his consulship, the priesthood of *pontifex maximus*, he won the right to be called defender of the Senate. But in public chains he gave up his breath and his body, mangled by the deadly hands of an executioner, he was seen lying on the Gemonian Steps to the great horror of the whole Forum.

---

Dio, *Roman History* 58.5.6

After Sejanus sacrificed on the Capitol, he was going down to the Forum, while the slaves who were attending him as bodyguards turned aside along the road leading to the prison, not having been able to follow him as a result of the crowd. Going down the flight of stairs from which condemned people were thrown, they slipped and fell.

## 11.16 Death of a Vestal

Vestal Virgins were priestesses tasked with the tending of the fire in Vesta's hearth, among other duties (cf. **6.3** in this volume). When the sacred flame of Vesta went out, it was seen as a bad sign for the city and the blame was placed squarely on the Vestal Virgins. The punishment was a very high one: the life of the woman deemed responsible. The authors below mention the area of the Colline Gate (Porta Collina) as the location where the Vestal was brought to die. The Campus Sceleratus, noted by Livy as the place of the burial of the condemned Vestal, is near the gate.

Further reading: Lindner 2015; Richardson 1992: 68, 302; Staples 1998: 129–56; Takács 2008: 87–90; Wildfang 2006: 55–9.

---

Dionysius of Halicarnassus, *Roman Antiquities* 2.67.3–5

[Prior to this passage, Dionysius describes the selection of the Vestal Virgins and their lives and duties] Strong punishments are set for their wrongs, of which the priests are the examiners and punishers according to law. The ones who have committed lesser wrongs they flog with rods, but the ones seduced they give over to a most shameful and pitiable death. Still alive, carried on a bier, they escort the procession displayed as for the dead, with their weeping friends and relatives accompanying them. Having been carried as far as the Colline Gate within the walls, they are placed with their funeral dress into a burial chamber furnished under the earth, but they obtain no grave monument nor offerings to the dead, no other customary funeral rites. Many other things seem to be indications of a Vestal not performing her rites in a holy way, especially the extinction of the fire, which the Romans feared above all terrible things, taking it as a sign of the destruction of the city.

---

Livy, *History of Rome* 8.15.7–8

In that year, the Vestal Minucia was suspected because her appearance was more elegant than is right. She was then charged by the priests based on a slave acting as a witness. She had been ordered by their decree to abstain from the sacred acts and to keep her household in her control. Once a judgment was made she was buried under the earth near the Colline Gate, beyond the paved road, in the Campus Sceleratus, that name created from her unchaste action.

---

Plutarch, *Life of Numa* 10.4–7

[Prior to this passage, Plutarch describes the lives, duties, and privileges of Vestal Virgins. Here he describes what happens to them as punishment for offenses] The woman having dishonored her virginity is buried alive in the earth near the Colline Gate, on which there is a hilltop within the city, stretching along at a distance. It is called a mound in the Latin language. Here a subterranean chamber, not a large one, is constructed, having a path of descent from above. In it are placed a covered couch, a lit lamp, some small things needed to live, such as bread, water in a jar, milk, and olive oil, as if they [the priests] were cleansing themselves of the guilt of destroying, by hunger, a body that had been consecrated for the greatest rituals. After they placed the condemned woman into a litter and covered it from the outside and held it down with straps so that not a sound is audible, they carry it off to the Forum. All the people stand aside in silence and, speechless, they escort it with a terrible sadness. There is no sight more awful nor does the city pass a day more hated than this. Whenever the litter has been taken to the place, the attendants release the bonds. The leader of the priests, after having said some secret prayers and having lifted his hands to the gods before the punishment, leads out the veiled woman and places her on the stairs going down to the chamber. Then he turns away from her, along with the other priests, as she goes down the stairs. The stairs are removed and the chamber is hidden, with much earth piled on it from above, so that the place is ground level with the rest of the mound. In this way are they punished, the ones who have let go of their sacred virginity.

## 11.17 Executing conspirators before nightfall at the Carcer

The Carcer was used for more than triumphal processions (see **9.10** in this volume): it was also the site of executions. In November of 63 BCE, the plans of Catiline and his fellow conspirators to set fires in Rome and assassinate their political enemies were betrayed to the government by a group of Gallic ambassadors, whom Lentulus and other ringleaders had tried to recruit in support of their cause. After this discovery, a heated debate in the Senate followed over the fates of these five leading conspirators. Roman citizens convicted of capital crimes were usually allowed to go into voluntary exile rather than face execution. Several spoke passionately, including Julius Caesar who argued strongly against the death penalty, but Cato the Younger was able to sway the Senate to approve this punishment. The executions took place on the evening of December 5 inside the Mamertine prison located at the base of the Capitoline Hill next to the Comitium and east of the Temple of Concord.

Further reading: Odahl 2010: 45–69; Pagán 2004: 27–49.

---

Sallust, *Conspiracy of Catiline* 55.1–6

After the Senate adopted Cato's proposal, the consul, thinking it best to take action before the approaching nightfall and in order to head off any new attempt, ordered the Board of Three to prepare the items that the execution demanded. Once the guards were stationed, he himself led Lentulus down to the prison; the same was done by the praetors for the rest of the conspirators. In the prison there is a chamber, which is called the Tullianum, where you go up gradually towards the left-hand side (the chamber is sunk deep in the ground about twelve feet). Walls are built up on all sides and it is roofed over with arches of stone. But because of neglect, darkness, and stench, its appearance is hideous and frightful. After Lentulus was sent down into that place, the executioners, to whom instructions had been given, strangled his neck with a noose. Thus, that patrician from the most illustrious Cornelian clan, who had held consular authority at Rome, met an end worthy of his character and deeds. For Cethegus, Statilius, Gabinius, and Caeparius, punishment was exacted in the same manner.

# Notes

## Introduction

1 For excellent discussions of this "spatial turn," in which monuments and urban space are active participants, see Laurence 2016: 175–6; Mignone 2016: 155–7; Östenberg, Malmberg, and Bjørnebye 2016: 2.

2 E.g., Dyson 2010: 1; Favro 1999: 205; Graham 2013: 278.

3 E.g., Gowers 1995: 23; Larmour and Spencer 2007: ix.

4 An excellent starting place to explore epigraphy in the city of Rome is Bruun 2014. In this chapter, he provides a breakdown of the contents of volume VI of the *Corpus Inscriptionum Latinarum* (normally abbreviated by scholars as *CIL* and referred to throughout this book as *Corpus of Latin Inscriptions*), a collection of Latin inscriptions. Volume VI is devoted solely to the city of Rome. In particular, for this number of inscriptions see Bruun 2014: 472.

5 http://www.perseus.tufts.edu/hopper/text?doc=Perseus:text:1999.04.0054 or http://penelope.uchicago.edu/Thayer/E/Gazetteer/Places/Europe/Italy/Lazio/Roma/Rome/_Texts/PLATOP*/home.html (organized by general topics, such as types of buildings).

6 Unfortunately, due to its recent publication date, we have not been able to include details from the work in this volume.

7 A good starting point for secondary sources on the city of Rome is the *Oxford Bibliography on the Topography of Rome* by Eve D'Ambra 2009.

8 Other books on the living city, such as Aldrete 2009, extend to Ostia and Pompeii.

9 A favorite edited collection of such works: Cahill 2005.

10 E.g. Johanson 2011 on the funerary cityscape and Favro 1998.

11 http://aarome.org/research/resources/maps-gis; http://dlib.etc.ucla.edu/projects/Forum; http://romereborn.frischerconsulting.com/about-current.php; http://digitalaugustanrome.org. Digital Augustan Rome is the digital successor of *Mapping Augustan Rome*, Haselberger 2002.

12 http://awmc.unc.edu/wordpress/.

13 https://sarahemilybond.com/2016/11/24/roma-aeterna-open-access-resources-for-mapping-the-city-of-rome/.

# Chapter 1

1   On this passage and its connection to memory, see Gowers 1995: 23; Jenkyns 2014: 15–16; O'Sullivan 2011: 104–5.

2   Anthony Boyle (2003: 15) notes that Ovid refers to Rome in *Tristia* 1.1 through the use of the word *urbs*, the Latin word for city, since for him Rome is the only city.

3   The *Lares* here refer to gods that protected the neighborhood.

4   See Carey (2003: 45–6) on how the use of measurements here is a display of Roman power.

5   Translation of the words in quotes is from Eichholz 1962: 79.

6   The Rostra is the speaker's platform located in the Roman Forum.

7   The Curia is the Senate house.

8   Sacra Via.

9   See Williams (2010: 324 n. 158) on *exoletus* as a technical term for a male prostitute.

10  The Velabrum was a neighborhood lively with markets and traffic, located between the Palatine and Capitoline.

11  See Gowers (2012: 245) on the word *divinus* as a fortune teller.

12  See Zetzel (1995: 167) on the translation of *accipere* as import and *reddere* as export in this context.

13  Ascanius is the son of Aeneas.

14  Father of Rhea Silvia, who was the mother of Romulus and Remus.

# Chapter 2

1   See Richardson (2006: 463) for the translation of *fugarit* as "panicked."

2   Text as in Goold 1990. There is a variant of line 59: *lumina* instead of *crimina*. Instead of proclaimed accusations, the line would read "raised torches."

3   Prochyta is an island, not far from Baiae in southern Italy. The Subura is a neighborhood in the city of Rome.

4   In the heat, when others may have left the city. On this see Courtney 2013: 130.

5   On *imperfectus* as undigested, see Courtney 2013: 157.

6   Drusus refers to the "drowsy emperor Claudius"; Courtney 2013: 158–9. See Braund (2004: 186 n. 43) on seals as animals who experience a deeper sleep than others.

7   On the distances in this poem, see Williams 2004: 38–9.

8   See Williams (2004: 38–9) on this phrasing.

9   According to Linderski (2001: 308), there are no other literary sources on such window gardens.

10  On this idea, see Lott 2013: 177.

11  On *cedere foro* as bankruptcy, see Courtney 2013: 438.

12  According to Oliver (1953: 909), Aelius Aristides is here talking about the multi-level *insulae* or apartment houses of the city of Rome.

13  The western end of the Esquiline.

14  On this building as "mixed-use" space, see Frier 1980: 29 n. 22.

15  The meaning of the seven hairs is unclear here. See Watson (2003: 296) on the possibility of this phrase referring to the wife's lack of hair or to locks of hair, rather than individual hairs.

16  A place for beggars. On this item, see Shackleton Bailey 1993: 117 n. 48.

17  Ancient writers describe the Subura as an active area of Rome with many artisans and full of life.

18  The Stagnum Neronis (the lake of Nero).

# Chapter 3

1  The imperial box at venues where spectacles were held such as the Circus Maximus.

2  This monument pictures a pair of human feet, one bare and the other wearing a boot.

3  Lucius Munatius Plancus, consul in 42 BCE.

4  Pamphilanus was a slave of the emperor Claudius. These warehouses, not far from the Galban warehouses, had been privately built and owned by the family of Lollius in the late Republic but came under imperial control at least by the reign of Claudius.

5  An early second-century BCE comedic playwright.

6  A Roman playwright of the 160s BCE.

7  The first three were towns on the coast of Campania, north of the bay of Naples; Laurentum was a town on the coast of Latium just south of Ostia. The elephants Speclator was in charge of would have been for use in the games as well as in parades and triumphal processions (on which see **9.4** and **9.9** in this volume).

8  The inscription is on a statue base, which once bore a statue of the Apolaustus.

9  The "rivals of the gods" refers to the deified emperors.

10  The Amphitheater is better known as the Colosseum; the Stadium refers to the one built by Domitian in the Campus Martius. See Chapter Five for these venues and the experiences of spectators there.

11  Phoebe: the moon. Three days in each month were specifically named: the Kalends—always the first of the month; the Nones—the fifth day, but the seventh in March, May, July, and October; and the Ides—the thirteenth day, but the fifteenth in March, May, July, and October.

12  A five-day festival for the goddess Minerva.
13  The Forum of Pallas was the Forum of Nerva or Transitorium.
14  I.e., they were genuine Corinthian bronze.
15  I.e., is nearly at the end of the work.
16  I.e., as a scarecrow.
17  For the purpose of introducing him to public life.
18  The Carinae or "Keels," so-called from its shape, was a fashionable residential district on the upper Sacra Via whose proximity to the Forum made it an ideal location for prominent public figures, particularly in the late Republic.

# Chapter 4

1  Rome's earliest written law code dating to the middle of the fifth century BCE.
2  The shoulder of the Capitoline Hill where embassies from foreign states were stationed while waiting to be called to speak before the Senate.
3  A period of five years.
4  The muse of comic poetry.
5  The laurel trees in the Campus of Marcus Vipsanius Agrippa.
6  I.e., if he inconveniences himself to come to Gallus's *salutatio*.
7  I.e., for dinner.
8  On the Quirinal Hill.
9  The Temple of Flora.
10  The *Capitolium Vetus*, a temple to Jupiter, Juno, and Minerva on the Quirinal Hill.
11  I.e., so that Martial can visit him at home.
12  A religious festival celebrated on August 23.
13  Eclipses were attributed to witches; the clashing of bronze vessels was intended to drive away evil spirits.
14  The Fates.
15  These were sacred banquets for female divinities at which their cult images were seated on chairs (*sellae*).
16  Greek goddesses of childbirth.
17  Special Greek sacrificial cakes.

# Chapter 5

1  On the translation of *cohaerenter* as "closely," as well as on the textual problems with *inominalibus* (inauspicious), see Boeft et al. 2011: 221.

2 See Bell (2014: 493) on the modern misperception of the Colosseum as attracting the largest audiences and having the "most partisan fans."
3 Tufa is a kind of stone.
4 Prize for victory.
5 Puteoli was a town on the bay of Naples.
6 The Marble Plan was a map covering a wall at the Temple of Peace that showed the architectural elements of the city. On the map and its surviving fragments, see Stanford's Digital Forma Urbis Romae Project: http://formaurbis.stanford.edu.
7 On the *regia* here as "main door," see Wardle 2014: 259.
8 The chair of a magistrate.
9 Another variant of line 15 has *et leviter nymphis*, instead of *et sonitus lymphis* as above.
10 At the Porticus of Pompey.
11 A *naumachia* is a place for mock sea battles.
12 See Coleman (2006: 22–7) on the *pegmata* as scaffolding and the *via* as the Sacra Via.
13 Baths of Titus.

# Chapter 6

1 July 10, 247 CE.
2 I.e., the Quinquatria festival for Minerva (known as Athena among the Greeks) held from March 19 to 23.
3 A building with four columns here used as a dining room.
4 White togas with a purple band along their bottom edges.
5 Priests in charge of the ceremonies whose Latin name was *quindecemviri sacris faciundis*.
6 This inscription was found on a marble altar base dating to around 7 BCE, recovered on the Tiber Island.
7 This inscription was found on the Quirinal Hill and dates to the period 101–5 CE.
8 June 2, 184 CE.

# Chapter 7

1 The *corona civica* (civic crown) was a wreath made of oak leaves traditionally given for bravery in saving the life of a citizen. Dio (*Roman History* 53.16.4) records that Augustus was awarded it for "saving the citizens."
2 The decemvirs (*decemviri*) were the presidents of the centumvirs (*centumviri*) who comprised the Centumviral Court.

3  An exedra is a semicircular apse, a projecting part of a building that is vaulted.

4  The Dog-Star, i.e., mid-summer.

5  Jupiter's temple on the Capitoline Hill.

# Chapter 8

1  On the *familia* mentioned here as Agrippa's own private crew of slaves, see Rodgers 2009: 265.

2  On the translation of *subiungam* as "list," see Rodgers 2009: 281.

3  Aqua Marcia.

4  Rodgers (2009: 300) refers to these as "routine repairs."

5  On the translation of *opera* as "tasks" here, see Rodgers 2009: 300.

6  On the translation of *fides* as "reliability" and *subtilitas* as "expertise," see Rodgers 2009: 307.

7  See Rodgers 2009: 308 on how this is a reference to all kinds of illegal activities.

8  On "unhealthy climate" as a translation for *gravioris caeli*, see Rodgers 2009: 250.

9  On "inferior" as further downstream, see Rodgers 2009: 255.

10 See Rodgers 2009: 176 on the meaning of the phrase "distinguished to touch." Rodgers notes that the water of the Virgo was good for bathing because of its "softness."

11 See Gaisser and McClain (2000: 151) on the new magnificence as the building projects of Augustus, during whose rule Livy was writing.

12 In chapter 110, Frontinus notes that "fallen" water refers to leaks from water tanks or overflow from pipes.

13 See Koloski-Ostrow (2015b: 36–7) on how these stories illustrate the size of the sewer openings.

14 The Latin word here used for the paving of the stone is *silex*. As Laurence (1999: 67) notes, this word can refer to any durable stone. Translators frequently refer to it as flint.

15 The Clivus Capitolinus was the road to the Capitoline Hill. See Richardson 1992: 89.

16 See Laurence 1999: 65.

17 The stade was an ancient Greek measurement of length.

18 Brundisium, the modern Brindisi, is a city in southern Italy.

19 Region on the right bank of the Tiber.

20 River god.

21 The Vestal Virgins.

22  While fortification of the city is most often cited as the reason for its construction, other possible reasons have been posited, such as pleasing the populace with a show of defense. On this idea and others, see Dey 2011: 112–16.

23  It should be noted that inscriptional evidence of such taxation is rare. On this, see Holleran 2012: 90.

24  On different sorts of customs taxes, see Holleran 2012: 90–1.

# Chapter 9

1  Men who accompany a Roman official and carry the *fasces*, the bundles of rods signifying power.

2  Unit for measuring currency.

3  The Latin word in the text is *opima*, a reference to the *spolia opima*, the armor or arms taken from an enemy killed. See Östenberg (2009: 19) on the three times the *opima* were "captured and dedicated."

4  Mary Beard (2007: 92) notes that "connecting the allusions to the route in ancient literature to the topography of the city on the ground has proved extremely difficult."

5  The emperor Domitian.

6  See Holloway (2008: 19–20) on how this ambiguous phrase refers to Constantine's Christian inspiration, but does not "compromise the pagan character of the monument."

# Chapter 10

1  A suburb north of the city.

2  A large building in the Campus Martius where votes were sorted and counted.

3  I.e., Domus Transitoria.

4  I.e., the Pantheon, Diribitorium, and Saepta Iulia.

5  The Pons Sublicius, on which see **8.20** in this volume.

6  These were towns in Latium.

7  It was also known as the Forum Transitorium.

8  Religious experts whose main responsibilities included interpreting the entrails of sacrificial victims for signs from the gods.

# Chapter 11

1  He delivered her funeral oration.
2  The Twelve Tables are early laws of the Romans.
3  Above Pomponia's name, there is a "v." Borbonus (2014: 89) notes that this suggests that she was alive when this inscription was made. On this inscription, see also Borbonus 2014: 239 n. 42.
4  One of seven officials involved in the preparation of sacred feasts.
5  There is another word in the inscription, *apparet*, but there are disagreements as to what it means.

# Bibliography

Aciman, A. (2002), "Roman Hours," in F. Mayes (ed.), *The Best American Travel Writing*, 1–10, New York: Houghton Mifflin.

Aicher, P. J. (1995), *Guide to the Aqueducts of Ancient Rome*, Wauconda: Bolchazy-Carducci Publishers.

Aicher, P. J. (2004), *Rome Alive: A Source-Guide to the Ancient City, Volume 1*, Wauconda: Bolchazy-Carducci Publishers.

Albertson, F. C. (1990), "The Basilica Aemilia Frieze: Religion and Politics in Late Republican Rome," *Latomus*, 49(4): 801–15.

Aldrete, G. S. (2007), *Floods of the Tiber in Ancient Rome*, Baltimore: Johns Hopkins University Press.

Aldrete, G. S. (2009), *Daily Life in the Roman City: Rome, Pompeii, and Ostia*, Norman: University of Oklahoma Press.

Aldrete, G. S. (2014), "Material Evidence for Roman Spectacle and Sport," in P. Christesen and D. G. Kyle (eds), *A Companion to Sport and Spectacle in Greek and Roman Antiquity*, 438–50, Malden, MA: Wiley-Blackwell.

Bablitz, L. (2007), *Actors and Audience in the Roman Courtroom*, London and New York: Routledge.

Ball, L. F. (2003), *The Domus Aurea and the Roman Architectural Revolution*, Cambridge: Cambridge University Press.

Balsdon, J. P. V. D. (1969), *Life and Leisure in Ancient Rome*, New York and San Francisco: McGraw-Hill.

Beacham, R. (1999), *Spectacle Entertainments of Early Imperial Rome*, New Haven: Yale University Press.

Beard, M. (1994), "The Roman and the Foreign: The Cult of the 'Great Mother' in Imperial Rome," in N. Thomas and C. Humphreys (eds), *Shamanism, History, and the State*, 164–90, Ann Arbor: University of Michigan Press.

Beard, M. (2007), *The Roman Triumph*, Cambridge, MA: Belknap Press of Harvard University Press.

Beard, M., J. North, and S. Price (1998), *Religions of Rome*, Cambridge: Cambridge University Press.

Bell, S. (2014), "Roman Chariot Racing: Charioteers, Factions, Spectators," in P. Christesen and D. G. Kyle (eds), *A Companion to Sport and Spectacle in Greek and Roman Antiquity*, 492–504, Malden, MA: Wiley-Blackwell.

Bergmann, B. and C. Kondoleon, eds (1999), *The Art of Ancient Spectacle*, New Haven: Yale University Press.

Betts, E. (2011), "Towards a Multisensory Experience of Movement in the City of Rome," in R. Laurence and D. J. Newsome (eds), *Rome, Ostia, Pompeii: Movement and Space*, 118–34, Oxford: Oxford University Press.

Bingham, S. (2013), *The Praetorian Guard: A History of Rome's Elite Special Forces*, London: I. B. Tauris.

Boatwright, M. T. (1989), *Hadrian and the City of Rome*, Princeton: Princeton University Press.

Boatwright, M. T. (2014), "Visualizing Empire in Imperial Rome," in L. Brice and D. Slootjes (eds), *Aspects of Ancient Institutions and Geography: Studies in Honor of Richard J. A. Talbert*, 235–59, Leiden: Brill.

Bodel, J. (1999), "Death on Display: Looking at Roman Funerals," in B. Bergmann and C. Kondoleon (eds), *The Art of Ancient Spectacle*, 259–81, New Haven: Yale University Press.

Bodel, J. (2011), "Dealing with the Dead: Undertakers, Executioners, and Potter's Fields in Ancient Rome," in V. Hope and E. Marshall (eds), *Death and Disease in the Ancient City*, 128–51, London and New York: Routledge.

den Boeft, J., J. W. Drijvers, D. den Hengst, and H. C. Teitler (2011), *Philological and Historical Commentary on Ammianus Marcellinus XXVIII*, Leiden: Brill.

Borbonus, D. (2014), *Columbarium Tombs and Collective Identity in Augustan Rome*, Cambridge: Cambridge University Press.

Boyle, A. J. (2003), *Ovid and the Monuments: A Poet's Rome*, Bendigo, Victoria: Aureal Publications.

Bradley, K. R. (1991), *Discovering the Roman Family*, Oxford: Oxford University Press.

Bradley, M. (2012), "The 'Sacred Sewer': Tradition and Religion in the Cloaca Maxima," in M. Bradley (ed), *Rome, Pollution and Propriety: Dirt, Disease and Hygiene in the Eternal City from Antiquity to Modernity*, 81–102, Cambridge: Cambridge University Press.

Bradley, M., ed. (2015), *Smell and the Ancient Senses*, London and New York: Routledge.

Braund, S. M., ed. (1996), *Juvenal* Satires *Book I*, Cambridge: Cambridge University Press.

Braund, S. M. (2004), *Juvenal and Persius*, Cambridge, MA: Harvard University Press.

Brilliant, R. (1999), "'Let the Trumpets Roar!' The Roman Triumph," in B. Bergmann and C. Kondoleon (eds), *The Art of Ancient Spectacle*, 221–30, New Haven: Yale University Press.

Brink, L. and D. Green (2008), "Housing the Dead: The Tomb as House in Roman Italy," in L. Brink and D. Green (eds), *Commemorating the Dead: Texts and Artifacts in Context. Studies of Roman, Jewish and Christian Burials*, 39–77, Berlin: Walter de Gruyter.

Brown, R. D. (1995), "Livy's Sabine Women and the Ideal of Concordia," *Transactions of the American Philological Association*, 125: 291–319.

Bruun, C. (1991), *The Water Supply of Ancient Rome: A Study of Roman Imperial Administration*, Helsinki: Societas Scientiarum Fennica.

Bruun, C. (2013), "Water Supply, Drainage and Watermills," in P. Erdkamp (ed.), *The Cambridge Companion to Ancient Rome*, 297–316, Cambridge: Cambridge University Press.

Bruun, C. (2014), "The City of Rome," in C. Bruun and J. Edmondson (eds), *The Oxford Handbook of Roman Epigraphy*, 471–94, Oxford: Oxford University Press.

Bruun, C. and J. Edmondson, eds (2014), *The Oxford Handbook of Roman Epigraphy*, Oxford: Oxford University Press.

Cadoux, T. J. (2008), "The Roman Carcer and Its Adjuncts," *Greece and Rome*, 55: 202–21.

Cahill, S., ed. (2005), *The Smiles of Rome: A Literary Companion for Readers and Travelers*, New York: Ballantine Books.

Cameron, A. (1976), *Circus Factions: Blues and Greens at Rome and Byzantium*, Oxford: Oxford University Press.

Canter, H. V. (1932), "Conflagrations in Ancient Rome," *Classical Journal*, 27(4): 270–88.

Carandini, A., ed. (2017), *The Atlas of Ancient Rome: Biography and Portraits of the City*, Princeton: Princeton University Press.

Carey, S. (2003), *Pliny's Catalogue of Culture: Art and Empire in the Natural History*, Oxford: Oxford University Press.

Carter, M. J. and J. Edmondson (2014), "Spectacle in Rome, Italy, and the Provinces," in C. Bruun and J. Edmondson (eds), *The Oxford Handbook of Roman Epigraphy*, 537–58, Oxford: Oxford University Press.

Casson, L. (2001), *Libraries in the Ancient World*, New Haven: Yale University Press.

Castriota, D. (1995), *The Ara Pacis Augustae and the Imagery of Abundance in Later Greek and Early Roman Imperial Art*, Princeton: Princeton University Press.

Champlin, E. (2003), *Nero*, Cambridge, MA: Harvard University Press.

Claassen, J. (1999), *Displaced Persons: The Literature of Exile from Cicero to Boethius*, Madison: University of Wisconsin Press.

Claridge, A. (2010), *Rome (Oxford Archaeological Guides)*, 2nd ed., Oxford: Oxford University Press.

Clarke, J. R. (1991), *The Houses of Roman Italy, 100 B.C.–A.D. 250: Ritual, Space, and Decoration*, Berkeley: University of California Press.

Coarelli, F. (2014), *Rome and Environs: An Archaeological Guide*, updated edition, Berkeley: University of California Press.

Coleman, K. (2000), "Entertaining Rome," in J. Coulston and H. Dodge (eds), *Ancient Rome: The Archaeology of the Eternal City*, 210–58, Oxford: Oxford University School of Archaeology.

Coleman, K. (2006), *Martial: Liber Spectaculorum*, Oxford: Oxford University Press.

Cooley, A. E. (2009), *Res Gestae Divi Augusti: Text, Translation, and Commentary*, Cambridge: Cambridge University Press.

Courtney, E. (2013), *A Commentary on the Satires of Juvenal*, reprint, Berkeley: California Classical Studies.

Dalby, A. (2000), *Empire of Pleasures: Luxury and Indulgence in the Roman World*, London and New York: Routledge.

D'Ambra, E. (2009), *Topography of Rome: Oxford Bibliographies*, Oxford: Oxford University Press.

Daugherty, G. N. (1992), "The *Cohortes Vigilum* and the Great Fire of 64 AD," *Classical Journal*, 87(3): 229–40.

Davies, P. J. E. (2004), *Death and the Emperor: Roman Imperial Funerary Monuments from Augustus to Marcus Aurelius*, Austin: University of Texas Press.

DeLaine, J. (2000), "Building the Eternal City: The Construction Industry of Imperial Rome," in J. Coulston and H. Dodge (eds), *Ancient Rome: The Archaeology of the Eternal City*, 119–41, Oxford: Oxford University Press.

Dey, H. W. (2011), *The Aurelian Wall and the Refashioning of Imperial Rome, AD 271–855*, Cambridge: Cambridge University Press.

Dillon, S. (2006), "Women on the Columns of Trajan and Marcus Aurelius and the Visual Language of Roman Victory," in S. Dillon and K. Welch (eds), *Representations of War in Ancient Rome*, 244–71, Cambridge: Cambridge University Press.

Dodge, H. (1999), "Amusing the Masses: Buildings for Entertainment and Leisure in the Roman World," in D. S. Potter and D. J. Mattingly (eds), *Life, Death and Entertainment in the Roman World*, 205–55, Ann Arbor: University of Michigan Press.

Dodge, H. (2000), "'Greater than the Pyramids': The Water Supply of Ancient Rome, in J. Coulston and H. Dodge (eds), *Ancient Rome: The Archaeology of the Eternal City*, 166–209, Oxford: Oxford University School of Archaeology.

Dodge, H. (2011), *Spectacle in the Roman World*, London: Duckworth Publishers.

Dodge, H. (2013), "Building for an Audience: The Architecture of Roman Spectacle," in R. B. Ulrich and C. K. Quenemoen (eds), *A Companion to Roman Architecture*, 281–99, Malden, MA: Wiley-Blackwell.

Dodge, H. (2014), "Amphitheaters in the Roman World," in P. Christesen and D. G. Kyle (eds), *A Companion to Sport and Spectacle in Greek and Roman Antiquity*, 545–60, Malden, MA: Wiley-Blackwell.

Dolansky, F. (2014), "Education in the Roman World," in M. Gibbs, M. Nikolic, and P. Ripat (eds), *Themes in Roman Society and Culture: An Introduction to Ancient Rome*, 117–38, Toronto: Oxford University Press.

Dunbabin, K. M. D. and W. J. Slater. (2011), "Roman Dining," in M. Peachin (ed.), *The Oxford Handbook of Social Relations in the Roman World*, 438–66, Oxford: Oxford University Press.

Duncan-Jones, R. (1996), "The Impact of the Antonine Plague," *Journal of Roman Archaeology*, 9: 108–36.

Dunkle, R. (2014), "Overview of Roman Spectacle," in P. Christesen and D. G. Kyle (eds), *A Companion to Sport and Spectacle in Greek and Roman Antiquity*, 381–94, Malden, MA: Wiley-Blackwell.

Dyson, S. L. (2010), *Rome: A Living Portrait of an Ancient City*, Baltimore: Johns Hopkins University Press.

Edwards, C. (1993), *The Politics of Immorality in Ancient Rome*, Cambridge: Cambridge University Press.

Edwards, C. (1996), *Writing Rome: Textual Approaches to the City*, Cambridge: Cambridge University Press.

Edwards, C. (2007), *Death in Ancient Rome*, New Haven: Yale University Press.

Edwards, C. and G. Woolf, eds (2003), *Rome the Cosmopolis*, Cambridge: Cambridge University Press.

Eichholz, D. E. (1962), *Pliny: Natural History Books XXXVI–XXXXVII*, Cambridge, MA: Harvard University Press.

Erasmo, M. (2008), *Reading Death in Ancient Rome*, Columbus: Ohio State University Press.

Erasmo, M. (2012), *Death: Antiquity and Its Legacy*, London: I. B. Tauris.

Erasmo, M. (2015), *Strolling Through Rome: The Definitive Walking Guide to the Eternal City*, London: I. B. Tauris.

Erdkamp, P. (2013), "The Food Supply of the Capital," in P. Erdkamp (ed.), *The Cambridge Companion to Ancient Rome*, 262–77, Cambridge: Cambridge University Press.

Evans, H. B. (1982), "Agrippa's Water Plan," *American Journal of Archaeology*, 86: 401–11.

Evans, H. B. (1997), *Water Distribution in Ancient Rome: The Evidence of Frontinus*, Ann Arbor: University of Michigan Press.

Fagan, G. G. (2011a), "Socializing at the Baths," in M. Peachin (ed.), *The Oxford Handbook of Social Relations in the Roman World*, 358–73, Oxford: Oxford University Press.

Fagan, G. G. (2011b), *The Lure of the Arena: Social Psychology and the Crowd at the Roman Games*, Cambridge: Cambridge University Press.

Fantham, E. (1996), *Roman Literary Culture: From Cicero to Apuleius*, Baltimore: Johns Hopkins University Press.

Favro, D. (1994), "The Street Triumphant: The Urban Impact of Roman Triumphal Parades," in Z. Çelik, D. Favro, and R. Ingersoll (eds), *Streets: Critical Perspectives on Public Space*, 151–64, Berkeley: University of California Press.

Favro, D. (1998), *The Urban Image of Augustan Rome*, Cambridge: Cambridge University Press.

Favro, D. (1999), "The City Is a Living Thing: The Performative Role of an Urban Site in Ancient Rome, the Vallis Murcia," in B. Bergmann and C. Kondoleon (eds), *The Art of Ancient Spectacle*, 205–20, New Haven: Yale University Press.

Favro, D. (2005), "Making Rome a World City," in K. Galinsky (ed.), *The Cambridge Companion to the Age of Augustus*, 234–63, Cambridge: Cambridge University Press.

Favro, D. (2011), "Construction Traffic in Imperial Rome: Building the Arch of Septimius Severus," in D. Laurence and D. J. Newsome (eds), *Rome, Ostia, Pompeii: Movement and Space*, 332–60, Oxford: Oxford University Press.

Favro, D. and C. Johanson, (2010), "Death in Motion: Funeral Processions in the
   Roman Forum," *Journal of the Society of Architectural Historians*, 69(1): 12–37.
Feldman, L. H. and M. Reinhold (1996), *Jewish Life and Thoughts Among Greeks and
   Romans: Primary Readings*, Edinburgh: T&T Clark.
Ferriss-Hill, J. L. (2011), "A Stroll with Lucilius: Horace, *Satires* 1.9 Reconsidered,"
   *American Journal of Philology*, 132(3): 429–55.
Flower, H. I. (1996), *Ancestor Masks and Aristocratic Power in Roman Culture*, Oxford:
   Clarendon Press.
Foubert, L. (2010), "The Palatine Dwelling of the *Mater Familias*: Houses as Symbolic
   Space in the Julio-Claudian Period," *Klio*, 92(1): 65–82.
Frier, B. (1977), "The Rental Market in Early Imperial Rome," *Journal of Roman Studies*,
   67: 27–37.
Frier, B. (1978), "Cicero's Management of His Urban Properties," *Classical Journal*,
   74(1): 1–6.
Frier, B. (1980), *Landlords and Tenants in Imperial Rome*, Princeton: Princeton
   University Press.
Fuhrmann, C. J. (2012), *Policing the Roman Empire: Soldiers, Administration, and Public
   Order*, Oxford: Oxford University Press.
Futrell, A. (1997), *Blood in the Arena: The Spectacle of Roman Power*, Austin: University
   of Texas Press.
Futrell, A. (2006), *The Roman Games: A Sourcebook*, Malden, MA: Wiley-Blackwell.
Gaertner, J. (2007), *Writing Exile: The Discourse of Displacement in Greco-Roman
   Antiquity and Beyond*, Leiden: Brill.
Gaisser, J. H. and T. D. McClain, eds (2000), *Livy: Book I*, Bryn Mawr, PA: Bryn Mawr
   Commentaries, Inc.
Gallia, A. B. (2016), "Remaking Rome," in A. Zissos (ed.), *A Companion to the Flavian
   Age of Imperial Rome*, 148–65, Malden, MA: Blackwell-Wiley.
Garnsey, P. (1988), *Famine and Food Supply in the Graeco-Roman World*, Cambridge:
   Cambridge University Press.
Gibson, R. K. and R. Morello, eds (2011), *Pliny the Elder: Themes and Contexts*, Leiden
   and Boston: Brill.
Goold, G. P. (1990), *Propertius: Elegies*, Cambridge, MA: Harvard University Press.
Gowers, E. (1993), *The Loaded Table*, Oxford: Oxford University Press.
Gowers, E. (1995), "The Anatomy of Rome from Capitol to Cloaca," *Journal of Roman
   Studies*, 85: 23–32.
Gowers, E. (2012), *Horace: Satires*, Cambridge: Cambridge University Press.
Graham, S. (2013), "Counting Bricks and Stacking Wood: Providing the Physical
   Fabric," in P. Erdkamp (ed.), *The Cambridge Companion to Ancient Rome*, 278–96,
   Cambridge: Cambridge University Press.
Grewe, K. (2016), "Urban Infrastructure in the Roman World," trans. J. K. Sandrock, in
   G. L. Irby (ed.), *A Companion to Science, Technology, and Medicine in Ancient Greece
   and Rome*, 768–83, Malden, MA: Wiley-Blackwell.

Griffith, A. B. (2009). "The Pons Sublicius in Context: Revisiting Rome's First Public Work," *Phoenix*, 63(3/4): 296–321.

Gruen, E. (1990), *Studies in Greek Culture and Roman Policy*, Leiden: Brill.

Gutierrez, D., B. Frischer, E. Cerezo, A. Gomez, and F. Seron, (2007), "AI and Virtual Crowds: Populating the Colosseum," *Journal of Cultural Heritage*, 8(2): 176–85.

Hales, S. (2009), *The Roman House and Social Identity*, Cambridge: Cambridge University Press.

Hallett, J. P. (1970), "'Over Troubled Waters': The Meaning of the Title *Pontifex*," *Transactions and Proceedings of the American Philological Association*, 101: 219–27.

Hartnett, J. (2011), "The Power of Nuisances on the Roman Street," in D. Laurence and D. J. Newsome (eds), *Rome, Ostia, Pompeii: Movement and Space*, 135–59, Oxford: Oxford University Press.

Haselberger, L. (2002), *Mapping Augustan Rome*, Portsmouth: Journal of Roman Archaeology.

Henderson, J. (2002), "A Doo-Dah-Doo-Dah-Dey at the Races: Ovid *Amores* 3.2 and the Personal Politics of the Circus Maximus," *Classical Antiquity*, 21(1): 41–65.

Hobson, B. (2009), Latrinae et Foricae: *Toilets in the Roman World*, London: Bloomsbury.

Hodge, A. T. (2002), *Roman Aqueducts & Water Supply*, London: Duckworth.

Holleran, C. (2011), "The Street Life of Ancient Rome," in R. Laurence and D. J. Newsome (eds), *Rome, Ostia, Pompeii: Movement and Space*, 245–61, Oxford: Oxford University Press.

Holleran, C. (2012), *Shopping in Ancient Rome*, Oxford: Oxford University Press.

Holloway, R. R. (2008), *Constantine and Rome*, New Haven: Yale University Press.

Hope, V. M. (2007), *Death in Ancient Rome: A Sourcebook*, London and New York: Routledge.

Hope, V. M. (2011), "Contempt and Respect: The Treatment of the Corpse in Ancient Rome," in V. Hope and E. Marshall (eds), *Death and Disease in the Ancient City*, 104–27, London and New York: Routledge.

Hopkins, K. and M. Beard (2011), *The Colosseum*, Cambridge, MA: Harvard University Press.

Humphrey, J. H. (1986), *Roman Circuses: Arenas for Chariot Racing*, Berkeley: University of California Press.

Huskey, S. J. (2006), "Ovid's (Mis)Guided Tour of Rome: Some Purposeful Omissions in *Tr.* 3.1," *Classical Journal*, 102(1): 17–39.

Jaeger, M. (1997), *Livy's Written Rome*, Ann Arbor: University of Michigan Press.

Jansen, G. C. M., A. O. Koloski-Ostrow, and E. M. Moormann, eds (2011), *Roman Toilets: Their Archaeology and Cultural History*, Leuven: Peeters.

Jenkyns, R. (1992), *The Legacy of Rome: A New Appraisal*, Oxford: Oxford University Press.

Jenkyns, R. (2014), "The Memory of Rome in Rome," in K. Galinsky (ed.), *Memoria Romana*, 15–26, Ann Arbor: University of Michigan Press.

Johanson, C. (2011), "A Walk with the Dead: A Funerary Cityscape of Ancient Rome," in B. Rawson (ed.), *A Companion to Families in the Greek and Roman Worlds*, 408–30, Malden, MA: Wiley-Blackwell.

Jones, B. W. (1992), *The Emperor Domitian*, London and New York: Routledge.

Joshel, S. R. (1992), *Work, Identity and Legal Status at Rome: A Study of the Occupational Inscriptions*, Norman: University of Oklahoma Press.

Joshel, S. R. and L. H. Petersen (2014), *The Material Life of Roman Slaves*, Cambridge: Cambridge University Press.

Kaiser, A. (2011), *Roman Urban Street Networks: Streets and the Organization of Space in Four Cities*, London and New York: Routledge.

Kaplow, L. (2008), "Redefining *Imagines*: Ancestor Masks and Political Legitimacy in the Rhetoric of New Men," *Mouseion: Journal of the Classical Association of Canada*, 8(3): 409–16.

Kaster, R. A. (2012), *The Appian Way: Ghost Road, Queen of Roads*, Chicago: University of Chicago Press.

Keppie, L. (1991), *Understanding Roman Inscriptions*, Baltimore: Johns Hopkins University Press.

Knapp, R. (2011), *Invisible Romans*, Cambridge, MA: Harvard University Press.

Koloski-Ostrow, A. O. (2015a), "Roman Urban Smells: The Archaeological Evidence," in M. Bradley (ed.), *Smell and the Ancient Senses*, 90–109, London and New York: Routledge.

Koloski-Ostrow, A. O. (2015b), *The Archaeology of Sanitation in Roman Italy: Toilets, Sewers, and Water Systems*, Chapel Hill: University of North Carolina Press.

Kraemer, R. S. (1992), *Her Share of the Blessings: Women's Religions among Pagans, Jews, and Christians in the Greco-Roman World*, Oxford: Oxford University Press.

Kyle, D. G. (2006), *Sport and Spectacle in the Ancient World*, Malden, MA: Wiley-Blackwell.

Lanciani, R. (1896), "The Sky Scrapers of Rome," *North American Review*, 162(475): 705–15.

Larmour, D. H. J. and D. Spencer, eds (2007), *The Sites of Rome: Time, Space, Memory*, Oxford: Oxford University Press.

Laurence, R. (1999), *The Roads of Roman Italy: Mobility and Cultural Change*, London and New York: Routledge.

Laurence, R. (2011), "Literature and the Spatial Turn: Movement and Space in Martial's *Epigrams*," in R. Laurence and D. J. Newsome (eds), *Rome, Ostia, Pompeii: Movement and Space*, 81–99, Oxford: Oxford University Press.

Laurence, R. (2013), "Traffic and Land Transportation in and Near Rome," in P. Erdkamp (ed.), *The Cambridge Companion to Ancient Rome*, 246–61, Cambridge: Cambridge University Press.

Laurence, R. (2016), "Towards a History of Mobility in Ancient Rome (300 BCE to 100 CE)," in I. Östenberg, S. Malmberg, and J. Bjørnebye (eds), *The Moving*

*City: Processions, Passages and Promenades in Ancient Rome*, 175–86, London: Bloomsbury.

Lim, R. (1999). "'In the Temple of Laughter': Visual and Literary Representations of Spectators at Roman Games," in B. Bergmann and C. Kondoleon (eds), *The Art of Ancient Spectacle*, 343–65, New Haven: Yale University Press.

Linderski, J. (2001), "*Imago Hortorum*: Pliny the Elder and the Gardens of the Urban Poor," *Classical Philology*, 96(3): 305–8.

Lindner, M. (2015), *Portraits of the Vestal Virgins, Priestesses of Ancient Rome*, Ann Arbor: University of Michigan Press.

Lindsay, H. (2000), "Death-Pollution and Funerals in the City of Rome," in V. Hope and E. Marshall (eds), *Death and Disease in the Ancient City*, 152–72, London and New York: Routledge.

Ling, R. (1990), "A Stranger in Town: Finding the Way in an Ancient City," *Greece & Rome*, 37(2): 204–14.

Littlewood, R. J. (1975), "Ovid's Lupercalia (*Fasti* 2.267–452): A Study in the Artistry of the *Fasti*," *Latomus*, 34: 1060–72.

Lott, J. B. (2004), *The Neighborhoods of Augustan Rome*, Cambridge: Cambridge University Press.

Lott, J. B. (2013), "Regions and Neighbourhoods," in P. Erdkamp (ed.), *The Cambridge Companion to Ancient Rome*, 169–89, Cambridge: Cambridge University Press.

Lovatt, H. (2016), "Flavian Spectacle: Paradox and Wonder," in A. Zissos (ed.), *A Companion to the Flavian Age of Imperial Rome*, 361–75, Malden, MA: Wiley-Blackwell.

Macaulay-Lewis, E. (2011), "The City in Motion: Walking for Transport and Leisure in the City of Rome," in R. Laurence and D. J. Newsome (eds), *Rome, Ostia, Pompeii: Movement and Space*, 262–89, Oxford: Oxford University Press.

Marshall, A. J. (1976), "Library Resources and Creative Writing at Rome," *Phoenix*, 30(3): 252–64.

Mattern, S. P. (2013), *The Prince of Medicine: Galen in the Roman Empire*, New York: Oxford University Press.

Mattingly, D. J., and G. S. Aldrete (2000), "The Feeding of Imperial Rome: The Mechanics of the Food Supply System," in J. Coulston and H. Dodge (eds), *Ancient Rome: The Archaeology of the Eternal City*, 142–65, Oxford: Oxford University School of Archaeology.

Mazzoni, C. (2010), *She-Wolf: The Story of a Roman Icon*, Cambridge: Cambridge University Press.

McGinn, T. A. J. (1998), *Prostitution, Sexuality, and the Law in Ancient Rome*, New York and Oxford: Oxford University Press.

McGinn, T. A. J. (2013), "Sex and the City," in P. Erdkamp (ed.), *Cambridge Companion to Ancient Rome*, 369–88, Cambridge: Cambridge University Press.

McGowan, M. M. (2009), *Ovid in Exile: Power and Poetic Redress in the* Tristia *and* Epistulae Ex Ponto, Leiden: Brill.

Meijer, F. (2010), *Chariot Racing in the Roman Empire*, trans. L. Waters, Baltimore: Johns Hopkins University Press.

Mignone, L. (2016), *The Republican Aventine and Rome's Social Order*, Ann Arbor: University of Michigan Press.

Miles, G. B. (1997), *Livy: Reconstructing Early Rome*, Ithaca: Cornell University Press.

Miles, M. (2008), *Art as Plunder: The Ancient Origins of Debate about Cultural Property*, Cambridge: Cambridge University Press.

Milnor, K. (2005), *Gender, Domesticity, and the Age of Augustus: Inventing Private Life*, Oxford: Oxford University Press.

Mitchell, S. (1987), "Imperial Building in the Eastern Roman Provinces," *Harvard Studies in Classical Philology*, 91: 333–65.

Moatti, C. (2013), "Immigration and Cosmopolitanization," in P. Erdkamp (ed.), *The Cambridge Companion to Ancient Rome*, 77–92, Cambridge: Cambridge University Press.

Morley, N. (2015), "Urban Smells and Roman Noses," in M. Bradley (ed.), *Smell and the Ancient Senses*, 110–19, London and New York: Routledge.

Newbold, R. F. (1974), "Some Social and Economic Consequences of the AD 64 Fire at Rome," *Latomus*, 33: 858–69.

Newsome, D. J. (2008), "Centrality in Its Place: Defining Urban Space in the City of Rome," in M. Driessen, S. Heeren, J. Hendriks, F. Kemmers, and R. Visser (eds), *TRAC 2008: Proceedings of the Eighteenth Annual Theoretical Roman Archaeology Conference*, 25–38, Oxford: Oxbow Books.

Newsome, D. J. (2011), "Introduction: Making Movement Meaningful," in R. Laurence and D. J. Newsome (eds), *Rome, Ostia, Pompeii: Movement and Space*, 1–56, Oxford: Oxford University Press.

Newton, F. G., and T. Ashby. (1910), "The *Columbarium* of Pomponius Hylas," *Papers of the British School at Rome*, 5: 463–71.

Nicholls, M. C. (2010), "Bibliotheca Latina Graecaque: On the Possible Division of Roman Public Libraries by Language," in Y. Perrin (ed.), *Neronia VIII: bibliothèques, livres et culture écrite dans l'empire romain de César à Hadrien*, 11–21, Brussels: Editions Latomus.

Nippel, W. (1995), *Public Order in Ancient Rome*, Cambridge: Cambridge University Press.

Noreña, C. F. (2013), "Locating the *Ustrinum* of Augustus," *Memoirs of the American Academy in Rome*, 58: 51–64.

North, J. A. (2000), *Roman Religion*, Oxford: Oxford University Press.

Noy, D. (1995), *Jewish Inscriptions of Western Europe*, Cambridge: Cambridge University Press.

Noy, D. (2000), *Foreigners at Rome: Citizens and Strangers*, London: Duckworth.

Odahl, C. M. (2010), *Cicero and the Catilinarian Conspiracy*, London and New York: Routledge.

Oleson, J. P. (2011), "*Harena sine calce*: Building Disasters, Incompetent Architects, and Construction Fraud in Ancient Rome," *Commentationes Humanarum Litterarum* 128: 9–27.

Oliver, J. H. (1953), "The Ruling Power: A Study of The Roman Empire in The Second Century After Christ through the Roman Oration of Aelius Aristides," *Transactions of the American Philosophical Society*, new series 43(4): 871–1003.

O'Neill, K. (1995), "Propertius 4.4: Tarpeia and the Burden of Aetiology," *Hermathena*, 158: 53–60.

Östenberg, I. (2009), *Staging the World: Spoils, Captives, and Representations in the Roman Triumphal Procession*, Oxford: Oxford University Press.

Östenberg, I., S. Malmberg, and J. Bjørnebye, eds (2016), *The Moving City: Processions, Passages and Promenades in Ancient Rome*, London: Bloomsbury.

O'Sullivan, T. (2011), *Walking in Roman Culture*, Cambridge: Cambridge University Press.

O'Sullivan, T. (2016), "Augustan Literary Tours: Walking and Reading the City," in I. Ostenberg, S. Malmberg, and J. Bjørnebye (eds), *The Moving City: Processions, Passages and Promenades in Ancient Rome*, 111–22, London: Bloomsbury.

Pagán, V. E. (2004), *Conspiracy Narratives in Roman History*, Austin: University of Texas Press.

Painter, B. W., Jr. (2005), *Mussolini's Rome: Rebuilding the Eternal City*, New York: Palgrave Macmillan.

Patterson, J. R. (2000a), *Political Life in the City of Rome*, Bristol: Bristol Classical Press.

Patterson, J. R. (2000b), "Living and Dying in the City of Rome: Houses and Tombs," in J. Coulston and H. Dodge (eds), *Ancient Rome: The Archaeology of the Eternal City*, 259–89, Oxford: Oxford University School of Archaeology.

Peachin, M. (2004), *Frontinus and the* Curae *of the* Curator Aquarum, Stuttgart: Franz Steiner Verlag.

Penner, L. (2012), "Gender, Household Structure and Slavery: Re-Interpreting the Aristocratic Columbaria of Early Imperial Rome," in R. Laurence and A. Strömberg (eds), *Families in the Greco-Roman World*, 143–58, London: Bloomsbury.

Petersen, L. H. (2003), "The Baker, His Tomb, His Wife, and Her Breadbasket: The Monument of Eurysaces in Rome," *The Art Bulletin*, 85(2): 230–57.

Petersen, L. H. (2006), *The Freedman in Roman Art and Art History*, Cambridge: Cambridge University Press.

Pittenger, M. R. P. (2009), *Contested Triumphs: Politics, Pageantry, and Performance in Livy's Republican Rome*, Berkeley: University of California Press.

Popkin, M. L. (2016), *The Architecture of the Roman Triumph: Monuments, Memory, and Identity*, Cambridge: Cambridge University Press.

Pratt, K. J. (1965), "Rome as Eternal," *Journal of the History of Ideas*, 26(1): 25–44.

Purcell, N. (2013), "'Romans, Play On!' City of the Games," in P. Erdkamp (ed.), *The Cambridge Companion to Ancient Rome*, 441–58, Cambridge: Cambridge University Press.

Putnam, M. C. J. (2001), *Horace's* Carmen Saeculare: *Ritual Magic and the Poet's Art*, New Haven: Yale University Press.

Quilici, L. (2008), "Land Transport 1: Roads and Bridges," in J. P. Oleson (ed.), *The Oxford Handbook of Engineering and Technology in the Classical World*, 551–79. Oxford: Oxford University Press.

Rainbird, J. S. (1986), "The Fire Stations of Imperial Rome," *Papers of the British School at Rome*, 54: 147–69.

Ramage, N. and A. Ramage (2009), *Roman Art: Romulus to Constantine*, 5th edn, Upper Saddle River: Pearson Prentice Hall.

Rawson, E. (1987), "*Discrimina Ordinum*: The *Lex Julia Theatralis*," *Papers of the British School at Rome*, 55: 83–113.

Rawson, B. (2003), *Children and Childhood in Roman Italy*, Oxford: Oxford University Press.

Rea, J. (2007), *Legendary Rome: Myth, Monuments and Memory on the Palatine and Capitoline*, London: Duckworth Publishers.

Rehak, P. (2006), *Imperium and Cosmos: Augustus and the Northern Campus Martius*, Madison: University of Wisconsin Press.

Reimers, P. (1989), "*Opus Omnium Dictu Maximum*: Literary Sources for the Knowledge of Roman City Drainage," *Opuscula Romama*, 17: 137–41.

Reitz-Joosse, B. (2016), "The City and the Text in Vitruvius's *de Architectura*," *Arethusa*, 49(2): 183–97.

Reynolds, P. K. B. (1926), *The Vigiles of Imperial Rome*, Oxford: Oxford University Press.

Richardson, L., Jr. (1980), "Two Topographical Notes," *American Journal of Philology*, 101(1): 53–6.

Richardson, L., Jr. (1992), *A New Topographical Dictionary of Ancient Rome*, Baltimore: Johns Hopkins University Press.

Richardson, L., Jr. (2006), *Propertius: Elegies I–IV*, Norman: University of Oklahoma Press.

Richmond, I. A. (1930), *The City Wall of Imperial Rome*, Oxford: Oxford University Press.

Ridley, R. T. (1992), "The Praetor and the Pyramid: The Tomb of Gaius Cestius in History, Archaeology and Literature," *Bollettino Di Archeologia*, 13: 1–29.

Rimell, V. E. (2009), *Martial's Rome: Empire and the Ideology of Epigram*, Cambridge: Cambridge University Press.

Robinson, O. F. (1992), *Ancient Rome: City Planning and Administration*, London and New York: Routledge.

Roche, P. (2011), *Pliny's Praise: The* Panegyricus *in the Roman World*, Cambridge: Cambridge University Press.

Rodgers, R. H. (2009), *Frontinus:* De Aquaeductu Urbis Romae, Cambridge: Cambridge University Press.

Roller, M. (2004), "Exemplarity in Roman Culture: The Cases of Horatius Cocles and Cloelia," *Classical Philology*, 99(1): 1–56.

Roman, L. (2010), "Martial and the City of Rome," *Journal of Roman Studies*, 100: 88–117.

Rose, P. (2005), "Spectators and Spectator Comfort in Roman Entertainment Buildings: A Study in Functional Design," *Papers of the British School at Rome*, 73: 99–130.

Rutledge, S. (2012), *Ancient Rome as a Museum: Power, Identity, and the Culture of Collecting*, Oxford: Oxford University Press.

Saller, R. P. (1982), *Personal Patronage under the Early Empire*, Cambridge: Cambridge University Press.

Salomies, O. (2014), "The Roman Republic," in C. Bruun and J. Edmondson (eds), *The Oxford Handbook of Roman Epigraphy*, 153–77, Oxford: Oxford University Press.

Scheidel, W. (2003), "Germs for Rome," in C. Edwards and G. Woolf (eds), *Rome the Cosmopolis*, 158–76, Cambridge: Cambridge University Press.

Scobie, A. (1986), "Slums, Sanitation, and Mortality in the Roman World," *Klio*, 68(2): 399–433.

Scobie, A. (1988), "Spectator Security and Comfort at Gladiatorial Games," *Nikephoros*, 1: 191–243.

Scott, M. (2013), *Space and Society in the Greek and Roman Worlds*, Cambridge: Cambridge University Press.

Scullard, H. H. (1981), *Festivals and Ceremonies of the Roman Republic*, London and Ithaca: Cornell University Press.

Sear, F. (1990), "Vitruvius and Roman Theater Design," *American Journal of Archaeology*, 94(2): 249–58.

Sear, F. (2006), *Roman Theatres: An Architectural Study*, Oxford: Oxford University Press.

Severy, B. (2003), *Augustus and the Family at the Birth of the Roman Empire*, New York and London: Routledge.

Shackleton Bailey, D. R. (1993) *Martial: Epigrams, Volume III, Books 11–14*, Cambridge, MA: Harvard University Press.

Shipley, F. W. (1933), *Agrippa's Building Activities in Rome*, St. Louis: Washington University.

Sobocinski, M. G. (2009), "Porta Triumphalis and Fortuna Redux: Reconsidering the Evidence," *Memoirs of the American Academy in Rome*, 54: 135–64.

Stambaugh, J. E. (1988), *The Ancient Roman City*, Baltimore: Johns Hopkins University Press.

Staples, A. (1998), *From Good Goddess to Vestal Virgins*, London and New York: Routledge.

Steinby, E. M., ed. (1993–2000), *Lexicon Topographicum Urbis Romae*, Rome: Quasar.

Storey, G. R. (2003), "The Skyscrapers of the Ancient Roman World," *Latomus*, 62(1): 3–26.

Storey, G. R. (2004), "The Meaning of *Insula* in Roman Residential Terminology," *Memoirs of the American Academy in Rome*, 49: 47–84.

Sumi, G. (2002), "Impersonating the Dead: Mimes at Roman Funerals," *American Journal of Philology*, 123: 559–85.

Takács, S. A. (2008), *Vestal Virgins, Sibyls, and Matrons: Women in Roman Religion*, Austin: University of Texas Press.

Taylor, R. (2001), *Public Needs & Private Pleasures*, Rome: L'Erma di Bretschneider.

Todd, M. (1978), *The Walls of Rome*, London: Elek.

Toner, J. P. (1995), *Leisure and Ancient Rome*, Cambridge: Polity Press.

Toner, J. P. (2009), *Popular Culture in Ancient Rome*, Cambridge: Polity Press.

Toner, J. P. (2013), *Roman Disasters*, Cambridge: Polity Press.

Toynbee, J. M. C. (1996), *Death and Burial in the Roman World*, Baltimore: Johns Hopkins University Press.

Trifilò, F. (2011), "Movement, Gaming, and the Use of Space in the Forum," in R. Laurence and D. Newsome (eds), *Rome, Ostia, Pompeii: Movement and Space*, 312–31, Oxford: Oxford University Press.

Tucci, P. L. (2008), "Galen's Storeroom, Rome's Libraries, and the Fire of A.D. 192," *Journal of Roman Archaeology*, 21: 133–49.

Tucci, P. L. (2011), "The Pons Sublicius: A Reinvestigation," *Memoirs of the American Academy in Rome*, 56/57: 177–212.

Tuck, S. L. (2013), "The Tiber and River Transport," in P. Erdkamp (ed.), *The Cambridge Companion to Ancient Rome*, 229–45, Cambridge: Cambridge University Press.

Tuck, S. L. (2016), "Imperial Image-Making," in A. Zissos (ed.), *A Companion to the Flavian Age of Imperial Rome*, 109–28, Malden, MA: Wiley-Blackwell.

Turcan, R. (1996), *The Cults of the Roman Empire*, Cambridge, MA: Blackwell.

Van den Berg, C. S. (2008), "The *Pulvinar* in Roman Culture," *Transactions of the American Philological Association*, 138(2): 239–73.

Van der Wal, R. L. (2007), "'Urbem, Urbem Cole!' Taking a Walk in Cicero's *Vestigia*," *Akroterion*, 52: 61–76.

van Tilburg, C. (2012), *Traffic and Congestion in the Roman Empire*, London: Routledge.

Vasaly, A. (1993), *Representations: Images of the World in Ciceronian Oratory*, Berkeley: University of California Press.

Versnel, H. S. (1970), *Triumphus: An Inquiry Into the Origin, Development and Meaning of the Roman Triumph*, Leiden: Brill.

Von Stackelberg, K. T. (2009), *The Roman Garden: Space, Sense and Society*, London and New York: Routledge.

Wardle, D. (2014), *Suetonius: Life of Augustus*, Oxford: Oxford University Press.

Watson, L. (2003), *Martial: Select Epigrams*, Cambridge: Cambridge University Press.

Welch, K. E. (2009), *The Roman Amphitheatre: From Its Origins to the Colosseum*, Cambridge: Cambridge University Press.

Welch, T. S. (2001), "*Est Locus Uni Cuique Suus*: City and Status in Horace's *Satires* 1.8 and 1.9," *Classical Antiquity*, 20(1): 165–92.

Welch, T. S. (2005), *The Elegiac Cityscape: Propertius and the Meaning of Roman Monuments*, Columbus: Ohio State University Press.

Welch, T. S. (2012), "Perspectives on and of Livy's *Tarpeia*," *Eugesta* 2: 169–200.

Welch, T. S. (2015), *Tarpeia: Workings of a Roman Myth*, Columbus: The Ohio State University Press.

White, P. (1993), *Promised Verse*, Cambridge, MA: Harvard University Press.

White, P. (2009), "Bookshops in the Literary Culture of Rome," in W. A. Johnson and H. N. Parker (eds), *Ancient Literacies: The Culture of Reading in Greece and Rome*, 268–87, Oxford: Oxford University Press.

Wildfang, R. L. (2006), *Rome's Vestal Virgins: A Study of Rome's Vestal Priestesses in the Late Republic and Early Empire*, London and New York: Routledge.

Williams, C. A. (2004), *Martial's Epigrams Book Two*, Oxford: Oxford University Press.

Williams, C. A. (2010), *Roman Homosexuality: Ideologies of Masculinity in Classical Antiquity*, Oxford: Oxford University Press.

Wiseman, T. P. (1995a), *Remus: A Roman Myth*, Cambridge: Cambridge University Press.

Wiseman, T. P. (1995b), "The God of the Lupercal," *Journal of Roman Studies*, 85: 1–22.

Witcher, R. (2013), "(Sub)urban Surroundings," in P. Erdkamp (ed.), *The Cambridge Companion to Ancient Rome*, 205–28, Cambridge: Cambridge University Press.

Woodhull, M. (2003), "Engendering Space: Octavia's Portico in Rome," *Aurora: Journal of the History of Art*, 4: 13–33.

Woolf, G. (2003), "The City of Letters," in C. Edwards and G. Woolf (eds), *Rome the Cosmopolis*, 203–21, Cambridge: Cambridge University Press.

Yavetz, Z. (1958), "The Living Conditions of the Urban Plebs in Republican Rome," *Latomus*, 17(3): 500–17.

Yegül, F. (2010), *Bathing in the Roman World*, Cambridge: Cambridge University Press.

Zanker, P. (1988), *The Power of Images in the Age of Augustus*, Ann Arbor: University of Michigan Press.

Zetzel, J. (1995), *Cicero: De Re Publica*, Cambridge: Cambridge University Press.

# Index